TRAVeler
touRest

BERMUDA GUIDE

BE A TRAVELER - NOT A TOURIST!

OPEN ROAD TRAVEL GUIDES SHOW YOU HOW TO BE A TRAVELER – NOT A TOURIST!

Whether you're going abroad or planning a trip in the United States, take Open Road along on your journey. Our books have been praised by ***Travel & Leisure, The Los Angeles Times, Newsday, Booklist, US News & World Report, Endless Vacation, American Bookseller, Coast to Coast,*** *and many other magazines and newspapers!*

Don't just see the world – experience it with Open Road!

ABOUT THE AUTHOR

Ron Charles is the author of Open Road travel guides to Bermuda, The Bahamas, Spain, Portugal and Holland. When he is not off on assignment, he lives in Montreal, Canada.

BE A TRAVELER, NOT A TOURIST - WITH OPEN ROAD TRAVEL GUIDES!

Open Road Publishing has guide books to exciting, fun destinations on four continents. As veteran travelers, our goal is to bring you the best travel guides available anywhere!

No small task, but here's what we offer:

• All Open Road travel guides are written by authors with a distinct, opinionated point of view – not some sterile committee or team of writers. Our authors are experts in the areas covered and are polished writers.

• Our guides are geared to people who want to make their own travel choices. We'll show you how to discover the real destination – not just see some place from a tour bus window.

• We're strong on the basics, but we also provide terrific choices for those looking to get off the beaten path and experience the country or city – not just see it or pass through it.

• We give you the best, but we also tell you about the worst and what to avoid. Nobody should waste their time and money on their hard-earned vacation because of bad or inadequate travel advice.

• Our guides assume nothing. We tell you everything you need to know to have the trip of a lifetime – presented in a fun, literate, no-nonsense style.

• And, above all, we welcome your input, ideas, and suggestions to help us put out the best travel guides possible.

BERMUDA GUIDE

BE A TRAVELER - NOT A TOURIST!

Ron Charles

OPEN ROAD PUBLISHING

OPEN ROAD PUBLISHING

We offer travel guides to American and foreign locales. Our books tell it like it is, often with an opinionated edge, and our experienced authors always give you all the information you need to have the trip of a lifetime. Write for your free catalog of all our titles.

**Catalog Department, Open Road Publishing
P.O. Box 284, Cold Spring Harbor, NY 11724**

Or you can contact us by e-mail at:
Jopenroad@aol.com

This third edition of the Bermuda Guide is dedicated to Lawrence Eliot Lamb, a great friend and an outstanding hôtelier.

The author wishes to thank the following people for their valued assistance in this project. Nicole Couture-Simard (Air Canada), David Allen (Minister of Tourism), David Dodwell (Shadow Minister of Tourism), Charles Webbe and Joy Sticca (Bda. Dept. of Tourism), Suzanne Chicoine (Lou Hammond & Associates), Anne Cousineau (Porter-Novelli Canada), Karen Bull (The Bermuda Collection), Laura Fairweather (Canadian Pacific Hotels), Sir John Swan (Former Premier of Bermuda), The Lamb Family (Pompano Beach), William Shoaf (Elbow Beach), Chris Baum (Sonesta Hotels), Perry Robinson (Elbow Beach), Michael & Susan Ternent (BerSalon), Richard Calderon (Elbow Beach), Mike Winfield (Cambridge Beaches), Trudy Mulder (Waterloo House), Neil Stephens (The Reefs), Alan Paris (Ariel Sands), Paul Mason (Bermuda Triangle Brewing), Donna Jenkins (Hamilton Princess), Abigail Outerbridge (Southampton Princess), David Penchon (Wheels), Joe Arnold (Wheels), Andrew Crisson, Delaey Robinson & Andrea Dismont (Aunt Nea's), and especially Gioacchino di Meglio (Little Venice Group).

3rd Edition

Cover photographs courtesy of Bermuda Government Tourism Board.
All prices, schedules, and details are subject to change, and we will not be held responsible for any such fluctuations, or other experiences, that travelers may encounter during their visit.

TABLE OF CONTENTS

SIDEBARS

1. INTRODUCTION

Close your eyes and imagine a beautiful island paradise with long stretches of pink sand beaches, pastel houses, great nightlife, and a climate that is never too hot or too cold. That paradise exists just a short airplane or boat ride away, and it's called Bermuda.

Once upon a time, this peaceful chain of islands was the favorite destination of jetset millionaires willing to pay any sum for the perfect stress-free vacation. Bermuda mastered the art of catering to demanding North Americans and Europeans, and supplying only the finest quality accommodations, cuisine, entertainment, and excursions. The warm, friendly locals became used to sun-worshiping foreigners, and tourism became a major factor in the local economy.

As the influx of tourists grew and grew, it became obvious that this fantastic vacation resort had to attract a wider range of visitors. Dozens of additional hotels and romantic inns in every price range sprouted up along the shoreline and in the rural countryside. Old fortresses and historic buildings were converted into museums and public parks. International investors created world class golf courses, beach clubs, and sporting facilities. Innovative Bermudians installed specialty boutiques, sea-based excursions, fine restaurants, and all sorts of adventurous activities. Now couples and families from all walks of life can experience the great beaches, attractions, and lodgings of Bermuda at affordable prices.

Be sure to mix in a little local culture by talking with locals, and asking them for their recommendations. As a Bermudian friend says: *"In this world there are tourists, and then there are travelers. A tourist leaves their vacation with a bag full of T-shirts and bumper stickers. A traveler leaves with a lifetime full of experiences."*

So travel to Bermuda with Open Road, and have the trip of a lifetime!

2. OVERVIEW

The lovely sub-tropical paradise of **Bermuda** is located in the Atlantic Ocean about 1040 kilometers (650 miles) east of the North Carolina coastline, and about 1238 kilometers (774 miles) southeast of New York City. Although often mistaken as part of the Caribbean, it is actually situated much further north. Once the exclusive playground for the rich and famous, these days Bermuda has worked hard to attract tourists of all ages and interests in all price ranges. Since it takes a mere two hours by plane, or only a day and a half by cruise ship to reach this beautiful nation from several major east coast cities, it has become a favored destination for North American visitors.

With its amazing collection of pink sand beaches, pastel colored cottages, world class seaside resorts, romantic bed and breakfast inns, superb restaurants, challenging golf courses, unique sporting facilities, exciting excursions, and typically British sensibilities, this fantastic chain of islands offers the perfect setting for an unforgettable vacation. Throughout the year, Bermuda is blessed with a tranquil climate, and an abundance of natural beauty.

From the moment you step off the ship or plane and walk off into the dramatic Bermuda landscape, you know you have arrived somewhere special. Almost all of the nearly 60,000 citizens here, from taxi drivers to shop keepers, seem to wear a big smile and are quite happy to tell you fantastic tales or point you towards almost unknown sights. If you're waiting at a bus stop, don't be surprised if a friendly stranger offers you a car ride into town. If you're asking a local's advice on a good restaurant for lunch, they may even invite you to their family seaside picnic. In general, Bermudians are some of the most friendly people I have ever met, and are quite used to sharing their paradise with others.

Things in Bermuda have changed drastically since the 16th century Age of Discovery when Spanish galleons on their way to the New World stayed clear of these so called Islands of the Devils. It was not until 1609 when the English vessel *Sea Venture* was shipwrecked here during a storm,

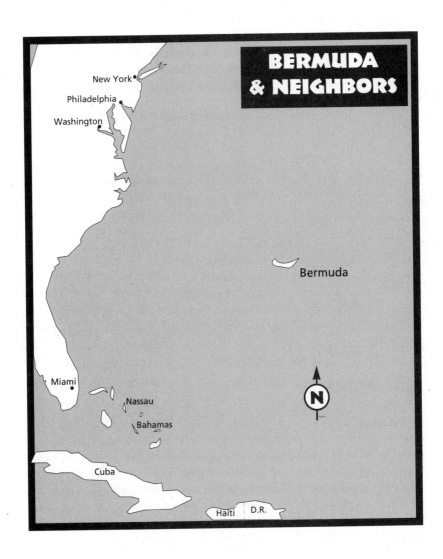

that Bermuda's amazing beauty and climate became known to the world. The adventurous spirit of these early settlers who persevered through countless hardships and an era of piracy on the high seas can still be felt in the presence of today's Bermudians. These rather polite but strong willed people have been able to retain their country's unique traditions, charm, and natural features while graciously welcoming visitors.

Now that over 600,000 tourists (mostly from America, Canada, and England) grace its shores each year, Bermuda has succeeded: tourism is the second major contributor to its rock solid economy. Since this nation has the second highest standard of living in the world, residents here live rather well, and don't have to pay for things like medical care and income tax.

Unemployment here is almost unheard of, crime is of minimal concern, and the family unit still plays an important role in society. Even though the country has seen an inevitable increase in the development of tourism facilities, it has been careful to preserve plenty of natural parks and public beaches for the benefit of residents, as well as visitors, to enjoy together. The majority of people here have a way of life that most of us can only dream about, and they work very hard to keep it that way.

While a fair amount of tourists come here for the sun and sea, there is always yet another impressive attraction to discover. As you will soon find out, getting to even the most remote corner of Bermuda will take less than an hour by public transportation or moped, and it is quite possible to see much of this nation in just the space of a one week vacation. I have summarized the highlights of Bermuda's parishes below to give you a basic idea of what each has to offer its visitors.

SANDYS PARISH

This is a quiet and tranquil area that is filled with historic sights, fine shopping possibilities, and adventurous sea faring excursions. Here you can spend at least one day touring a 19th century British naval base, learn about Bermuda's history at dramatic museums, and see local crafts being made by hand.

You can take an exciting submarine ride or snorkeling trip, go scuba diving, rent a Boston Whaler or a Sunfish, suntan in privacy on long sandy beaches, dine in English style pubs and popular seaside restaurants, hike along coastal nature paths, view old defensive forts, cross the world's smallest drawbridge, stay in a charming cottage colony, and shop till you drop – even on Sundays!

SOUTHAMPTON PARISH

In this large parish there is an abundance of things to see and do. In just one day you can play a round on a championship golf course, climb to the top of a beautiful lighthouse, suntan and socialize in the warm waters of Bermuda's most popular beaches, snorkel amidst schools of tropical fish, learn to scuba dive, walk along high bluffs and fortress walls, enjoy a refined afternoon tea, dine high atop the ocean on an open air terrace, enjoy a dinner show, and spend your nights in a room with an unforgettable view.

WARWICK PARISH

This part of Bermuda contains a good mixture of traditional residential neighborhoods, as well as more modern commercial zones. Warwick has some of the Bermuda's most magnificent secluded cove beaches, quaint historic churches, fine horseback riding, wild woodlands, great birdwatching, family fun activities, seagoing excursions, and accommodations in all price ranges.

PAGET PARISH

Paget is a wonderfully beautiful area in the heart of Bermuda. Its north coast is dotted by small harbors lined with pretty pastel colored mansions and cottages, and its south coast lined with even more fine beaches. This is one of the best places to visit for fantastic gardens, art galleries, sports facilities, boat rentals, cute boutiques, shipwreck diving and snorkeling cruises, action packed nightlife and entertainment, some of the islands' best restaurants, and an endless supply of hotels, inns, and apartments.

PEMBROKE PARISH

As home to the capital city of Hamilton, Pembroke parish is the heart of Bermuda. You can easily spend several days in this parish just exploring both its cosmopolitan and rural sights. Here you can take a carriage ride past the pastel colored storefronts, hop on a glass bottom boat ride, shop for great bargains on imported goods, view internationally renowned artwork, dance in the streets during festivals, visit museums, watch Parliamentary proceedings, witness traditional skirling ceremonies, head to the seaside nature reserves, indulge in participant and spectator sports, enjoy exotic restaurants, and party all night long.

DEVONSHIRE PARISH

Now you are in a delightfully tranquil area of the country. Here you won't find many of the same distractions and development which is common elsewhere. This is the perfect place to go and enjoy rural Bermuda and its lush terrain. Besides wonderful walking trails, here your kids can learn English style horseback riding, play an inexpensive round of golf, hit the squash courts, bird watch in an Audubon sanctuary, picnic in peaceful seaside parks, and tour the windswept hamlets of the north coast.

SMITH'S PARISH

This parish has a vast array of unusual geological wonders, natural beauty, and a few quiet beaches. You can wander through an old pirate haven, witness strange checkerboard rock formations, see inscriptions left by early European explorers, tour an opulent 18th century mansion, take an exciting helmet dive to the bottom of the sea, walk cliffside trails at water's edge, and stumble upon unusual creatures in nature reserves.

HAMILTON PARISH

In this part of Bermuda there are dozens of memorable sights and attractions, many of which are within easy walking distance of each other. There is a wonderful aquarium, an impressive zoo, several museums, a perfume factory, a glass blowing workshop and studio, amazing caves with stalactites and stalagmites, fun places to stop for anything from a milk shake to a rum swizzle, excellent world class resorts and golf courses, tons of watersports activities including jet skiing and scuba diving, fine beachfront fishing areas, and perhaps the finest restaurant in all of Bermuda.

ST. GEORGE'S PARISH

This easternmost part of Bermuda was where this nation was first settled. Some of the many great things to see in both the old city of St. George and its surroundings include fine examples of early Bermudan architecture, boutique-laden historic lanes, magnificent beaches, posh residential areas, hilltop defensive batteries, museums depicting life in the old days, fine art galleries, beautiful seaside parks, a wonderful old lighthouse, a state of the art biological research facility, a couple of the most authentic Bermudan restaurants, challenging golf courses, and great pubs and taverns.

3. SUGGESTED ITINERARIES

Since most people unfortunately do not have the time to see everything here during their vacation, I have selected a few easy-to-follow itineraries to help you plan your stay. These are only suggestions, and careful reading of this book will help you to customize your own schedule of activities and relaxation.

THE 3 DAY GETAWAY

Day 1

Arrive by plane as early as possible.
Take a taxi to your hotel.
Check into your hotel relax for an hour or so.
Grab a beach towel and head over to Horseshoe Bay Beach.
Enjoy a late al fresco snack at the beach house.
Return to your hotel to relax and change.
Call a restaurant in Hamilton for a reservation.
Head into Hamilton for great dinner.
Visit one of the local pubs in Front Street.
Go back to your hotel and rest up for tomorrow

Day 2

Enjoy an early breakfast at your hotel.
Grab a beach towel and head over to Tobacco Bay Beach.
Head into St. George for shopping, sightseeing, and a pub lunch.
Purchase your in-bond duty free liquor products.
Return to your hotel to relax and change.
Call to reserve dinner at one of the al fresco beachview restaurants.
Go back to your hotel and rest up for tomorrow.

Day 3

Head into Hamilton as early as possible.
Enjoy an early breakfast in Hamilton.

Walk to the shops and attractions in Hamilton.
Return to your hotel.
Pack and take a taxi back to the airport.

THE CRUISE SHIP PASSENGER'S 5 DAY TOUR
Day 1

Arrive at your scheduled port of call in Bermuda.
Grab a beach towel and Head over to Elbow Beach.
Enjoy a light meal at the beach snack bar.
Get some more sun at the beach.
Return to your ship relax, change, and enjoy dinner.
Depart the ship and head to the nearest club.
Party until you have had enough.
Return to your ship to rest up for tomorrow.

Day 2

Enjoy an early breakfast on the ship.
Depart the ship and head into Hamilton for sightseeing.
Call an excursion company and make a reservation for tomorrow.
Enjoy a pub lunch in Hamilton.
Tour the museums, art galleries, and historic buildings in Hamilton.
Enjoy a light dinner with a strong coffee in Hamilton.
Party in one of Hamilton's clubs.
Return to your ship to relax, change, and enjoy the midnight buffet.
Rest up for tomorrow.

Day 3

Enjoy breakfast on the ship.
Head out for the morning departure of an exciting excursion.
Return to your ship to relax and change.
Enjoy a lunch on the ship.
Call to reserve an optional round of golf tomorrow.
Head out for St. George for shopping and sightseeing.
Make your duty free purchases today!
Enjoy a nice afternoon swim at Tobacco Bay Beach.
Head back into St. George for a light meal.
Hang out and play pool or darts in a local St. George pub or tavern.
Return to your ship to relax, change, and enjoy the midnight buffet.
Get some rest for tomorrow.

Day 4

Enjoy breakfast on the ship.
Head out to Hamilton parish to sightsee and shop.

Visit the perfumery, glass blowing studio, and caves.
Enjoy a lunch at the Swizzle Inn.
Play an optional round of Golf.
Return to your ship to relax, change, and enjoy dinner.
See the show on the ship.
Party into the night at the ship's disco or lounge.

Day 5

Enjoy breakfast on the ship.
Grab a towel and head for the nearest beach for a last swim
Return to the ship for a late lunch.
Enjoy your last views of Bermuda while cruising away.

THE 7 DAY BERMUDA VACATION
Day 1

Arrive by plane as early as possible.
Take a taxi to your hotel.
Check into your hotel and relax.
Grab a beach towel and head over to Horseshoe Bay Beach.
Enjoy a late al fresco snack at the beach house.
Return to your hotel to relax and change.
Call a recommended nearby restaurant for a reservation.
Head out for great dinner.
Go back to your hotel and rest up for tomorrow

Day 2

Enjoy an early breakfast at your hotel.
Grab a beach towel and some sneakers and head to the Dockyard.
Enjoy the museums, crafts displays, shops, and sights.
Enjoy a fine pub lunch at the Dockyard.
Head over to Somerset Long Bay beach for a swim.
Change back into casual clothing and head to Somerset Village.
Enjoy a casual dinner in Somerset Village.
Go back to your hotel and rest up for tomorrow

Day 3

Head into Hamilton as early as possible.
Enjoy an early breakfast in Hamilton.
Walk to the shops in Hamilton.
Call an excursion company and make a reservation for tomorrow.
Enjoy an exotic or traditional lunch in Hamilton.
Call a restaurant in Hamilton for a dinner reservation.
Tour the museums, art galleries, and historic buildings in Hamilton.

Enjoy a great dinner in Hamilton.
Visit one of the local pubs in Front Street.
Go back to your hotel and rest up for tomorrow

Day 4

Enjoy an early breakfast at your hotel.
Grab a beach towel and head over to Elbow Beach.
Enjoy a light meal at the beach snack bar.
Call to reserve dinner at one of the al fresco beachview restaurants.
Head out for the afternoon departure of an exciting excursion.
Return to your hotel to relax and change.
Go back to your hotel and rest up for tomorrow.

Day 5

Head into St. George as early as possible.
Enjoy an early breakfast in St. George.
Walk around St. George for shopping and sightseeing.
Make your duty free purchases today!
Call to reserve an optional round of golf for tomorrow.
Enjoy a nice afternoon swim at Tobacco Bay Beach.
Head back into St. George for a great dinner.
Hang out and play pool or darts in a local St. George pub or tavern.
Go back to your hotel and rest up for tomorrow.

Day 6

Enjoy an early breakfast at your hotel.
Head out to Hamilton parish to sightsee and shop.
Visit the perfumery, glass blowing studio, and caves.
Enjoy a lunch at the Swizzle Inn.
Play an optional round of Golf.
Head over to tour the Bermuda Botanical Gardens.
Call a restaurant in Hamilton for a reservation.
Enjoy a great dinner in Hamilton.
Party in one of Hamilton's clubs.
Go back to your hotel and rest up for tomorrow.

Day 7

Head into Hamilton as early as possible.
Enjoy an early breakfast in Hamilton.
Walk to the shops and attractions in Hamilton.
Return to your hotel.
Pack and take a taxi back to the airport.

4. LAND & PEOPLE

LAND

Bermuda is located in the Atlantic Ocean about 970 kilometers (600 miles) due east of Cape Hatteras, North Carolina at 32 degrees latitude and 64 degrees longitude. The country is made up of a collection of over 200 limestone-based islands and islets, many of which remain uninhabited, that were created by a prehistoric volcanic eruption.

Its single largest landmass is known as **Great Bermuda Island**, which is where you will find the capital city of **Hamilton**. Several of its adjacent islands have been connected together with a series of bridges and some landfill to create the archipelago which most people refer to as Bermuda. Together, this fish-hook shaped chain of connected islands forms a land area of 52 square kilometers (20.6 square miles) and extends for some 35.4 kilometers (22 miles) in length, and has a maximum width of 3.3 kilometers (2 miles). This means that no matter where you stand in this nation, you are never far from the seashore.

The most famous feature of Bermuda is its wonderful pristine beaches. The sand here has a delightful pink hue, due to the unusual composition of calcium carbonate remains of marine invertebrates and red *Foraminifera* shell particles washed up from the extensive reefs that surround most of the islands. Many of these beaches have sheltered coves, and some are extremely isolated.

Among the most notable visitors to the shallow waters are hundreds of small colorful sub-tropical fish species that often will come right up to you. One of the least desired visitors to the seafront are the blue colored Portuguese man o' war that wash up between March and July and can give you one hell of a sting with its long tentacles. About half an hour's boat ride from Bermuda are huge fishing banks, reefs, and pelagic fisheries which host an abundant amount of jacks, marlin, tuna, shark, wahoo, snapper, grouper, mackerel, barracuda, parrotfish, grunt, triggerfish, chub, porgy, blue marlin, and all sorts of species. For scuba divers, snorkelers, and fishermen, these areas are a source of endless adventure.

Much of Bermuda's coastline features high bluffs, bizarre geological formations, haunting caves, and limestone boulders. Here you can find an array of land crabs, lizards, and seabirds such as the famous Longtail which visits here between March and October.

The interior lands of Bermuda range from flat open spaces, to hilly areas which can reach altitudes of up to 80 meters (261 feet) above sea level. Although agricultural and commercial development have altered some of the wild lands, there are still several marsh areas, brackish ponds, subterranean caves, and nature preserves. The landscape once was dominated by natural forests – the famed Bermudian Cedar – but these hearty trees were all but completely destroyed by a blight in the early part of this century.

Nowadays you will find hundreds of different imported and indigenous plants, flowers and trees which have prospered in the sub-tropical climate here. In addition to such common flora as hibiscus, oleander, bay grape, yucca, and poinsettia, you will also come across paw-paw, loquat, easter lily, screw pine, cassava, banana, and natal plum.

FAUNA

Some of the most common birds and amphibians you'll find in Bermuda include: **cahows, kiskadees, cardinals, eastern bluebirds, giant toads,** *and the wonderful little* **tree frogs** *which can be heard singing on any given night between April and November. There are also an assortment of small insects, but their numbers are fairly limited.*

PEOPLE

Bermudians are among the nicest people you can ever imagine. Since its founding by the English crew and passengers of the shipwrecked *Sea Venture* in 1609, Bermuda has maintained a strong link with all things British. Most people here tend to be on the conservative side and speak with a mixture of American and English accents. They tend to address strangers in a friendly but formal tone, and take pride in their community.

As with any other country, the richer and more connected families do tend to stick together and become members of private yacht clubs and exclusive golf courses. There is an elite class here, although they are hard to identify in the crowd. Since cars and gasoline are rather expensive, even the richest Bermudians can be seen driving compact Japanese cars socializing with people from all classes. Bermudians are not at all snobby, and tend to know not only their neighbors, but almost all of the 60,000 other residents of these islands.

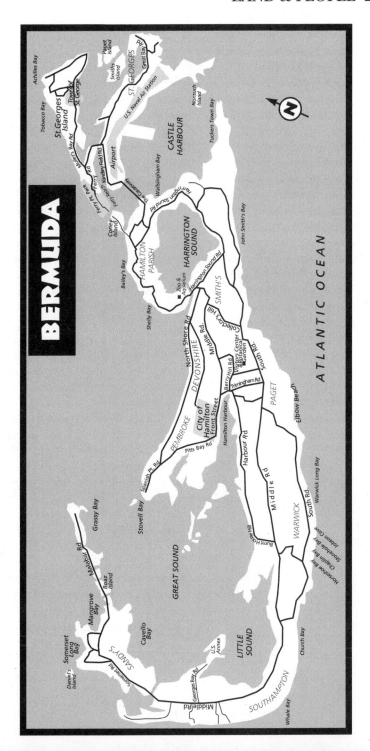

The most popular houses of worship are the Anglican Churches (Church of England) although immigrants and slaves brought with them an assortment of other faiths. As black slaves became part of the work force here in the 17th through early 19th centuries, they brought with them several religions and sects including the popular African Methodist Episcopal Church. When the Portuguese farmers came here from the Azores in the 19th century, they brought with them Roman Catholicism. There are also growing Jewish, Muslim, Seventh Day Adventist, Presbyterian, and Baptist communities.

Although racial harmony is easily witnessed in the younger generations of Bermudians, the older and more affluent white population has often been accused of minor degrees of racism. I have seen a few cases of this myself, but overall things are relatively harmonious. Since education is based on American and British systems, black Bermudians have been taught little about their roots and heritage, leading to a new interest in finding their identity.

The Portuguese population sticks rather closely together, and continue to be somewhat distrusted by many Bermudians, even though they have never done anything to deserve it. Currently, the population of Bermuda is about 61% black and 39% white. The average age of the 60,000 citizens is about 34 years old, and most people here have achieved at least a high school education. Although there is a fine campus at the Bermuda College, many Bermudians come to the United States and Canada for university education.

Bermuda enjoys one of the highest standards of living in the world. There is no poverty, unemployment, illiteracy, major crime, or serious public health issues. With the relocation of the reinsurance industry from London to Bermuda in the 1980's, billions more dollars poured into the economy. Due to its favorable tax laws, Bermuda has also become a magnet for American companies looking for tax exempt status. Anybody who is educated and needs a job can easily find with one of these businesses, the huge tourism industry, or an offshoot service related field. However, an onslaught of crack cocaine is beginning to take its toll on some residents.

One of the most controversial discussions these days centers around the separation of Bermuda from England and the Commonwealth. While many Bermudians feel that they deserve total independence, the old guard still opposes this transition in fear of losing their privileged trade links.

5. A SHORT HISTORY

THE ISLANDS OF DEVILS

In the days of the Spanish and Portuguese **Age of Discovery** – in the early 1500's – it was not uncommon for Iberian sailing vessels to be sent searching for yet another route to reach the reputed gold and spice riches of the New World.

On one such voyage in 1503, **Juan de Bermudez**, captain of the Spanish vessel *La Garza*, was the first to discover this small chain of islands now has known as Bermuda. Since it first made it on to the maps in 1511, his name has ever since been identified with what is now called Bermuda. At that time the only residents of these islands were wild birds and sea creatures.

Throughout the early and middle 16th century, other Spanish and Portuguese ships were temporarily stranded on the hidden reefs that line much of the Bermuda Islands. Shipwrecked sailors from these vessels would venture ashore, only to be scared to their wits by the noises they heard after nightfall, actually the calls of wild birds, which at that time were thought of as the sounds of the Devil and his evil spirits.

For many decades, Bermuda was known as **The Islands of Devils**. Almost no relics exist from these early visits, except for the so-called **Spanish Rock** on Bermuda's south shore where the initials R.P., a cross, and the date 1543 have been engraved by visiting Portuguese sailors. Word quickly spread back to Europe that these evil, haunted, and treacherous islands should be avoided at all costs. After **Henry Maye** was stranded here for a brief period in 1593, he returned safely to England and described what he saw to all who would listen.

THE BRITISH SETTLEMENT

In 1609, the new British colony in Jamestown, Virginia was struggling to survive with few supplies and food remaining to support its early settlers. The London based **Virginia Company** had then decided to help secure the future of this dwindling colony by sending supplies and additional settlers aboard a fleet of nine ships from Plymouth, England on May 15, 1609 under the direction of **Admiral Sir George Somers**. It was literally smooth sailing until the fleet encountered a sudden tempest of high seas and strong winds which struck without warning. During the storm, the 300 ton flagship known as the *Sea Venture* became separated from the rest of the pack.

Over the course of the next few days, the *Sea Venture* developed a growing leak in its hull as it was carried far to the south. The strong-willed crew spent hour upon hour pumping water from the ship's hold, which had been filled to the depth of three meters (nine feet) with sea water. As Sir George sat upon the half deck and pondered how long it would take for the vessel to sink, he spotted a small island nearby, and cried out "Land!" He then pointed the sinking wooden ship towards the coast of this nearby island, and unexpectedly ran it aground between two huge rocks not far from the shore. The wind almost immediately began to calm down, and the 150 or so men, women, and children of the ill-fated *Sea Venture* were placed along with their possessions and ship's provisions into the skiffs, and sent forward to land at what is now the coast of **St. George's**. The only thing they lost was the ship itself, and at this point Sir George knew for certain that they had landed upon the beaches of the dreaded Islands of the Devil.

Upon arrival on this warm and tranquil island, the accidental settlers found a paradise laden with wild pigs, birds, and fish which were so tame that they could be easily captured and fed upon. With the help of nearby palmetto leaves and cedar trees, several cabins were built, and fresh water was brought up from a hole dug into the ground. It has been said that William Shakespeare had written *The Tempest* based on reports of this incident, although some historians disagree.

A small makeshift settlement was soon created, and its inhabitants were easily overcome with an air of lazy relaxation during which time a couple got married, a couple of children were born, and unfortunately one sailor was killed. The officers almost had to force discussion on how the stranded yet carefree settlers could safely reach their original destination of Jamestown. A group of 14 men soon set sail on a small hand made boat, hoping to soon return with a rescue ship, but were never seen or heard from again.

After about nine more months, a pair of larger cedar ships called *Deliverance* and *Patience* were built, and the displaced settlers soon sailed away to finally reach Jamestown, which was in desperate need of the provisions brought from Bermuda. Only two people, **Christopher Carter** and **Robert Walters**, had decided of their own free will to stay here and settle in. Sir George Somers promised that he would soon return to bring them supplies. When he did come back to Bermuda about a month or so later with another ship and crew, he found the two alive and well. As he began to help in the creation of a plantation, he became gravely ill and died here on November 9, 1610. His heart and entrails were buried under a simple cross in what is now the town of **St. George**. The rest of his body was secretly stowed aboard his ship which was then sent to England.

THE SETTLEMENT OF BERMUDA

Upon returning to England, Sir George Somers' body was appropriately buried near Dover, while the ship's crew told enchanting stories of this beautiful semi-tropical island paradise. It was not long before the top officers of the Virginia Company decided that Bermuda could easily become a profitable new colony to exploit, and provide an excellent trans-Atlantic rest station for its ships heading towards the Americas.

After obtaining a grant for Bermuda from King James I, the Virginia Company sent a group of some 60 volunteers (who were probably expecting to get rich quick) to set sail aboard a small ship called the *Plough*. They appointed the ship's master carpenter, **Richard Moore**, as their trusted commander and first Governor of this new settlement, and finally landed in St. George's harbor in 1612.

During the last two years of isolation, Christopher Carter had become rather upset and distrustful of the other two men stuck on the island with him. Although they were successful in planting crops such as corn, building sturdy huts, and finding an immensely valuable 45 pound chunk of ambergris, it seems that they had begun to fight each other and were not exactly the best of friends. As soon as the *Plough* became visible to these three poor souls, they seemed to forget about their personal differences, and anxiously went over to greet their fellow countrymen, still wearing what remained of their tattered clothing.

Soon after his arrival, Governor Moore took Christopher Carter aside and inquired about what fortunes they may have discovered during their two years here. Although a plan had already been concocted to smuggle the rare ambergris aboard the ship and sell it upon arrival in England, Carter broke down and told the Governor the truth. The plotters were briefly imprisoned and sent back to England (except for Carter who was rewarded with his own island, where the Carter House now stands).

As the new settlers began to plant additional crops like tobacco and grains, they decided that it would also be prudent to build a defensive fortresses to repel any Spanish incursions. Governor Richard Moore decided to rule Bermuda from near his home on Smith's Island, although the lack of fresh water eventually brought them all back to St. George.

One of the most amusing stories about the early settlers is the so-called **Skirmish of 1614**. After passing Spanish galleons loaded with treasures from the New World noticed that their long-time foes, the British, had colonized Bermuda, they wanted to attack it. Governor Moore had earlier ordered the construction of a fortress near St. George at nearby **Castle Island**, but the only armament available was a cannon with just three cannon balls.

Upon the sighting of two Spanish vessels, the settlers fired two shots at the galleons (two-thirds of their total defensive power) and they promptly retreated. The Spaniards would never return again, fearing what they mistakenly assumed was the massive firepower and armory of the Bermudians. This was one of the great bluffs of all time. When the ship carrying the imprisoned ambergris smugglers, as well as the prized ambergris itself, returned to Britain, some serious deal making began.

THE SETTLEMENT GROWS

A powerful group of investors from London, called the **Bermuda Company**, bought the rights to Bermuda for about 2000 pounds sterling by 1615. Dreaming of riches from pearls and ambergris, the company's principal investors sent more and more ships full of hundreds of additional settlers, as **Daniel Tucker** became the next Governor. Soon after, Bermuda's first coins (known as **Hog Money**) were stamped with a wild hog on one side, and the likeness of the *Sea Venture* on the other, to commemorate the original shipwrecked settlers and the hogs which they found upon arrival.

By about 1617, the Bermuda Company ordered the islands west of what is now St. George's to be divided into a series of eight tribes (now known as parishes) with each tribe being named after one of the company's principal officers. Each tribe would have 50 shares, consisting of 25 acres each, and a dividing road would soon span each tribe's border. Later on that year, a ship called the *Edwin* returns from the West Indies, bringing with it a Negro (the first on Bermuda) and an Indian who were to become the islands' first two slaves.

Although the Spanish never returned to directly attack Bermuda, its galleons still sailed in the general vicinity. Since pirates were a common threat to any vessel in open seas, many English and European boats were savagely attacked. Now the English government did not hesitate to make it worth the while of Bermudians to plunder the riches of their enemies. Profiteering (officially sanctioned and otherwise) and piracy became an important part of life of some of the more adventurous early settlers.

It even became an important topic of the Governor's speech during the settlement's first ever House of Assembly meeting at **St. Peter's Church** in St. George's in 1620. As then **Governor Butler** rose to speak at the meeting, he even added the following statement which reflects rather well the general mood of the era:

"You hear by this barke ... of the rumors and likelihood of great wars in Christiandom. If it should fall out that any saudine breach happen between England and Spain, (and who knows how soon this may be), there is not any place that it will break out sooner than here. The pirates, likewise, have a longing eye for these islands .... let us, therefore, so provide for ourselves, that come an enemy ... we may be able to give hime a brave welcome." Additional forts were soon added to further protect Bermuda's coastline.

It is also about this time that the typical maze-like limestone Bermudian roofs became to appear. It became common for local settlers to hut large blocks of limestone into whatever shape was desired, and leave them to harden in the heat. A lime-based whitewash was also used on these blocks, thus creating a waterproof building material. Due to the scarcity of fresh water to supply the ever growing residents, a system was devised to construct a maze like water trap atop each building. The trap then collected rainfall which would in turn fill a cistern in the structure's lower floor, thus providing a constant supply of drinking water for each house. Since water is still a somewhat limited commodity, the roofs are still in use on even the newest homes built in present-day Bermuda.

While Bermuda was enjoying a reasonable level of prosperity, emerging as a whale hunting and boat building center by about 1650, trouble was lurking just around the corner. Back home in England, **Oliver Cromwell** and the Puritans had just beheaded **King Charles I**, and took over the English government. This did not sit very well with Bermudians who were fiercely loyal to the crown, and supported **Charles II** as their new King.

The Puritans who were, until that point, living in harmony with their fellow Bermudians, felt discriminated against. They were eventually to leave these islands with former **Governor William Sayles** to form the new settlement of **Eleuthera** in what is now the **Bahamas**. Under the Cromwellian English Parliament Bermuda suffered from a trade embargo with Britain. During this era of great confusion and divided loyalties in the British Isles, Cromwell sent Scottish and Irish opposition members to Bermuda as slaves and indentured servants. In 1660, Charles II would finally persevere and be crowned as the next King of England, and things got back to near normal as the embargo ceased.

At about this time, an immense fear of witchcraft embroiled much of Bermuda in horrid witch trials for over 40 years. A favorite test was to dump suspected witches into the sea to find out if they would sink or float. If they floated, they were burned or hanged; if they sunk, they would often drown before rescue attempts were made.

THE COLONY OF BERMUDA

After years of disastrous economic policy and mismanagement, in 1684 England successfully sued the Bermuda Company and canceled its rights to Bermuda. The English government now steps in and officially creates the new self-governing Crown colony of Bermuda.

During this period, Bermudian merchants and seafarers had been raking in fortunes by sailing to **Turk's Island** (about 1450 kilometers or 900 miles south of Bermuda) to create huge salt ponds. Massive ships were constructed from local cedar wood, and long range trade was undertaken, with great success, with the Americas and the West Indies. The unusually designed and rigged sloops which were produced here became known throughout the world as the finest made anywhere, and boat building became an even greater part of the local economy. Through a series of new Governors, both good and bad, Bermuda continued to grow.

AMERICA'S WARS & THEIR IMPACT ON BERMUDA

During the 18th century, Bermuda had close ties with the American colonies. For years these islands had found a beneficial supplier for the supplies which were all but essential for their survival. Many Bermudians had close friends, associates, and relatives now living in Virginia and the South.

When the **American Revolution** began, some Bermudians were split between their loyalties to the Crown and their need to continue trading with the revolting colonies. The Philadelphia-based **Continental Congress**, looking for support for their actions, declared an embargo on all English colonies who continued to be loyal to the Crown. The thought of being deprived of their essential supplies began to sink into the minds of some Bermudians with strong contacts to America.

An attempt was made by a few prominent Bermudians to go to the Continental Congress and plead for a lifting of the embargo. Although the offer was rejected, soon after a letter from **George Washington** arrived with a counteroffer. It essentially stated that the Americans were in desperate need of gunpowder to fight the English. If the highly prized, and poorly guarded stockpile of gunpowder in St. George could somehow be diverted to America, the embargo would not be enforced. Without any permission from the government, a band of men including members of the well-known Tucker family, broke into the armory and stole several dozen kegs of gunpowder, and loaded it onto nearby ships headed for Boston. Although the so called **Gunpowder Plot** infuriated the Governor and most other politicians, the result was that Bermuda was able to continue receiving supplies from America.

In the 1780's, the British Royal Naval Engineers begin to develop a large harbor in the middle of Bermuda, building a series of defensive forts to secure the area, and created what is now **Hamilton**. Soon after, the government soon was relocated from St. George to Hamilton.

In 1809, the Royal Engineers began their next massive project, the construction of the heavily defended **Royal Naval Dockyard** in **Sandys**. Through the toil of imported slaves (slavery continued until 1834) as well as thousands of English convicts that were transfered here, the new regional headquarters of the Royal Navy fleet and administration came to Bermuda. It was during the **War of 1812** that the British fleet departed Bermuda and successfully burned Washington D.C. to the ground.

With so many Bermudians having relatives and trading partners in the southern American states, most Bermudians favored the the Confederacy during the **Civil War**. Hundreds of local sea venturers made huge profits by sailing into Confederate ports, running the blockade that was part of an attempt of the Union's navy to enforce an embargo on the south. There were even agents of the rebel army like **Major Norman Walker** who were stationed in St. George to assist in the south's procurement of supplies and guns in exchange for cotton that would then be shipped to England at a large profit to the Bermudian-based blockade runners.

Once the Union finally won the war, another source for additional income was needed to revive the Bermudian economy. At this point, hundreds of Portuguese farm hands were brought in from the **Azores** to help plant and harvest vegetables, especially the famed Bermuda onions.

THE SEEDS OF TOURISM DEVELOPMENT

It all started innocently enough back in 1883, when **Princess Louise of England** (who was married to the Governor General of Canada) decided to come to Bermuda for a few months to escape the cold. After the international press printed stories about how wonderful she thought this nation was, sophisticated English and North American travelers started to develop an interest in taking their winter vacations here.

In 1884, the opulent **Princess Hotel** opened to receive this new influx of visitors. Many of these early tourists arrived via the *Orinoca* steamship from New York. With the addition of tennis, and then golf, the island began to attract huge numbers of foreigners throughout the year. Since prohibition was at its height in America during the 1920's, even more Americans came here to drink and enjoy the warm sunshine and pink sand beaches. Sensing a potential landmine, the English steamship company of **Furness-Withy** decided to build a huge hotel in England, and then have it shipped piece by piece to Bermuda as a stately resort and golf club for the increasing number of high-end British and American tourists. The resulting structure, now known as the **Castle Harbour Resort**, was completed in 1931. The first scheduled air service to Bermuda from New York landed here in 1937. It all snowballed into what has become a major tourism industry, which now attracts over 550,000 people each year.

Some of the most unusual visitors to Bermuda were the 1200 British and allied intelligence officers who stalked the basement corridors of the Princess Hotel during World War II. They played an important role in the defeat of the Nazis, as they intercepted countless secret messages en route to German spies. They even went as far as to distract air mail pilots going from Europe to America, and confiscate suspicious letters which were then opened, inspected, decoded, resealed, and sent back on the plane before its departure.

It was during this time that the U.S. Navy was given a 99 year lease by Winston Churchill to construct a military base on three islands in St. George's that were filled in and connected together to create the **U.S. Naval Air Station** on what is now **St. David's Island**. Although the British military closed its bases here in 1957, the American bases are still active.

RECENT EVENTS

As life continued to improve for Bermudians in the postwar era, there were still dramatic occurrences that shaped the future of this tiny country. Social changes begin to take place starting with the right to vote for women land owners in 1944, racial integration of public places in 1959, the right to vote for all citizens in 1963, racial integration of public schools in 1971, and the 1971 election of Bermuda's first black leader, **Edward Richards**. In 1973, **Governor Richard Sharples** and his aide were assassinated while walking on the grounds of Government House by a militant revolutionary, later tried and hung.

These days, things are quiet and harmonious in Bermuda. It is a rather stable country trying to decide if they will separate from the Commonwealth and grappling with other regional issues. It has grown to become a country with one of the highest standards of living in the world, with no personal income tax, free education, health insurance coverage, and plenty of foreign tax sheltered companies.

6. PLANNING YOUR TRIP

BEFORE YOU GO

One of the first things that I suggest you do before even planning your vacation to Bermuda is to give a call to the nearest **Bermuda Department of Tourism Office**. This tiny country spends a fortune on producing some of the finest and most informative brochures and booklets about the services and facilities available in Bermuda for tourists and sports enthusiasts.

The polite hard working people who answer the phone at the tourist department's offices, many of whom are Bermudian by birth, will be more than glad to send you a free packet of updated information and maps. You can expect to receive a few booklets such as *Where to Stay*, *What to Do*, *Sports and Sightseeing*, *Golf Guide*, and *Hotel and Guesthouse Rates*. If you have specific questions on another subject, they will answer you over the phone in many cases.

BERMUDA TOURISM OFFICES IN NORTH AMERICA

- *310 Madison Avenue, Suite 201, New York City, NY 10017. Tel. 212/818-9800; 800/223-6106*
- *44 School Street, Suite 1010, Boston, MA 02108. Tel. 617/742-0405*
- *245 Peachtree Center Ave NE, Suite 803, Altanta, GA 30303. Tel. 404/524-1541*
- *150 N. Wacker Drive, Suite 1070, Chicago, IL 60606. Tel. 312/782-5486*
- *Tetley/Moyer & Associates, 3151 Cahuemga Blvd. West, Suite 111, Los Angeles, CA 90010. Tel. 213/436-0744; 800/421-0000*
- *1200 Bay Street, Suite 1004, Toronto, Ont. M5R 2A5 . Tel. 416/923-9600; 800/387-1304*

All prices in this book are in US dollars unless otherwise noted.

WHEN TO VISIT BERMUDA

Bermuda has two different seasons, both enjoyable – High Season and Low Season. Both are described below:

High Season

The high season is typically **April through October**. It is the warmest, most expensive, and busiest time of year to stay in this beautiful country. Although the summer is fantastic in Bermuda, it does have both its advantages and drawbacks. During the day you can usually be more than comfortable with Bermuda shorts, sun dresses, polos, T-shirts, and perhaps a light water-repellant jacket in the evenings.

The beaches are full, the seawater is warm, everything is open, restaurants can have long lines, the bars and nightclubs are packed to capacity, and the hotels and inns charge their highest rates. Some other holiday time periods such as Christmas and Thanksgiving time may also be considered high season.

While July and August can become somewhat hot for many people, September and October can bring occasional tropical storms and the odd hurricane. In general, high season is when Bermuda really comes to life.

Low Season

The low season usually is thought of as **November through March** and is when the nation is peaceful, the temperature is a bit cooler, you won't have to wait on long lines for restaurants, and bargains can be found everywhere. This time of year you can look forward to spring-like weather during the days, and chilly but refreshing winds in the evenings.

The beaches are empty, the sea is a bit too cold to swim in, most hotels charge a fraction of their full rates, almost 50 restaurants slash their prices for a special dine around program, and a few tourist related businesses (such as a couple of hotels, restaurants, and most of the sea going excursions) close down. Now you may find some days where shorts are enough, or other days when you should consider wearing long pants, warm socks, a comfortable long or short sleeve shirt, and have a medium-weight water-repellant jacket handy.

This is still the perfect time of year for golf, tennis, hiking, museum, culture, and nature enthusiasts. It can also be rather enjoyable for those visitors who don't mind leaving without a guaranteed sunburn. There are also many special activities which are offered only during this time of year such as free guided tours, social events, and open houses to private estates and their formal gardens. This is my favorite time to visit Bermuda, and I have been rather surprised at how warm the weather can actually be.

AVERAGE WEATHER CONDITIONS

	High Air Temp.	Low Air Temp.	Rainfall
January	67.8 F/19.9 C	58.8 F/14.9 C	5.85"
February	67.4 F/19.7 C	58.0 F/14.4 C	5.50"
March	68.3 F/20.2 C	59.2 F/15.1 C	4.55"
April	69.8 F/21.0 C	60.2 F/15.6 C	3.82"
May	74.7 F/23.7 C	65.9 F/18.8 C	3.19"
June	79.2 F/26.2 C	71.6 F/22.2 C	5.15"
July	83.9 F/28.8 C	74.6 F/23.7 C	4.75"
August	85.0 F/29.5 C	75.8 F/24.3 C	5.12"
September	83.1 F/28.4 C	74.0 F/23.3 C	5.76"
October	79.2 F/26.2 C	70.8 F/21.6 C	5.91"
November	74.1 F/23.4 C	66.3 F/19.1 C	4.23"
December	70.1 F/21.1 C	61.5 F/16.4 C	4.98"

The 68 Degree Temperature Guarantee

The Bermuda Department of Tourism in conjunction with many of the islands' hotels, inns, retail stores, museums, attractions, and the public transportation board, has come up with a great way to promote more tourism in the low season. Valid between January and March, this new program, known as the **Temperature Guarantee**, offers a 10% refund on accommodations at participating properties if the temperature fails to reach 68 degrees F at any day during your stay here.

Also included would be a **free unlimited bus and ferry pass** for the next day, **retail store discounts**, and best of all would be the **free admission** passport to the Bermuda Aquarium, Museum and Zoo, the Bermuda National Gallery, Crystal Caves, Bermuda National Trust properties, the Maritime Museum, Fort St. Catherine, the Bermuda Journey show, and the *Deliverance II*.

WHAT TO PACK

Besides the appropriate clothing, you should bring several items which you may normally take for granted. Almost anything you need can be purchased in Bermuda, but at a premium.

Consider bringing along personal hygiene items, a sweater for winter nights, a rainproof umbrella and jacket, a few good books, comfortable walking shoes, sneakers, appropriate golf or tennis shoes, swimming suits, beach towels, suntan lotion, a normal or video camera and perhaps a disposable underwater camera. You might also want to bring along an alarm clock, a travel iron, batteries, a walkman, plenty of film, sports equipment such as golf clubs and tennis balls and racquets, snorkeling gear, a copy of any necessary prescriptions, an extra pair of contact lenses or glasses, sunglasses with UV coating, a money pouch, a waterproof key necklace, travelers checks, your ATM bank card, cigarettes (if you smoke, they are $4.50 a pack here), and if you are staying in an apartment you should bring allowable packaged and sealed food supplies.

Since the electric current is the same as in North America, adapters and converters will be unnecessary.

WHAT TO WEAR IN BERMUDA

This really depends on when you are going, and what you expect to do while you're here. To begin with, you should remember that Bermuda is a fairly conservative nation. Many hotels and restaurants have dress codes which have been somewhat relaxed over the past few years. Here are some of the commonly used terms which will be found in this book, and at many establishments:

Informal Dress means that you can wear just about anything you like. If women are wearing a bathing suit, they should put on a cover up before entering a hotel, restaurant, or a public area besides the beach. Jeans, shorts, T-shirts, and sneakers are acceptable.

Casual Dress usually indicates that shoes are preferred over sneakers, Bermuda shorts are preferred over regular shorts, no halter tops, no bathing suits, and no offensive T-shirts.

Smart Casual Dress has become rather commonplace, and it usually advises men to wear cotton or linen shirts with collars and neck buttons, shoes, Bermuda shorts with knee high colored socks, or long pants (not jeans). For women it can be slacks, skirts, blouses, dresses, sun dresses, and fashionable sandals or shoes.

Formal Dress has several different connotations. In most cases this refers to men wearing a button down shirt, sports jacket, tie, and dress shoes. For women it can include full length dresses, fashionable suits, blouses, and dress shoes. In rare cases, you may find that black tie suits or business attire is expected, but I have rarely seen this be the case except for state dinners and official functions.

AVERAGE NON-STOP JET FLIGHT TIMES

New York to Bermuda	2 hours 20 minutes
Boston to Bermuda	2 hours 15 minutes
Toronto to Bermuda	2 hours 50 minutes
Halifax to Bermuda	2 hours 10 minutes
Atlanta to Bermuda	2 hours 35 minutes
Philadelphia to Bermuda	2 hours 25 minutes
Baltimore to Bermuda	2 hours 5 minutes
Charlotte to Bermuda	2 hours

SCHEDULED NON-STOP FLIGHTS TO BERMUDA FROM NORTH AMERICA

Air Canada
• *in the US and Canada, Tel. 800/361-6340; within Bermuda, Tel. 441/293-2121*

Air Canada offers superb non-stop flights daily from Toronto and weekly from Halifax to Bermuda aboard their modern fleet of comfortable Airbus A-320 jet aircraft. They also offer stress-free same day connecting service to Bermuda via other major Canadian cities such as Montreal, Calgary, Edmonton, Winnipeg, Ottawa, and Vancouver. Air Canada offers the best service in the business, and is also well known for having excellent safety and on-time records. If you call in advance, either your travel agent or the staff at Air Canada can reserve great discounted promotional fares starting at just $399 CD round-trip, plus taxes, to Bermuda.

This famous Canadian-based international carrier can provide exceedingly comfortable seating in their spacious non-smoking Hospitality Class and Executive (Business) Class sections where you may enjoy first run in-flight movies, several channels of great high fidelity music programming, impressive culinary delights and wines (including a wide variety of special meals available with advance notice), on-board duty-free shopping, complimentary snacks and beverages, and an assortment of current periodicals. Your travel agent can also book special packages to Bermuda including round-trip airfare, hotels, and transfers from Air Canada Vacations.

Every mile you fly with Air Canada will earn you valuable points with the Aeroplan frequent flyer program. After taking every major carrier to Bermuda at least twice during the past decade, I highly recommend that you first contact Air Canada.

American Airlines
• *in the US, Canada, and Bermuda, Tel. 800/433-7300*

American Airlines offers as many as two daily non-stop flights via wide body DC-10 and 757 jet aircraft from New York's John F. Kennedy international airport, and new high season only daily service from Boston, directly to Bermuda. They can also arrange connections to several dozen US gateways, and will be pleased to help reserve special hotel packages with extra added features.

Prices for their more restrictive promotional fares start at about $289 plus taxes round-trip, while high season rates begin at about $419. Their in-flight service is quite good, their typical prices are in line with most other carriers, and you can easily connect to other American Airline flights via major North American airports and receive frequent flyer points for the whole trip.

Continental Airlines

• *in the US and Canada, Tel. 800/525-0280; within Bermuda, Tel. 800/231-0586*

Continental can fly you daily on non-stop 737 jets planes between Newark, New Jersey and Bermuda. They also offer connecting flight service from over 35 other US cities, and can arrange complete vacation packages. Continental has an impressive staff, nice new aircraft, a full array of special services, a wonderful frequent flyer program called OnePass, and special low season promotional fares starting at just $248 round-trip plus taxes.

Delta Airlines

• *in the US and Canada, Tel. 800/241-4141; within Bermuda, Tel. 800/221-1212*

Delta Airlines has daily non stop service year round from their hubs in Boston and Atlanta to Bermuda via jet aircraft. They also have an extensive array of connecting flights from various points throughout North America and Europe. Non-refundable low season promotional fares start at $218 round-trip plus taxes. Delta has a well maintained fleet of planes, a nice on board staff, and a generous frequent flyer program called SkyMiles.

USAir

• *in the US and Canada, Tel. 800/622-1015; within Bermuda, Tel. 800/423-7714*

USAir has daily scheduled non-stop jet service to Bermuda year round from Baltimore and Philadelphia, as well as additional non-stop flights from New York, Boston, and Charlotte during the high season only. Their lowest off season promotional fares start at $269 plus tax round-trip.

USING TRAVEL SPECIALISTS

Although it is fairly easy to book a vacation in Bermuda on your own, it may be a wise idea to call your favorite travel agent and compare prices and information. Travel agents generally work through wholesale tour operators who often have special package deals on specific hotels. Usually these tour operators pre-book an allotment of dozens of rooms in assorted categories at different hotels and inns. This bulk purchase allows them to sometimes offer substantial savings on advance purchase air/land bookings.

The vast majority of these tour operators will deal only with travel agencies and do not deal directly with the public. One exception to this rule are the major North American airline companies who run their own tour operations departments, and will be glad to sell directly with the general public as well as to travel professionals.

Tour operators who will also deal direct to consumers in North America include:
- **American Airlines Fly Away Vacations,** *Tel. 800/321-2121 USA and Canada*
- **Bermuda Travel Company,** *Tel. 800/323-2020 USA*
- **Delta Airlines Dream Vacations,** *Tel. 800/872-7786 USA and Canada*
- **Continental Airlines Grand Destinations,** *Tel. 800/634-5555 USA*
- **USAir Vacations,** *Tel. 800/455 0123 USA*

LUGGAGE REGULATIONS

Most airlines have a luggage limit of 70 pounds per person which must fit into two standard sized (under 62" Length + Width + Height) suitcases. You are also allowed to carry aboard one piece of luggage if it will fit under your seat or in the overhead luggage compartments. Most will allow you to exceed these limits, although additional surcharges may apply.

CRUISING TO BERMUDA

During the high season only (roughly May through October) there are up to five different luxury liners docked at the Bermudian ports of Hamilton, St. George's, and King's Wharf. The vast majority of these cruise ships depart the major cities on America's eastern seaboard (such as New York and Boston) for five-to-seven day adventures. They include an average of four days in Bermuda and one and a half days at sea in each direction to get to and from their points of departure.

While these vessels' state rooms, pricing policies, and clientele vary between cruise lines, they all offer some of the same basic features. Once at sea on these floating resorts, you can enjoy formal dinners and massive midnight buffets, exciting casino action, live music and entertainment, fully supervised children's activity programs, plenty of duty-free shopping, on-board movie theaters, seaview lounges, optional baby sitting services, free 24 hour room service, sporting events, theme parties, sun bathing, socializing, and plenty of other fun-filled scheduled activities each day. Their rates include as many as eight meals per day ranging from formal gala dinners to massive casual midnight buffets (even when you are docked at port), and for a small surcharge a number of optional day trips and excursions in Bermuda may be arranged.

Staterooms (cabins) come in several different sizes and categories depending on how much money you are willing to spend. While cruise ship staterooms are generally smaller than typical hotel rooms, they are furnished in a similar way with private bathrooms, cable television, in-room phones, and an assortment of bedding configurations to accommodate between one and four guests each. The less expensive of these accommodations are usually referred to as **Inside Cabins** since they have no window to let in any natural sunlight, while the better units are usually larger and may include nicer **Outside Cabins** with either windows or portals, and even spacious suites that in some cases feature private seaside terraces and separate sitting rooms.

I advise reserving a state room or suite that is located close to the center of the ship so that the inevitable rocking caused by the sea and its waves is much less noticeable. Another suggestion is to insist on "Late Seating" dining reservations at the time of booking so that you may enjoy an extra hour or two of exploring Bermuda before returning to the ship for dinner.

Keep in mind that a port charge and departure tax of around $145 per person (including children) is not included in most ship's advertised prices, so ask for details when you reserve your space. You should also anticipate the need to hand out tips to various ship staff members that can add up to a total of more than $60 per passenger per cruise. The following is a listing of the major cruise lines operating to Bermuda. Make sure to call around and compare prices between travel agencies, cruise-only discount agencies, and directly with each cruise company.

Royal Caribbean Cruise Lines, *Tel. 800/327-6700, serving the US and Canada*

RCCL continues to run some of the most comfortable and luxurious cruise liner vacations to Bermuda. Known throughout the world for its fine gourmet cuisine, personalized service, exciting entertainment, and superb spacious state rooms, their medium sized 37,584 ton *Song of America* vessel carries some 1,400 discriminating passengers and departs each Sunday afternoon from New York City on superb seven day cruises. All RCCL cruises to Bermuda dock in St. George's for a little more than one day before continuing along the coast to Hamilton where it will dock for another two and a half days prior to its return back to New York on Sunday morning.

Cruise-only prices for this wonderful adventure at sea start at about $799 per adult in double occupancy. If you book far enough in advance there may be special rates available starting at just $99 for the third and fourth adult sharing the same stateroom, or perhaps even free passage for children under 12 sharing a cabin with two adults, plus $124.50 in port charges and departure taxes per person (including children!). They also have great excursions, perhaps the best staff in the business, as well as add on airfares from most major American and Canadian cities. Highly Recommended.

Norwegian Cruise Lines, *Tel. 800/327-7030, serving the US and Canada*

NCL offers great seven day Bermuda cruises from New York aboard their almost brand new 41,000 ton *Dreamward* ship between late April and late September each year. You and another 1,241 fortunate passengers will depart from New York City on Saturday afternoon and spend a day and a half at sea before arriving at St. George for a day, and then Hamilton for two and a half days, until departing for the return voyage towards to New York. This is a beautiful modern luxury liner with some of the nicest staterooms and suites in this market.

Cruise-only prices start at just $799 per adult in double occupancy, with a limited number of special $199 fares available per third and fourth child or adult sharing the same cabin, plus $124.50 US per person in port charges and departure taxes. The crowd is a good mix of first time and repeat cruisers of all ages, and is heavily favored by couples and families looking for high quality cruise experience. Add on air fare is available from most major North American cities for a reasonable surcharge. Highly Recommended.

Cunard Cruise Lines, *Tel. 800/528-6273, serving the US and Canada*

For the most deluxe-minded passengers, contact the reservations department at Cunard and asking about their once a year five day cruise from New York to Bermuda aboard the impeccable 70,327 ton *Queen Elizabeth II*. This is the world's most famous ship and has recently been renovated to accommodate 1,498 passengers. The cruise dates change each year, but in the recent past this special sailing has departed late August and spent two days in Hamilton before returning to New York.

Cruise-only prices begin at $970 per person double occupancy, $485 per for a third and fourth person in the same stateroom, and $134.50 per occupant in port charges and taxes. Keep in mind that Cunard often offers a 20% early booking discount on advance reservations, and can arrange special add on airfares and land excursions. Since there are several fine restaurants on board, you are generally assigned a dining room depending on how deluxe your cabin is. Highly Recommended.

Majesty Cruise Lines, *Tel. 800/222-1003, serving the US and Canada*

Majesty schedules nice relaxing six and seven day cruises to Bermuda from Boston aboard the lavish 32,400 ton *Royal Majesty* luxury liner which can accommodate 1,056 passengers. This impressive ship departs each

Sunday from Boston and spends either three or four days docked in St. George's before returning back to Boston.

Cruise-only prices start at about $749 per person double occupancy, with special $199 third and fourth adult or child fares when they stay in the same room as two full fare passengers, plus $169.50 per occupant in port fees and departure taxes. Besides add on airfares and a good selection of excursions, Majesty has first class service and a friendly staff that await you. Note: It has been recently announced that this vessel will be sold to Norwegian Cruise Lines and may eventually be pulled from the Bermuda market.

Celebrity Cruise Lines, Tel. 800/437-3111, *serving the US and Canada*

Celebrity has two different luxury liners that service Bermuda, each with rather different specifications, ports of call, and clientele bases. Their deluxe modern 47,000 ton 1,410 passenger *Zenith* vessel is by far the better choice of the two and departs New York to spend just under two days each in both Hamilton and St. George before returning to the Big Apple. Their older, smaller, and less impressive 36,970 ton *Meridian* ship takes 1,004 passengers to King's Wharf all the way out near the Royal Naval Dockyard for a four day stop before returning to New York.

Cruise-only rates with Celebrity's two ships begin at around $899 per adult in double occupancy, with special $649 companion fares for third and fourth adult, or $549 third and fourth companion child fares, plus $135 per person in departure taxes and port charges. Add-on air fare is available from most major North American cities. I have been told that the Meridian will soon be sold to an Asian shipping concern and may eventually be pulled from the Bermuda market.

Special Cruise Discount Agencies

These days there are a growing number of travel agencies and wholesalers who deal only in providing discounted, special event, and last-minute cruise packages to the general public. The following companies have great reputations for giving honest first hand advice, the highest levels of customer service, and being able to access special unpublished cruise fares on selected voyages:

• **The Cruise Line Inc.**, *Tel. 800/777-0707, serving the US and Canada*
• **Cruises of Distinction**, *Tel. 800/634-3445, serving the US and Canada*
• **CruiseShipCenter**, *Tel. 800/707-7327, serving Canada*

TRAVEL EMERGENCY & MEDICAL INSURANCE

One of the most important issues of any trip abroad is what to do in case of an emergency. Since the possibility of a medical problem or accident is always a factor of risk, it is strongly advised that you take out an insurance policy. The best types of travel insurance are in the "Primary Coverage" category.

In an emergency, most of these policies will provide 24 hour toll free help desks, lists of approved local specialist doctors,airlifting you to a hospital with the proper facilities for your condition, and much more valuable assistance including refunds on additional expenses and unused hotel nights.

TRIP CANCELLATION & INTERRUPTION INSURANCE

Many special policies also cover vacation refunds if a family member gets ill and you must cancel your trip, if the airline you were supposed to be flying on goes out of business, if you must depart early from your trip due to sickness or death in the family, if the airline fails to deliver your baggage on time, if the cruise ship which you are on comes back too late for you to catch your flight home, if your luggage is stolen, if your stay is extended due to injury, etc. Not normally covered are airplane schedule changes, missed connections, and flight cancellations. Please check with your travel agent, tour operator, or the insurance companies for further details.

Travel Insurance Companies in North America
- **Mutual of Omaha (Tele-Trip)**, *Tel. 800/228-9792 in the US; (402) 351-8000 in Canada*
- **Travel Guard**, *Tel. 715/345-0505 in the US and Canada*
- **Voyageur Insurance**, *Tel. 905/793-9666 in Canada*
- **Access America**, *Tel. 800/284-8300 in the US and Canada*

ENTRY REQUIREMENTS

There are a few necessary items and documents that all North American visitors must have to be admitted to Bermuda. Upon arrival at the airport or cruise ship terminal, you must be able to present your return flight or cruise ticket, proof of accommodations for the entire length of your stay, sufficient funds to cover your expenses, and proof of citizenship (see below). If you intend to stay for over 30 days, you must also register with the Bermudian immigration officials.

For American citizens who wish to enter Bermuda, one of the following items must be presented as proof of US citizenship to the immigration officials upon arrival in Bermuda: a valid or recently expired US passport, or any of the following with a corresponding photo ID – an original birth certificate with a raised seal, a certified copy of your birth certificate with an official seal, a signed US voter's registration card, a US alien registration card, a US naturalization certificate, a US re-entry permit. Of these items, a valid passport is by far the best choice.

For Canadian citizens who are coming to Bermuda, one of the following documents must be available to the immigration officials as proof of Canadian citizenship. A valid Canadian passport, or any of the following with a corresponding photo ID, an original birth certificate with a raised seal, a certified copy of your birth certificate with an official seal, a Canadian certificate of citizenship, or a landed immigrant status certificate.

Customs Upon Entry

North American visitors to Bermuda are permitted to bring with them (duty free) for personal use items such as clothing, jewelry, cameras, film, books, video cameras, laptop computers, sporting equipment, etc. They may also bring up to 50 cigars, 200 cigarettes, 1 pound of unrolled tobacco, 1 quart of liquor, 1 quart of wine, and gifts of less than $30 in value.

Most canned and packaged foodstuffs may also be brought in duty free, but for some items (including meats) you may be charged a minimum of a 22.25% duty. All plants, live seafood, and fresh fruits and vegetables may be confiscated. The importation of illegal drugs, and firearms with the proper police license, is a criminal offense and will be punishable by up to 5 years in jail and a $10,000 penalty.

After arriving at the **Kindley Field** international airport in St. George's parish, you will have a few (sometimes long) lines to wait on before clearing customs and immigration. Follow the signs for non-Bermudian resident lines, go through immigration, pick up your luggage from the proper carousel, walk past the customs officers, and you will be directed to the airport exit. If you are suspected of some type of illicit activity, you will be brought to a special area and your luggage and documents may be further inspected.

FROM THE AIRPORT TO YOUR HOTEL

Once you have departed the airport, you can either take a taxi from the airport to your hotel, or meet up with your prearranged transfer provider. Since there is only one exit, you will have no difficulty in finding anyone who has been sent to pick you up. The average price for a taxi to hotels in the east end of the country is about $9.50, to Hamilton for around $18, to the south shore hotels for about $23, and to the west end hotels at about $29.50. See the taxi subheading in this chapter for further information.

If you are arriving by ship, the passenger terminals also have customs and immigration officials awaiting your arrival and departure from the ship on a daily basis. Please bring your cruise ship boarding pass, and your proof of citizenship with you.

Since almost none of the cruise passengers are staying in hotels while in Bermuda, taxi rates will depend on where you wish to go.

Airport Bus Transfers

One of the only ways to avoid a costly taxi ride from the airport to your selected hotel is to call a few days in advance and pre-reserve space on one of Bermuda's two private airport transfer companies. Although few tourists are aware of these companies and their services, they offer great rates on a per person basis that in many cases are much more economical than taxis for individual travelers and couples. If you contact **Bee Line Transportation**, *Tel. 441/293-0303*, or **Bermuda Hosts Ltd.**, *Tel. 441/293-0303*, you will be quoted a flat per person transfer rate of between $8 and $33.50 round trip from the airport to your hotel (depending on how far away the property is from the international airport).

For example, at press time the round trip per person rate from the airport to Grotto Bay Beach Hotel is $8, to Marriott's Castle Harbour is $12, to downtown Hamilton or the Elbow Beach Hotel is $20.50, to the Reefs or the Southampton Princess is $25.50 and to Cambridge Beaches or the Pompano Beach Club is $33.50 (a savings of up to 40% off on normal taxi rates for one passenger). They will greet you in the arrival's lounge of the airport and will direct you to either mini-van style taxis or air conditioned buses, and may also require that you wait just a few additional minutes until the vehicle has several additional passengers going your way.

When booking these discounted round-trip transfers, make sure to reconfirm your departure directly with the transportation company at least 24 hours prior to your departing flight!

GETTING AROUND BERMUDA

Since rental cars are not available on Bermuda, there are several alternative forms of transportation available for use during your vacation. Almost all of the sights and beaches that visitors may wish to access can be easily reached by a combination of buses and ferries. Another popular way of zipping around the islands is to rent a moped or scooter. For those of you who would like a bit of pleasant exercise, renting a normal 10 or 12 speed bicycle might be more desirable.

Although not particularly inexpensive, it is also possible to take taxis from place to place during the course of your vacation. The following section will offer all of the current information needed to arrange your transportation needs while in Bermuda.

By Bus

The government of Bermuda's **Public Transportation Board** (**PTB**) has created an excellent public transportation system with 11 separate bus routes that crisscross the entire country. The PTB uses a zone system to divide Bermuda into 14 separate transit zones, each roughly two miles in length, which are used to determine what fare will be applicable to specific bus rides. To travel from one part of Bermuda to another it may often be necessary to travel through a few or more zones per ride in each direction. Currently the cash price (in coins only) for all bus rides from one through three zones is $2.50 per person while any ride between four through fourteen zones will cost $4 per person.

Since bus drivers are not permitted to accept dollar bills or to make change, it is prudent to purchase either single use discounted tokens, bulk ticket booklets, or multiple day transportation passes depending on how much public transportation you expect to utilize during your stay here. The price for single ride one through three zone tokens is $2.25 each, while the four through fourteen zone tokens cost $3.75 each. The bulk 15 ticket booklets cost $15 each for use on rides up to three zones each, and the bulk ticket booklets for use on rides up to fourteen zones cost $24 each.

For an even better price break I suggest that you consider the purchase of an unlimited use one through fourteen zone pass which is available at $10 for one day, $21 for three days, $34 for seven days, $40 for one month, and $105 for three months (reduced prices for kids are available upon request). The above mentioned tokens, booklets, and passes are also valid for use on Bermuda's ferry system, described below, and can be purchases at the Central Bus Terminal just off Church Street in downtown Hamilton, as well as at several other sights including most post offices, Visitor's Service Bureaus, and leading hotels.

All PTB busses can be easily identified by their wide blue and pink striped exteriors and route number signs. Bus stops are located on various points throughout each route, and are marked with a pink and blue striped pole, and often contain a stone block waiting shelter. When looking for a bus stop, make sure that you are on the side of the street which will lead the bus in the desired direction. If the top color of the bus stop indication pole is painted pink then the bus is heading in the direction of Hamilton; if the top color of the pole is blue then the bus is traveling away from Hamilton. As you board the bus, tell the driver your final destination, pay the required fare, and ask the driver to notify you when the bus is about to get to your stop. If you already know what stop to get out on, push one of the well marked "STOP" buttons located between the windows on the inside of the bus and the driver will pullover at the next stop.

NEW PTB PUBLIC BUS FARES & RULES

These new rates are effective as of April 1, 1997.

For Adults:

FARE CATEGORY	3 ZONE	14 ZONE
Cash	$2.50	$4
Tokens	$2.25	$3.75
Tickets (15 per booklet)	$15	$24
1-Day Transportation Pass		$10
3-Day Transportation pass		$21
7-Day Transportation Pass		$34
Monthly Pass		$40
3-Month Pass		$105
Local Senior Citizens		FREE

For Local Students & Children

FARE CATEGORY	14 ZONE
Cash - children ages 5-16	$1
Tickets (15 per booklet)	$6
Visitor 3-Day Transportation Pass	$10
Visitor 7-Day Transportation Pass	$15
Term Pass	$38
Children Under Age 5	FREE

Rules

Transfers are free where appropriate upon request from bus operator.

• *Exact Change Only. Dollar Bills not accepted.*

• *Tokens and Passes are honored on buses and ferries.*

• *Tickets are sold in booklets of 15, and are for use on buses only. Tickets are sold at the Central Terminal in Hamilton, and many sub-post offices. Check the post office near you.*

• *Valid Passes are good for unlimited journeys through all zones on buses and ferries. Passes may be obtained at the Central Terminal in Hamilton, and at the PTB Headquarters at Palmetto Road, Devonshire and at many sub-post offices. The one, three, and seven day Transportation Passes may be obtained at the Visitors Service Bureau and many hotels and guest houses.*

All of the PTB buses start or finish their routes at the Central Bus Terminal in the heart of Hamilton (just next to the city hall). In some cases it might be necessary to make a transfer at this station to complete your journey. If you have to transfer to another bus, when you first board the bus and announce your final destination, the driver will provide a free transfer pass valid only for the next possible connection.

Keep in mind that public buses do not operate late at night, and have limited Sunday and holiday schedules. In fact there are several bus routes that do not even operate after 6:40pm, so pay close attention to the timetables or you may get stuck taking a rather expensive long haul taxi ride (I got hit with an unexpected $34 one way taxi fare from St. David's to Somerset because I was one minute late for the last bus).

Bus drivers are not permitted to allow passengers with luggage to board their buses, so don't even think about saving some money by getting to the airport via the bus system. The best source for detailed bus timetables and route maps is the free PTB bus and ferry schedule/map, available at major bus terminals, the Visitors Service Bureau, or the front desk of most hotels.

Additional information can be obtained directly from the PTB, Tel. 441/ 292-3851 on weekdays during normal business hours.

By Private Mini-Bus Shuttle

Additional private mini-bus companies run in the extreme east and west ends of the island. Although typically used by commuting residents, they provide excellent service, and are sometimes less expensive than the public bus system.

On the west end of Bermuda, the **West End Mini-Bus** service runs between the Royal Naval Dockyard and the Somerset Bridge. The fare is about $1.50 in either direction between the Dockyard and the Watford Bridge area, $2 in either direction between the Dockyard and the Somerset Village area, and $3 in either direction between the Dockyard and the Somerset Bridge. *You must call them to reserve a scheduled pick up time in advance, Tel. 441/234-3444; the normal operating hours of this shuttle are from 7:30am until 7pm daily.*

On the east end of Bermuda, the **St. George's Mini-Bus** service runs between the town of St. George (and its outskirts) onto both the Ferry Reach area, and at night only to St. David's. The fare is about $1.50 within the St. George area (including the Fort St. Catherine area), $2 between St. George and the Ferry Reach area, and $2.50 between St. George and St. David's Island.

You must call them to reserve a scheduled pick up time in advance, Tel. 297-8492; the normal operating hours of this shuttle are from 7am until 7pm daily, with extended evening hours in the high season.

By Ferry

A wonderful alternative to buses, scooters, or expensive taxi fares is the exceptional network of government operated ferries that connect much of Bermuda. The nation's **Main Ferry Terminal**, *Tel. 441/295-4506*, on Front Street in Hamilton. You can pick up the handy foldout schedules, purchase tokens, or ask questions. Most multiple day bus passes and some types of bus tokens are usable on the ferry system.

Different routes can take you either way between the city of Hamilton and Paget Parish (either Lower Ferry, Hodsdon's, or Salt Kettle) for just $2.25 per person each way, either way between the city of Hamilton and Warwick Parish (Darrell's or the Belmont Hotel) for $2.25 per person each way, and either way between the city of Hamilton and The Royal Naval Dockyard (or interim stops at Somerset Bridge, Cavello Bay, Watford Bridge, and Boaz Island) for $3.75 each way per person. There is also a new Tuesday through Thursday "Summer Only" express ferry service between Dockyard and Hamilton (on Wednesday and Thursday it will also service St. George's) with just one, two, or in some cases even three departures on those days for a fee of $5 each way. Bicycles are usually permitted aboard ferries for free, but mopeds and scooters are only permitted along the city of Hamilton to Somerset to Royal Naval Dockyard route and each one costs an additional $3.75 per direction.

The ferries run from about 7:00am until either 5:00pm, 7:00pm or 11:00pm depending on the exact route and day of the week you wish to travel. Keep in mind that in rough seas and other forms of bad weather the ferries be canceled.

THE HIGH SPEED FERRY IS HOPEFULLY ON ITS WAY!

As this edition was being prepared, Bermuda's Ministry of Transportation announced that plans are well under way to introduce high speed ferry service between Hamilton and distant points along the island. These American-built passenger craft are expect to cut commuter times in half, and will most likely cost around twice the price of a normal ferry ticket. For more details, contact the Hamilton Ferry Terminal, Tel. 441/295-4506.

By Taxi

Bermuda has a large supply of 600 or so independently owned taxis, the majority of which are part of radio dispatch systems. For the most part, the taxi drivers are hard working, polite, typically humorous, and full of all sorts of helpful hints and recommendations. In the summer, it is never a long wait to find a vacant taxi, or you can summon one by phone.

During the low season, drivers will often take other jobs, leading to a shortage of available taxis during rush hours and inclement weather. Most taxis are either converted late model sedans or station wagons which are licensed to take up to 4 passengers at a time. Many new van-size taxis can take up to 6 passengers at a time.

Many, but not all, taxis now accept most major credit cards. To catch a cab, look for an empty taxi and simply flag it down. If it is going on a pre-scheduled pickup it may not stop, but just try again.

Now that taxis have been granted a fare change after many years without increases, the way the meters work is as follows: as soon as you enter a taxi, a digital meter begins to tick away. The newly calibrated taxi meters start at $3.15 and add about $1.68 for each mile traveled. This rate only applies to one through four passengers occupying the same taxi between 6:00am and 12 midnight from Monday through Saturday. If there are more than four people in the same taxi, the rate increases by a surcharge of about 25%. For each piece of normal luggage there will also be a 25 cent surcharge added to the meter. If you enter a taxi on Sundays, holidays, or any night between the hours of 12:01am and 5:59am the rate is also surcharged by an additional 25% or so. Taxi tour rates are $30 per hour for up to four passengers, and $42 per hour from five to six passengers. Be advised that trying to find a taxi to take you back to your hotel after the clubs on Front Street close down at 3am or so is, at times, just impossible.

To call a taxi for a pick-up, contact one of the following companies:
• **Bermuda Radio Taxis**, *Tel. 441/295-4141, 24 hours a day*
• **Sandys Taxis**, *Tel. 441/234-2344, 8:00am until 11:00pm*
• **B.I.U. Taxis**, *Tel. 441/292-4476, 7:00am until 12:01am*

If you intend to do a lot of running around it may be best to hire a taxi driver as a tour guide by the hour at a flat rate of $30 per hour for one through four passengers, or $42 per hour for five or six passengers. Since so many of Bermuda's taxis are converted air conditioned maxi-vans, usually six people can easily fit in comfort. This is a great way for you to find out about the islands and get to lesser known attractions that may fit your specific interests. Almost every full time taxi driver is licensed and qualified as a tour guide.

The following is a list of taxi-guides that I can recommend for half- and full-day sightseeing trips anywhere in Bermuda. Just call at least a day or two in advance and they can arrange everything from intensive specialty tours to sightseeing trips or private airport transfers:
• **Lenny Holder**, *Taxi Van # 1826, Tel. 441/234-8709*
• **Kingsford Bean**, *Taxi # 1244, Tel. 441/234-2344*
• **Eugene Evans**, *Taxi Van # 1195, Tel. 441/234-7151*

• **Tim Flood**, *Taxi Van # 1528, Tel. 441/295-3589*
• **Dennis Hollis**, *Taxi Van # 1340, Tel. 441/234-8062*

Let them know what you need, or if there is a tour or an airport run needed, and they will usually be right on time. After finding a driver that you really like, you may ask him for his direct cellular phone number for future use.

Note: Several taxis will refuse to pick up passengers at the beaches, supposedly to avoid getting sand and water on their seats. The reality is that the smart drivers will have plastic seat covers for this very situation, but some refuse to spend the 30 seconds needed to put them on. Occasionally a few drivers are quite rude in this situation and just blow off passengers. Tell the dispatcher from that company the story and give the cab's licence plate number.

By Horse & Carriage Ride

Horse-drawn carriages are available for sightseeing and special event purposes in several locations throughout Bermuda. The most typical tours are given by the friendly operators on Front Street in Hamilton. Their rate is $20 per half hour for up to 4 passengers at a time, and they can take you just about anywhere you wish to go. Local law prohibits them from going out when it gets too cold.

Additional special services can be arranged by calling **Terceira's Stables** *in Devonshire, Tel. 441/236-3014*.

By Bicycle

For those of you who wish to keep fit while touring this beautiful country, I suggest renting a sturdy bicycle for use during some of your stay. The typical price structure for a 15 or 18 speed mountain bike is around $15 for 1 day, $24 for 2 days, $32 for 3 days, and $5 for each additional day. Expect to also get hit with a non-refundable repair waiver of $5 and a refundable deposit of around $10.

The best places to rent bicycles include:
• **Dowlings Cycles** *in St. George, Tel. 441/297-1614*
• **Smatts Cycle Livery** *in Hamilton, Tel. 441/295-1180*
• **Eve's Cycle Livery** *in Paget, Tel. 441/236-6247*
• **Georgiana Cycles** *in Somerset, Tel. 441/234-2404*

Or you can contact your hotel's front desk. Make sure to wear your helmet!

By Moped & Scooter

Moped and scooter rental agencies are located in hotels and branch offices throughout most parishes in Bermuda. The most common of these are gasoline-powered and tend to utilize a 50cc engine which gets about 52 miles to each gallon. If transportation for only one person is needed, a 3 horsepower moped will certainly do the trick.

The least expensive of these one passenger mopeds have kick start pedals, and no electric turn signals. For bit more money, I suggest that you consider renting the fancier models that feature electronic ignition and electronic turn signals. If there are two people that would like to ride together, or a single person wants double the power and comfort of a moped, the 2 passenger scooters are the way to go. Capable of reaching speeds well over the legal limit, these 6 horsepower scooters have better brakes, stronger headlights, locking helmet storage compartments, lots of footroom, and a rear mounted metal basket to hold towels and personal items.

All of these mopeds and scooters come with a helmet that must be worn with its chin strap tightened.

Prices on moped and scooter rentals tend to be fixed on Bermuda, so don't even waste your time looking for a better deal. Although credit cards are not mandatory for rentals, most companies will gladly accept them for payment. One major difference between the dozens of rental agencies is that each one of them offers different qualities of equipment and instruction.

GO SPEED RACER!

Unless otherwise indicated, there is a Bermuda-wide 35 kilometer (22 mile) per hour speed limit, although no one seems to drive this slow. Some people will tend to pass on blind curves, and several people are injured in avoidable accidents each season. Many of these accidents occur because the driver either didn't keep on the left side the street, or was looking at the bikini-laden beaches instead of the road. Children under 16 are not permitted to drive.

The wearing of safety helmets is mandatory at all times, and I strongly suggest that you also wear sunglasses or eye protection since scooters and mopeds don't have windshields and small bugs and flying pebbles may hit your face. Make sure to obey all traffic signs and regulations, be extremely careful when attempting to pass another car, truck, moped, or scooter, and pay extra attention to the right of way at rotary traffic circles. Driving at night or while it is raining is not suggested for all but the most seasoned drivers.

An important issue that the moped or scooter must be locked, and the key and helmet must be secured. Although third party liability insurance is included in all rates, and a one time non-refundable repair and vehicle damage waiver of $15 will be added to your bill, this does not usually cover you against the theft of either the vehicle or helmet(s). Unfortunately the theft of mopeds, scooter, bicycles, and helmets are not covered by any available insurance, and are becoming commonplace in Bermuda (just take a peek at the *Royal Gazette's* "Weekly Stolen Scooters" listings each Monday), so be careful. Don't park your scooter or moped next to cars on windy days since they are easily tipped over and may damage other adjacent vehicles.

Keep in mind that most of these vehicles have a maximum tank capacity of only 1 gallon. After some 50 or so miles, you will need to fill up at one of the many gas stations. Expect to pay about $5 per gallon and use normal gasoline. The typical business hours for gas stations are from about 7am until 7pm daily, but some stations stay open until 11pm. Bermuda has only one 24 hour gas station, and this Esso station is located on Bermudiana Road at the edge of the city of Hamilton.

The following is a list of recommended moped and scooter rental agencies in order of preference:

Wheels Cycles Group Ltd., *Main Office - 117 Front Street, Hamilton-Pembroke. Tel. 242/292-2245. Internet: www.bermuda.com/wheels. Eleven branch offices in Hamilton, Southampton, Smith's, St. George's, and Warwick.*

Wheels is both the biggest and best full service supplier of rental scooters in all of Bermuda. Their friendly staff will be happy to provide you with a sparkling new (and rather powerful) 50cc Peugeot scooter that can seat either one or two passengers in complete comfort. Besides offering intensive driver training to all clients, they also have free hotel pick-up services anywhere on the island, radio controlled emergency repair trucks, and hassle free rental policies.

Their branch offices are conveniently located near Victoria Park in the city of Hamilton, at Devil's Hole near Tucker's Town, on the Southampton Princess estate, at the Sonesta Beach Resort, the Hamilton Princess Hotel, Flatts Village, and in Marriott's Castle Harbour resort. A $20 refundable deposit and a $18 non-refundable repair and third party liability waiver will be added to your bill. Most of their branches are open from 8:30am until 5:00pm every day of the week. Wheels accepts all major credit cards, has locking helmet compartments on all their scooters, and includes free rental helmets and baskets. Wheels is where I go to supply all my two wheeled transportation needs on the island, and I recommend you do the same!

Oleander Cycles, *Main Office - Valley Road-Paget, Tel. 441/236-5235. Six branch offices in Pembroke, Devonshire, Southampton, and Sandys.*

The most serious supplier of high-quality late model mopeds and scooters in all of Bermuda. Most of their mopeds are made by Liberty-Daelim, while their scooters are Suzuki. The people here are honest, patient, and quite helpful. All clients are given a detailed lecture and lesson before being sent out to a large practice area.

One of their most impressive instructors is Mr. Quentin Tuzo who who makes absolutely sure that each driver takes the safety issue seriously. One of Oleander's added benefits is that they offer a complimentary client pick-up and drop off shuttle to any hotel in Bermuda. They can also arrange for clients to pick up their scooter at one location, and return it to another of their offices.

You can pay by cash, traveler's check, or any major credit card. A $20 refundable deposit and a $15 non-refundable repair waiver will be added to your bill. Their branches are all open from 8:30am until 5:30pm daily.

Eve Cycle Livery, *Main Office - Middle Road, Paget, Tel. 441/236-6247. One branch office in St. George's.*

Eve's is a small local former livery company which has transported tourists around Bermuda since the 1920's. They stock a selection of high end mopeds and scooters from Honda. The training program is pretty good, and they have a fleet of 5 radio controlled trucks which are used for emergency roadside service.

All rentals can be paid with cash, traveler's check, or any major credit card. A $20 refundable deposit and a $18 non-refundable repair waiver will be added to your bill. *Their branches are open from 8:30am until 5:30pm daily.*

TYPICAL PRICES FOR MOPED/SCOOTER RENTALS

	1 Day	2 Days	3 Days	4 Days	5 Days	Extra Days
Moped *(One Person–Kick Start)*	$27	$46	$61	$73	$84	@$9
Moped *(One Person–Electronic Ignition)*	$35	$59	$79	$95	$108	@$12
Scooter *(Two Persons–Electronic Ignition)*	$44	$81	$112	$135	$155	@$15

LODGING PARTICULARS

Most of the accommodation reviews included in this book use descriptive phrases like *Cottage Colony, Resort Hotel, Hotel, Inn, Cottages, Apartment Complex,* and *Guesthouse.* These do not always relate to the official status which the Bermudan government gives to these properties.

The reason I have used these terms is to better explain the type of accommodations and facilities that you can expect from these establishments. The following is a breakdown of my terminology for these diverse places to stay while in Bermuda:

Cottage Colonies

These uniquely Bermudan deluxe resorts usually are comprised of several detached multiple occupancy lodges which are referred to as cottages. The cottages themselves may contain somewhere between two and 12 independent guest rooms or suites, each with their own private entrance, private bathroom, and in most cases a nice patio as well. It is most common for these cottages to surround a main clubhouse which usually houses a restaurant, bar, library, TV room, and the reception desk.

All cottage colony rooms and suites are fully air conditioned, and have private phones, daily maid service, and offer a wide range of on premises facilities. In some cases your room or suite may have a small refrigerator to store cold drinks and snacks. Most cottage colonies offer special dine around programs, access to private beaches, outdoor pools, an excursion desk or concierge, safe deposit boxes, and privileges to most major golf courses. Many cottage colonies prefer not to accept children under 5 unless accompanied by a full time nanny. These are fantastically enjoyable places to stay, and offer visitors a chance to experience Bermuda at its finest.

Resort Hotels

These properties are usually large hotels located either on the sea or near a golf course which offer a full range of facilities and services. Most resort hotels have one or more large wings, which can contain up to 300 rooms each. This type of accommodation is perfect for people who want to spend plenty of time on site, and take advantage of the many on premises facilities which can include golf, tennis, boat rides, pools, discos, show lounges, social desk, boutiques, business meeting rooms, and multiple restaurants. All resort hotels are fully air conditioned and each room or suite generally contains a private bathroom, cable television, hair dryer, mini safe, and a host of other amenities.

Children of all ages usually welcome at these hotels, and several offer great kids programs. Although not particularly Bermudan by nature, this type of property is what most North Americans are used to staying in while on vacation or business.

Hotels

While generally smaller and less deluxe than resort hotels, these establishments tend to be located further away from the beaches and golf courses. All hotels are air conditioned, and have rooms which contain private bathrooms. The front desk of these properties can arrange excursion reservations, dinner reservations, and tee-off times and several area golf courses.

Not all hotels offer a complete range of facilities, in-room televisions, or room service. Hotels may also be located far away from the beaches and major attractions that you may wish to visit. Children of all ages are usually accepted. These properties offer a lower price than the resort hotels and can help you to save some money.

Inns

This category is not recognized by the Bermuda Department of Tourism, which unfortunately lists even of the most deluxe of these properties as guest houses. I have utilized the inn category in many of my reviews. To me, an inn represents a private home or mansion that has been converted into a B&B type of establishment. These properties offer great Bermudan charm and uniquely personalized service.

All inns are air conditioned, and have an assortment of cute guest rooms with private bathrooms in either a main building or an adjacent cottage. Facilities and room quality differ greatly from one in to the other, but almost all of them have a breakfast room, TV room, home style living room, and access to off site facilities. Some of the inns have rooms with kitchenettes, while others may offer their guests use of the main house's kitchen. Most inns will gladly accept children and can arrange babysitting. Inns are a great way to keep your budget reasonable, and still enjoy romantic accommodations and first rate Bermudan service.

Cottages

This type of accommodation can come in many different varieties. I have used this term to describe small properties which may offer independent cottages or rooms located inside 2-4 unit private cottage style lodges. Several cottages look almost like small deluxe summer houses, and even have superb views over secluded beaches.

Most come with daily maid service, kitchenettes, air conditioners, a common garden and pool area, and a part time property manager. Since most of these cottages allow children, they are perfectly designed for families and couples who will be doing a fair amount of their own cooking.

If you don't need much in the way of fancy on site facilities, and prefer a bit of privacy, this is the perfect choice.

Apartment Complexes

Once again, properties which fit into this category are rather varied. The one thing they all have in common is that you will have a private entrance, fully equipped kitchen, and a good price. Some apartment complexes are comprised of a series of small 4-12 unit Bermudan style lodges, while others are in less imaginative modern complex buildings which on occasion seem a bit out of place here. Your location depends on the specific apartment complex you select, but many have splendid water and city views.

These places have plenty of long stay guests, and are busy throughout the year. Facilities are minimal, but in most cases you will at least have air conditioning, an outdoor swimming pool, vending machines, coin operated laundry machines, and telephones. Most apartment complexes are happy to welcome children and families. If you pick the right apartment complex, you can save a fortune and accommodate up to six people per apartment, depending on how many bedrooms your apartment has.

Guest Houses

I use this final category to describe converted manors and houses which offer minimal services, facilities, and basic inexpensive accommodations. Even though the government may consider all inns as guest houses, I don't.

Guest houses are usually run by nice Bermudians who enjoy hosting visitors in their own private homes. Some units have kitchenettes, air conditioners, views of the water, and a private bathroom. Some guest houses prefer not to accept small children. Considering the fact these are the least expensive and facility-laden accommodations available in Bermuda, if you carefully pick the right guest house you can have a great time and get a little local culture at the same time.

Hotel Price Listing Details

For all hotels, resorts, cottages colonies, guest-houses, and inns I have reviewed in this book, the prices listed have been based on the most recently available 1997/8 rack rate prices (the full retail price) of their least expensive room for two people with a private bathroom. Special discounted rates are also often available upon request. This means that you may easily find lower package prices by calling each hotel directly, or by visiting a travel agent. Of course you should expect to pay additionally for suites, deluxe seaview rooms, optional meal plans, spa therapies, excursions and tips.

Also keep in mind that in most cases the **7.5% government hotel occupancy tax**, a 10% to 15% service charge (in lieu of tipping), and other nonsense surcharges will be added on to the listed prices. If your hotel does not add service charges to its room rates and restaurant(s), you should expect to leave tips for the bell-man, concierge, waiters, wine stewards, and chamber maids.

You'll also see initials next to a reviewed hotel's rate that will help you to understand what is included in the lowest listed price in both high and low seasons. Keep in mind that while most hotels and inns consider April through October to be high season, and November through March to be low season, some properties do not necessarily follow this rule and may consider holiday time periods as high season as well.

The letters *E.P.* next to a hotel price indicate that no meals are included (**European Plan**). The initials *C.P.* means that a small breakfast is included (**Continental Plan**). The letters *B.P.* suggests that a typical Bermudan breakfast will be served each morning (**Bermuda Plan**). The initials *M.A.P.* generally explains that a full breakfast and a full dinner will be included (**Modified American Plan**). And in the rare case that you'll find the letters *A.I.* next to a hotel price, this will point out that a full breakfast, a small lunch, a full dinner, and drinks are included in the listed price (**All Inclusive**). It is often possible to arrange for optional meal plans including fine dine around programs at many hotels and inns in Bermuda for a reasonable surcharge.

RESTAURANT PARTICULARS

For every restaurant that I have reviewed in this book, I have used a simple formula to calculate the price of a typical meal for two. The approximate bill for two is based on the current 1999 cost for two people ordering a multiple course meal from a restaurant's normal lunch and/or dinner menu, not including either a well indicated 15% service charge, or a 15% tip in lieu of any service charge. Gratuities, wine, drinks, and the most expensive al la carte menu selections have not been included in this formula.

Also keep in mind that many special programs may be available to further reduce your meal price, including early bird specials (offered by some 25 different establishments), low season discounts, hotel M.A.P. and dine-around meal plan packages, and other special promotions.

DINE AROUND PROGRAMME

*There are now over 15 restaurants that participate in Bermuda's **November through March Dine Around Programme** that allows visitors to enjoy up to a 55% savings at many fine establishments. Sponsored by the Bermuda Department of Tourism, details regarding this special program can be found in a free brochure available at all of the island's guest accommodations. The average price per person for a dine-around program dinner is about $24 plus tips and beverages. Among the many 1999 participants are the Bombay Bicycle Club, The Carriage House, Chopsticks, Coconut Rock, Colony Pub, Fisherman's Reef, Flanagan's, Fourways Inn, Freddie's Pub in the Square, Freeport Seafood, Frog & Onion Pub, Harbourfront, Henry VIII, Hog Penny, La Trattoria, Little Venice, Lobster Pot, M.R. Onions, Newport Room, Paw Paws, Portofino, Robin Hood, Rosa's Cantina, Tio Pepe, The View, Waterlot Inn, Wharf Tavern, and Windows on the Sound.*

There are no vouchers required to enjoy these selected discounts. Advance reservations are strongly suggested as this program is extremely popular, and when making reservations you must notify the restaurant that you will be ordering from the special dine around program menu.

FESTIVALS & SPECIAL EVENTS

Since the exact dates and listings for these events change yearly, please contact your local Bermuda Department of Tourism office for specific dates, prices, schedules, and eligibility requirements.

JANUARY

• **ADT Bermuda Race Weekend** (Mid-January)

A world class running event with a marathon, 10K, and 1 mile race.

• **The Bermuda Festival** (January and February)

For 6 weeks Bermuda hosts a variety of special theater, music, and dance performances hosted by internationally known artists and stars.

• **Annual Bridge Tournament** (Late January)

A regional tournament sponsored by the local chapter of the American Contract Bridge League.

FEBRUARY

• **National Badminton Tournament** (Early February)

Held in Pembroke parish for local players only.

• **Bermuda Chess Tournament** (Early February)

A 5-round test of skills sponsored by the Bermuda Chess Association.

• **Lobster Pot Golf Tournament** (Mid February)
  A Pro Am invitational held at the Castle Harbour Golf Club.
• **Bermuda Rendezvous Bowling Tournament** (Mid February)
  This A.B.C. and W.I.B.C. sponsored event is held at Warwick Lanes.
• **Bermuda Amateur Golf Festival** (Late February)
  Several events for enthusiasts of all ages held all over Bermuda.
• **Valentine's Mixed Golf Foursomes** (Late February)
  An invitational tournament held at St. George's Golf Club.

MARCH
• **All Breed Championship Dog Shows** (Early March)
  These dog shows and obedience trails are held at the Botanical
Gardens in Paget with Bermudian and International champions.
• **Bermuda College Weeks** (Early March)
  Spring break sports activities for North American university athletes.
• **Annual Hamilton Street Festival** (Mid March)
  Located on Front Street, this event includes street vendors, live
music, dancing, fashion shows, and fun for the whole family.
• **Easter Lily Ladies Golf Tournament** (Mid March)
  A special Pro Am event at the St. George's Golf Club.
• **Bermuda Horse & Pony Show** (Late March)
  This event included humping, flat, driving, and western exhibitions.
• **Bermuda Youth Soccer Cup** (March and April)
  Soccer teams from all over the world participate in this competition.
• **Bermuda Men's Amateur Golf Championship** (Late March)
  Held at the famous Mid Ocean Golf Club.
• **Hasty Pudding Club Show** (Late March)
  Harvard University's comedic show is presented in Hamilton.

APRIL
• **Palm Sunday Walk** (Early April)
  A scenic walking tour organized by the Bermuda National Trust.
• **Easter Rugby Classic** (Mid April)
  A well attended international sporting event held at the National
Sports Club in Devonshire.
• **Open Houses & Gardens** (April and May)
  Some of Bermuda's finest private homes and gardens are open to the
public with the help of the Bermuda Garden Club.
• **Agricultural Exhibition Show** (Late April)
  Bermuda's own version of a regional county fair takes place at the
Bermuda Botanical Gardens in Paget.
• **Peppercorn Ceremony** (Late April)
  Amidst this nation's best display of pomp and circumstance, a single

peppercorn is presented by the local chapter of the Grand Lodge of Scotland to top officials as rent for the Old State House in St. George.

MAY
• **Beating Retreat Ceremonies** (May through October)
  Military reenactments and performances by the Bermuda Regiment band are held in several locations in Bermuda.
• **Bermuda Game Fishing Tournament** (May through November)
  Open to all fishing enthusiasts, prizes are awarded for top catches.
• **Bermuda Heritage Month** (May)
  A full month of cultural events, marathons, boat races, cycle races, and other activities throughout Bermuda culminating with the fabulous Heritage Parade on Bermuda Day (May 24).
• **Open Badminton Tournament** (Early May)
  This international event takes place at the Bermuda Athletic Association's facilities in Pembroke.
• **Invitational International Race Week** (Early May)
  The Royal Bermuda Yacht Club in Hamilton hosts this competition.
• **Trans-Atlantic Bermuda Race** (Odd Numbered Years)
  Several yachts race here from Ponce de Leon, Florida.

JUNE
• **President's Choice Open Air Pops Concert** (Mid June)
  Presented by the Bermuda Philharmonic Society.
• **Gibbons Ironkids Triathlon** (Mid June)
  A great race for kids 7 to 14 years old at the U.S. Naval Air Station.
• **Bermuda Duathlon** (Mid June)
  This race is sponsored by the Bermuda Triathlon Association.
• **Men's Amateur Stroke Play Golf Championship** (Late June)
  This 72 hole event takes place at the Port Royal Golf Course.
• **Queen's Birthday Parade** (Late June)
  Front Street in Hamilton becomes the sight of this exciting parade.
• **Newport-Bermuda Race** (Even Numbered Years)
  Yachts race single handedly from Newport, Rhode Island and return double handed from Bermuda.
• **Bermuda Ocean Race** (Even Numbered Years)
  Dozens of yachts race from Annapolis, Maryland to Bermuda.

JULY
• **Marine Science Day** (Mid July)
  The Bermuda Biological Research center hosts an open house with lectures, demonstrations, and exhibits for the whole family.

• **American Independence Day** (July 4)
   Fireworks and celebrations are hosted by the U.S. Naval Air Station.
• **Cup Match Cricket Festival** (July or August)
   A fantastic and festive 2 day cricket match attended by most of Bermuda at the Somerset Cricket Club in Sandys.

AUGUST
• **Non Mariners Race** (Early August)
   An amusing test of home made boats in Mangrove Bay, Somerset.
• **Bermuda Reggae Sunsplash Concert** (Mid August)
   Jamaican Reggae bands display their talents in Bermuda.
• **Bermuda Field Hockey Festival** (August and September)
   The finest international field hockey teams participate in this event.

SEPTEMBER
• **Bermuda Triathlon** (September and October)
   Sponsored by the Bermuda Triathlon Association.
• **American-Bermudian Friendship Festival** (Mid September)
   The U.S. Naval Air Station hosts an air show and other events.
• **Member's Flower Show** (Late September)
   A wonderful exhibition by the Bermuda Garden Club at the Arts Centre at the Royal Naval Dockyard.

OCTOBER
• **Columbus Day Weekend Regatta** (Early October)
   The Great Sound is filled with keel boats racing for the title.
• **Ladies Amateur Golf Championship** (Early October)
   A major golf event held at various locations in Bermuda.
• **Men's Open Golf Championship** (Mid October)
   This world class event is held at the Port Royal Golf Course.
• **Omega Gold Cup Match Race** (Late October)
   America's Cup and Bermudian yachtsmen race in Hamilton Harbour.
• **Bermuda Horse & Pony Show**
   This event included humping, flat, driving, and western exhibitions.
• **The Convening of Parliament** (October or November)
   The Governor of Bermuda hosts this ceremonial event at the Cabinet Building in Hamilton.

NOVEMBER
• **Guy Fawkes Night** (Early November)
   An afternoon of enjoyable fairs and fireworks at the Bermuda Maritime Museum at the Royal Naval Dockyard.
• **International Flower Show** (Early November)

The world's top flower arrangers compete in this event.
• **World Rugby Classic** (Early November)
The National Sports Club hosts teams of Bermudan and International rugby players in Devonshire.
• **All Breed Championship Dog Shows** (Mid November)
These dog shows and obedience trials are held at the Botanical Gardens in Paget with Bermudian and International champions.
• **Remembrance Day Parade** (Mid November)
Bermudians help honor their war dead by witnessing this parade of international military marching bands on Front Street in Hamilton.
• **Bermuda Equestrian Festival** (Some Years Only)
A 2 day international horse show at the Botanical Gardens in Paget.
• **Lawn Tennis Club Invitational** (Late November)
Teams of visiting and local players participate in this 2 week event.
DECEMBER
• **XL Tennis Classic** (Early December)
International tennis greats participate in this A.T.P. sponsored event
• **Goodwill Golf Tournament** (Mid December)
A prestigious Pro Am foursomes event at several golf courses.
• **The Santa Claus Parades** (Late December)
The Jaycees host 3 gala parades, with floats, throughout Bermuda.

DEPARTING FROM BERMUDA

Leaving Bermuda is a fairly easy task. The first thing you must do is to be promptly at the airport, or aboard the ship when you are asked to check in (usually about 90 minutes before departure). If you are flying out of Bermuda, present your ticket at the check-in counter, and pay the mandatory departure tax in cash. This tax for airline passengers is never included in the ticket price, and is $15 per adult, $5 per child between 2 and 11 years old, and is exempted for infants under 2.

A few overpriced souvenir shops, telephones, and snack bars can be visited while waiting for the boarding announcements at the airport. If you are leaving by boat, the $60 cruise departure tax should have been included in your prepayment to the cruise line.

CUSTOMS REGULATIONS FOR YOUR RETURN

For US Citizens

All US citizens can return to America with up to $600 in purchased goods without paying duty if you have left the US for over 48 hours and haven't made another international trip within the last 30 days. Each family member is eligible for the same limits, and these amounts may be pooled together. Normally a 10% duty will be assessed on goods which

have exceeded the $600 value, but are below $1600 in total value. Above this point the duty will vary with the specific merchandise being imported
Each adult may also bring in up to two liters of wine or alcohol and either 100 cigars (except from Cuba) or 200 cigarettes. There is no duty on antiquities or works of art which are over 100 years old, or on General System of Preference (G.S.P.) items that have been manufactured in Bermuda. Bring all receipts with the merchandise to customs to avoid problems. In most cases you will actually clear US customs and immigration at the departure lounge of Bermuda's Kindley Field International Airport instead of having to wait until arriving in America.

For Canadian Citizens
All Canadian citizens can return to Canada with up to $500 CD once each year if you have left Canada for over seven days, up to $200 CD several times each year if you have left Canada for over 48 hours, or up to $100 CD several times each year if you have left Canada for over 24 hours. Each family member is eligible for the same limits per person. Normally a combination of federal and provincial taxes will be assessed on goods which have exceeded the duty free values depending on the specific items involved and your length of stay.
Each adult can also bring in 1.14 liters of alcohol, or 8.5 liters (24 cans or bottles each with 12 ounces) of beer. Also allowed for those at least 16 years old are up to 50 cigars (including Cuban cigars!), 200 cigarettes, and 400 grams of tobacco. Bring all receipts with the merchandise to customs to avoid problems.

THE INTERNET IN BERMUDA
Both the government and private industry in Bermuda have begun to embrace the Internet as a marketing tool for its various hotels, restaurants, banking and insurance interests, and tourist attractions. There are in fact a few Bermuda based Internet access providers such as **ibl**, but they only offer long term subscriptions and are not geared for traveling businessmen and computer freaks that are here for brief time periods.
While some of the major resorts offer computer station rentals with Internet links, their typical price can be as much as $40 per hour with a one hour minimum usage charge, and that's a lot of money to spend for sending a five minute E-mail message. My best suggestion is pay a visit to the nice folks at Print Express on Burnaby Hill, *Tel. 441/295-3949 during normal retail business hours,* just off downtown's Hamilton's bustling Front Street. Their rates are just $15 per hour and all computers are loaded with Netscape Navigator as well as several other current word processing and graphics software.

In terms of getting accurate details about Bermuda from the Internet while still at home, there has been some good progress. A recent search on my regular net service provider via the Netscape, Lycos, Wahoo, AltaVista, and Microsoft Explorer browsers led me to well over 450 pages of text and images of tourism related topics and establishments. I was able to pre-plan several aspects of my last trip using the available maps, weather charts, hotel and restaurant descriptions, history, and general island information found via links at some of the web sights listed below.

The first web-site below is a wonderful new service provided by the Bermuda Department of Tourism and has good links to other great sites. Happy surfing:

http://www.gobermuda.com
http://microstate.com/cgi-win/mstatead.exe/bolcat,14
http://www.odci.gov/cia/publications/95fact/bd.html
http://www.bermuda-best.com/Bermuda-Best.html
http://www.travelfile.com
http://www.bermudareservations.com
http://www.bermudaweb.net/tourism/index.html
http://emporium.turnpike.net/D/diving/sites.html
http://tile.net/tile/news/bermudat.html
http://www.caribb.com/bermuda.htm
http://www.bbsr.edu/weather.html
http://www.bermudaweb.net/onion/weather.html
http://www.ibl.bm/cgi-bin/mailsearcher
http://www.bercol.bm/Bermuda/facts_and_figures.html
http://www.bermudasun.org
http://tile.net/news/bermudai.html
http://www.bbsr.edu/
http://www.bercol.bm/Bermuda/bermuda_pictures.html
http://www.bermuda.com/travel.html
http://www.gcb.com/catalog/t/t11/5622.html
http://www.bermudacommerce.com/
http://geology.smith.edu/marine/albook.html

7. BASIC INFORMATION

AIRLINE OFFICES IN BERMUDA

If you need to alter your return flight reservation, request special assistance at the airport, check on the on time status of a plane, or track down missing baggage, you should call your airline.

- **Air Canada,** *18 Queen Street, city of Hamilton, Tel. 441/293-2121*
- **American Airlines,** *18 Queen Street, Hamilton, Tel. 800/433-7300, Tel. 441/293-1556*
- **British Airlines,** *89 Front Street, city of Hamilton, Tel. 441/295-4422*
- **Continental Airlines,** *Bermuda (Kindley Field) Airport, Tel. 800/231-0856; Tel. 441/293-3092*
- **Northwest Airlines,** *Bermuda (Kindley Field) Airport, Tel. 800/225-2525; Tel. 441/293-8592*
- **Delta Airlines,** *85 Front Street, city of Hamilton, Tel. 800/221-1212; Tel. 441/293-1022*
- **US Air,** *89 Front Street, city of Hamilton, Tel. 800/423-7714; Tel. 441/293-3072*

BABYSITTING SERVICES

Almost every hotel and inn offers some sort of babysitting and child care service. Some of the major resorts offer in-house full day programs, others call in outside expert babysitters and nannys. You can also call **Busybodies** babysitting *in Hamilton at Tel. 441/234-1031.*

BANKS, CREDIT CARDS, & CURRENCY

To begin with, the Bermudian dollar is exactly equivalent in value to the US dollar and is divided by 100 cents. While you can interchangeably use either currency (both are legal tender here) in Bermuda, you will have difficulties converting Bermudian dollars back into US or Canadian dollars once you have returned home. You can usually request that all change from purchases be given to you in US dollars only, thus avoiding the reconverting problem back home.

Fortunately, a brand new currency exchange office in the international airport's newly renovated departure terminal makes it much easier to exchange any unused Bermudian bills and coins into US, Canadian, British, Japanese, or other major monetary units. Operated by Randy Masters, **The Exchange** offers competitive rates on all sorts of currency services. They also sell Bermudian Monetary Authority's beautiful gold and silver mint coins that make for great gifts. *The Exchange's normal hours are Monday, Wednesday, and Friday from 11:00am until 4:30pm, as well as Tuesday, Thursday, and Saturday from 11:00am until 7:30pm, and is often open for the early morning flights that arrive and depart from the airport.* For more details call them at 441/297-4663.

I strongly suggest that you consider using travelers checks for added peace of mind. Now that American Express has doubled its fee to at least 2%, you should ask your bank if they offer another major brand such as Visa, Thomas Cook, Bank of America, or Barclays (sometimes banks will even waive the fee on these). In any case, you may be told that photo ID is unnecessary to cash these at shops, restaurants, hotels, and banks, but don't count on it! Make sure you have at least one piece of photo ID with you whenever attempting to use this method of payment.

There are no surcharges imposed for cashing travelers checks at most banks. Try to avoid getting denominations over $50 to make your life easier. Be sure to keep your serial number sheet separated from the checks in a safe place, and keep the 24-hour emergency refund number handy in case of theft or loss.

Bermuda has several large full service banks including the **Bank of Bermuda**, **Bank of Butterfield**, and **Bermuda Commercial Bank**. These banks offer several branch offices which are usually open from 9:30 am until 3pm from Monday to Thursday, and 9:30 am until 4:30pm on Fridays. These banks can exchange most international currencies for a small fee, provide money orders, arrange emergency wire transfers, and cash travelers checks.

There are also a variety of 24-hour **ATM banking machines** linked with the Cirrus, Plus, and Visa international networks for withdrawals from connected accounts (if you remember your PIN number). You can also find a bank at the airport that can be accessed from 11am until 4pm on weekdays.

Credit cards pose an unusual problem in Bermuda. First of all, several hotels, inns, and cottage colonies refuse to accept any credit cards at all. They have their reasons (chargebacks, disputed accounts, and up to 4% in fees), and have a clientele base growing increasingly unhappy with this situation. On the other hand, many resorts, shops, restaurants, and even some taxis will gladly accept Visa, Mastercard, and in some cases American Express and Diners Club. If you desire to pay your bill at a restaurant by credit card, please try to use cash for tips.

Neither American Express or Western Union offer money wire services for tourists in Bermuda. You must make an arrangement with a local bank for this type of transaction.

BARS & NIGHTCLUBS

The minimum drinking age in Bermuda is 18 years old. If you look somewhat younger than this, expect to be asked for picture ID. Expect to pay a cover charge of up to $15 per person at most discos and dance clubs. Most pubs and bars have licenses that forbid them to stay open after 1am. Most nightclubs have special permits to stay open until 3am.

A few private clubs and after hour clubs can be found to be open until sunrise, but you may have to be a member or an invited guest to get in. Please check each parish chapter for specific listings on Bermuda's best bars.

BUSINESS HOURS

Although this is beginning to change for the better, currently most stores in cosmopolitan areas such as Hamilton and St. George are usually open from about 9am until 5:30pm from Mondays to Saturdays. In the high season some tourist shops may open to at least 7pm, and during Harbour Night festivals until 9pm. Many of the shops at the Clocktower Mall near the Royal Naval Dockyard in Sandys are also open on Sundays.

CABLES, TELEXES, & TELEGRAMS

To send or receive a telexes and other types of cables, please contact the **Cable & Wireless** offices *at 20 Church St., Hamilton, Tel. 441/297-7000, from 9am until 5pm Monday through Saturday.*

CHURCHES & HOUSES OF WORSHIP

This is a brief listing of some of the most popular churches and houses of worship in Bermuda. Check the **Bermuda Yellow Pages** for a more complete listing.

• **African Methodist Episcopal,** *St. John's Church, St. Paul's Church, 68 Harrington Sound Road, Smiths Court Street, city of Hamilton. Tel. 441/ 293-8606; Tel. 441/292-0505*

• **Anglican (Church of England),** *Cathedral of the Most Holy Trinity, St. Peter's Church, Church Street, city of Hamilton, York Street, St. George Tel. 441/292-2967; Tel. 441/297-8359*

Apostolic Faith, *Rehoboth Church, United Apostolic Church, Khyber Pass, Warwick, Hartle Drive, Somerset Tel. 441/236-8607; Tel. 441/234-1141*
• **Baptist**, *Emmanuel Baptist Church, First Baptist Church, 35 Dundonald Street, city of Hamilton Middle Road, Devonshire Tel. 441/295-6555; Tel. 441/236-7212*
• **Brethren**,*Calvary Gospel Chapel, Cobbs Hill Gospel Chapel, Rose Hill, Southampton, Cobbs Hill Road, Warwick Tel. 441/234-3250; Tel. 441/236-9413*
• **Church of God**, *First Church of God, First Church of God, Church Lane, Pembroke, Sound View Road, Somerset Tel. 441/295-6080; Tel. 441/234-0973*
• **Methodist**, *Wesley Methodist Church, Grace Methodist Church, Church Street, city of Hamilton, North Shore Road, Pembroke Tel. 441/292-0418; Tel. 441/292-1821*
• **Roman Catholic**, *St. Teresa's Cathedral, St. Michael's Church, Elliot Street, city of Hamilton, South Shore Road, Paget Tel. 441/292-0607, Tel. 441/236-2166*

CONSULATES & EMBASSIES

If you have a major problem that may necessitate a call to your government's representative for Bermuda (lost passport, crime, immigration difficulty, or arrest) these are the best contact numbers:
• **American Consulate General and Canadian Consulate General**
Both are located at 16 Middle Road, Devonshire Tel. 441/295-1342; New York City offices (212) 768-2400.

DOCTORS & HOSPITALS

When an emergency comes up, call the **King Edward VII Memorial Hospital**, *7 Point Finger Road in Paget at Tel. 441/236-2345.* They are open 24 hours per day and can also advise you on how to get a referral for specialists and outside doctors. The **Government Health Clinic** *on Victoria Street in the city of Hamilton Tel. 441/236-0224* may also be of some asistance in less urgent medical and dental matters.

You may find that your North American insurance policy may not cover all related expenses here. Please check with your insurance carrier for details.

ELECTRICITY

Electric current in Bermuda is the same as in North America. All outlets have 2 prongs, carry 120 volt - 60 hertz power, and do not require adapters or converters for consumer products from North America. If you're arriving from Europe, converters will be needed.

EMERGENCIES

Bermuda has just one number to contact the fire department, police department, and ambulances. In case of emergency, *call 911.*

FAXES

Almost any hotel in Bermuda will gladly send or recieve a fax for their guests. Although the cost may vary, expect to pay around $5 per page for a fax to North America. If you want a better price, contact **Cable & Wireless** in the city of Hamilton *at Tel. 441/297-7000,* **Busycomm Ltd.** in the city of Hamilton *at Tel. 441/295-8571,* or **Mailboxes Unlimited** in the city of Hamilton *at Tel. 441/292-6563.*

There are also credit card operated fax machines at several Visitors Service Bureaus and tourist areas.

LAUNDRY SERVICES & DRY CLEANING

While most hotels and resorts offer their own in-house laundry and dry cleaning, the prices are extremely high. Since some of these places can pick up and deliver, a better idea may be to call or visit one of the following laudromats and dry cleaners:

- **Devonshire Laundromat**, *17 Watlington Rd., Devonshire, Tel. 441/236-7117*
- **Duds & Suds**, *63 Middle Rd., Southampton, Tel. 441/234-2824*
- **Quality Dry Cleaners**, *Reid Street, Hamilton, Tel. 441/292-8193*
- **Paget Dry Cleaners**, *Lover's Lane, Paget, Tel. 441/236-5142*
- **Warwick Laundromat**, *Middle Rd., Warwick, Tel. 441/238-9692*
- **West End Laundry**, *57 Somerset Rd., Somerset, Tel. 441/234-3402*

LIBRARIES

The **Bermuda Public Library** has its main location *on Queen Street in the city of Hamilton and can be reached at Tel. 441/295-2905.* Their hours are from 9:30am until 6pm Monday through Friday, and 10am until 5pm on Saturdays. There are branch offices in both Somerset and St. George's, open from 10am until 5pm on Monday, Wednesday, and Saturday.

Visitors may make special arrangements to take out books during their stay; call for details.

MAIL

Bermuda has an excellent postal service with rather reasonable rates. You will only pay about 60 cents to send a post card or light letter to North America via air mail, 75 cents to Europe. The many branch post offices are generally open from 8am until 5pm weekdays only, but the **General Post Office** *on Queen St. in the city of Hamilton* is open from 8am until 12 noon on Saturdays. The friendly postal employees can also sell many nice collectable commerative stamps.

There are also several private parcel and express package and document services in Bermuda including:
- **DHL**, *Church Street in the city of Hamiton at Tel. 441/295-3300*
- **Federal Express**, *Church Street in the city of Hamilton at Tel. 441/295-3854*
- **UPS**, *Par-la-Ville Road in the city of Hamilton at Tel. 441/292-6760*
- **IBC**, *Church Street in the city of Hamilton at Tel. 441/295-2467*

MOVIE THEATERS

Bermuda has a few cinemas usually showing first or second run American and English movies twice a day for about $7.50 each, although matinees may cost less. Exact listings and show times appear in the daily newspapers.

Theaters include:
- **Liberty Theatre**, *49 Union Street, Hamilton Tel. 441/292-7296*
- **Liberty Theatre**, *30 Queen Street, Hamilton Tel. 441/292-2135*
- **New Somers Playhouse**, *37 Wellington St., St. George Tel. 441/297-2821*
- **Neptune Cinema**, *Royal Naval Dockyard, Sandys Tel. 441/234-2923*

NEWSPAPERS

Locally produced newpapers include the *Royal Gazzette* (published Monday through Friday), the *Mid Ocean News* (published on Friday), the *Bermuda Sun* (published Friday), and the *Bermuda Times* (published bi-weekly). These are all available at hundreds of stores throughout the nation.

For those of you who crave news from back home, a selection of international newspapers are flown in daily including the *Wall Street Journal*, *The New York Times*, the *Boston Globe*, *USA Today*, the *London Times*, the *International Herald Tribune*, and an assortment of other well-known periodicals.

PHARMACIES

There are many pharmacies scattered throughout Bermuda. You might be not be able to refill most prescriptions written by non Bermudian doctors. Late night pharmacies include:
- **The Phoenix Center**, *Reid Street, Hamilton Tel. 441/295-3838*. Open 8am until 6pm Monday through Saturday; 12 noon until 6:30pm on Sundays.

• **Peoples Pharmacy**, *Victoria Street, Hamilton Tel. 441/292-7527.* Open 10am until 6pm Monday through Saturday; 10am until 6pm on Sundays.

• **Collector's Hill Apothecary**, *Collector's Hill, Smiths Tel. 441/236-8664.* Open from 8am until 8pm Monday through Saturday; 2pm until 9pm on Sundays.

PHOTO SHOPS & FILM DEVELOPING

Film, camera supplies, and developing are all fairly expensive in Bermuda. The best bets for cameras and film development are:

• **Bermuda Photocraftsmen**, *Reid Street, Hamilton, Tel. 441/295-2698*

• **Sprint Prints**, *Middle Road, Southampton, Tel. 441/238-3267*

• **True Color Minilab**, *Duke of York Street, St George, Tel. 441/297-8024*

• **Jiffy 2 Hour Photo**, *Burnaby Street, Hamilton, Tel. 441/295-4436*

PHYSICALLY-CHALLENGED TRAVELERS

Accessibility laws do not exist for hotels, restaurants, shops, and public buses in Bermuda. Although some of these businesses do try and design a few special entrances and accommodations for wheelchair-bound clients, it is not that common.

My best suggestion is to first contact the **Bermuda Physically Handicapped Association** *at Tel. 441/292-5025.* They may be able to help by providing a specially designed bus, pointing you to hotels and restaurants that have special facilities, and advising you on current conditions. There is also a special transportation service offered by **London Taxi** *at Tel. 441/292-3691*; they maintain a hydraulic lift shuttle. Or you can try one of the following organizations:

• **Society for The Advancement of Travel for the Handicapped**, *New York, N.Y. Tel. 212/447-7284.* A members only service with basic information about travel needs for the physically challenged. Yearly membership is $45 for adults and $25 for students.

• **MossRehab Travel Information Services**, *Philadelphia, Pennsylvania. Tel. 215/456-9600.* A free information and referral service with valuable hints and suggestions on companies which offer travel services for the physically challenged.

• **Flying Wheels Travel**, *Owatonna, Minnesota Tel. 800/535-6790.* A great full service travel agency and group tour operator that can provide helpful information and reservations for the physically challenged. Services include all forms of special transportation and accommodation reservations, and guided group tours.

PUBLIC HOLIDAYS

On these days, most public and private offices, as well as many stores and business, do not open. The exact dates of these holidays vary each year, and may be slightly altered to create a three-day weekend. Public holidays include New Years Day, Good Friday, Easter, Bermuda Day (24 May), Queen's Birthday (late June), Cup Match (late September), Somers Day (August), Labour Day, Rememberance Day (11 November), Christmas Day, and Boxing Day (26 December).

RADIO & TELEVISION

Besides receiving several radio and TV stations from the east coast of America, Bermuda has several of its own. These include **ZBM** at 1340 AM, **ZFB** at 1230 AM, **ZBM** at 89 FM, **ZFB** at 95 FM, **Channel 7 ZFB (ABC)**, and **Channel 9 ZBM (CBS)**. Most resorts offer a full range of additional cable and satellite stations from around the globe.

SAFETY

Just like anywhere else in the world, Bermuda is not immune to crime. Since visitors laden with cash and jewelry make the easiest targets, I strongly suggest taking some logical precautions. Try not to leave your valuables, passport, airplane ticket, or cash anywhere but in a mini safe or safety deposit box. Lock your moped each time you leave it. Carry a money pouch instead of a wallet. Keep your windows and patio doors locked at all times, even when you are sleeping in your room. Bring traveler's checks instead of cash, and try not to walk around the back side of Hamilton late at night.

SERVICE CHARGES

In the vast majority of cases, a service chrge of 10% is added to your accommodations bill. This charge is divided up by the hotel's employess and eventually gets to people like bellmen, chamber maids, and other staff. Please try to leave a bit more for those who have gone out of their way to asist you. Additional charges like the so-called energy surcharge or resort levy may also be imposed on hotel bills.

Restaurants will often impose a 15% service charge at the bottom of your bill. This also gets divided between the staff, but if the service is excellent, you may wish to leave a bit more.

SMOKING

While smoking in Bermuda is not heavily regulated by shops, restaurants, bars, and offices, it is still somewhat impolite to light up in many establishments without first asking for permission. Most restaurants have dedicated non-smoking areas, and prefer that you avoid using pipes and cigars while indoors.

Americans tend to go cigar crazy here and purchase Cuban products for their consumption while in Bermuda. While these cigars are illegal to import back to the US, many people have been known to replace the original labeling with stickers from cheaper Dominican Republic cigars and attempt tricking the customs officials back home. Cuban cigars range in price from about $9 to over $28 a piece, and can be found at the **Tienda del Tobacco** and the **Chatham House** (both on Front Street in downtown Hamilton), as well as at many trendy restaurants, bars, and tobacconists.

Those looking for American and Canadian name-brand cigarettes will find them for between $4.50 and $5.75 per pack at almost any hotel, restaurant, bar, gas station, or grocery shop.

TAXES

The only taxes in Bermuda relevant to your visit are the 7.5% government **hotel occupancy tax**, which is added to your hotel bill, and a $20 per person **airport departure tax** (waived for infants up to two years old) that is now usually included in all airline ticket prices. Cruise ship passengers will be notified about any pending port charges when they book passage here.

TELEPHONES

This is one area where Bermuda is more advanced than just about any other destination I have visited. There are payphones all over the islands, and they come in different types. The older style phones require that you first dial the local number, and then drop in 20 cents after the party answers. You may also be able to dial collect and credit card calls with operator assistance from these older phones.

The newer digital display phones allow you to call locally or internationally by depositing coins before you make your call. You can aslo use the Bermuda Telephone Company cash cards (available at their offices and Visitors Service Bureaus), and make operator assisted collect and credit card calls. To call North America you must first dial the country code (1), the area code and the number. If you require operator assistance for a collect or credit card call you must dial the operator (0), then the country code (1), then the area code and number you wish to reach. International calls are cheapest between 11pm and 7am on weeknights. If you need to get through to an 800 number not in service from Bermuda, you may dial 900, instead of 800, and pay the normal long distance international rates to reach that line.

USING PRE-PAID CALLING CARDS IN BERMUDA

One way to get around the high cost of calling your home or office from Bermuda is to buy one of the new pre-paid international calling cards. Offered by local Bermuda-based companies such as **Bermuda Cable & Wireless** and **TeleBermuda International**, these plastic disposable cards can be bought in denominations from $10 to $50 each and can be used from almost any payphone in Bermuda. A typical call to North America will cost around $1 per minute or so with these cards, which you can buy at many gift shops, some pharmacies, the Elbow Beach snack shop, or from either of the two companies mentioned above directly. While not all that easy to use at first, after a few attempts they can save you plenty of money and frustration. These cards expire 90 days after their first usage, and have instructions listed on their backside.

Contact:

• **Cable & Wireless**, Customer Service Desk, Church St., Hamilton. Tel. 441/297-7022.

• **TeleBermuda**, Customer Service Desk, Front St., Hamilton. Tel. 441/292-7853

The Bermuda Telephone Company also offers an extensive selection of 976 exchange audiotext 24 hour information services which are the price of a local call. These include recorded messages on such topics as stock reports, international news stories, sports scores and profiles, current weather in major cities, horoscopes, soap opera updates, science reports, childrens stories, music and entertainment reviews, health suggestions, TV listings, recipes, legal advice, and environmental news. Please check the red colored pages of the *Bermuda Telephone Directory* for more information and specific exchange numbers in this 976 program.

If you decide to call anywhere from your hotel, you'll be in shock when you get the bill. Besides charging as much as a 350% surcharge on calls made from your room, some hotels can really rip off its clients. In one case, a large resort in Bermuda will charge an additional $5 surcharge for every attempt at making an overseas call. Even if you call collect, use a calling card, get a busy signal, or hang up, you will have to pay $5 to this hotel for each attempt (this is a real ripoff). You may also need to add an extra digit or two to get an outside line. My best advice is to leave your room, walk downstairs to the lobby, and use a pay phone for any long distance calls. I have included a list of impotant phone numbers and access codes for your reference.

Useful Telephone Numbers

• Local Operator	0
• International Operator	01
• USA Country Code	1
• Canada Country Code	1
• Directory Assistance	411
• Emergencies	911
• Hamilton Police Station	295-0011
• St. George's Police Station	297-1122
• Somerset Police Station	234-1010
• Air Sea Resque	297-1010
• King Edward VII Hospital	236-2345
• Bermuda Government	292-5998
• What's On in Bermuda	974
• Weather Forecast	977
• Current Weather	977-1
• Marine Forecast	977-2
• Storm Warnings	977-3
• Dial a Prayer	975
• Time and Temperature	909
• ATT Calling Card Access Code	800/872-2881
• MCI Calling Card Acess Code	800/623-0484

TIME

The clocks here are set at Greenwich Mean Time minus 4 hours. This makes Bermuda one hour ahead of the Eastern time zone in North America. Each year, Bermuda follows daylight savings time between April and October.

TIPPING

This is a matter of personal opinion, but I will give you mine. Even if your hotel posts a 10% service charge, I would still give a $1 per bag tip to a porter or bellman, $1.50 per night tip for the chambermaid, and a $3 tip to the concierge each time he reserves a tee off time or restaurant reservation for you.

In the bars and clubs it is usual to leave a $1 tip per drink. At restaurants that do not impose service charges, leave about 15% of the total bill. If they do impose a service charge, and you are rather impressed with their service, leave another 5% to 10% tip. If a sommelier (wine steward) is at all helpful, give him 5% of the bottle's cost.

Taxi drivers should get about a 10% tip on the metered rate, unless they are not nice. For those of you on cruise ships, check with the cruise director for suggestions on tipping your service staff.

TOURIST INFORMATION

The following are the locations and contact numbers for the Visitors Service Bureaus throughout Bermuda. Their hours vary from season to season, but you can usually reach them from 9am until 4pm Monday through Saturday.

- **Visitor Service Bureau**, *8 Front Street, Hamilton, Tel. 441/296-1480*
- **Visitor Service Bureau**, *Kings Square, St. George, Tel. 441/297-1642*
- **Visitor Service Bureau**, *Royal Naval Dockyard, Tel. 441/234-3824*
- **Visitor Service Bureau**, *Somerset Branch, Tel. 441/234-1388*
- **Visitor Service Bureau**, *Bermuda Airport, Tel. 441/293-0736*
- **Bermuda Departnent of Tourism**, *43 Church Street, Tel. 441/292-0023*

WEDDINGS

Visitors who wish to get married while in Bermuda must contact your local office of the Bermuda Department of Tourism to obtain a Notice of Intended Marriage. This form must be appropriately completed, and sent several weeks in advance to the **Registrar General of Bermuda**, *Government Registration Building, 30 Parliment Street, Hamilton HM12, Tel. 441/ 297-7709*. Along with the paperwork, you must send a bank check for $150 to cover the cost of the registration, license, and printed notices that will appear in Bermudian newspapers.

Civil weddings can be performed at the Registry General's office for an additional $150, or at any number of churches, halls, and private estates. For more information about private functions, contact **The Wedding Salon**, *51 Reid Street, Hamilton, Tel. 441/292-5677* or **The Bridal Suite**, *Southampton, Tel. 441/238-0818*.

8. SPORTS & RECREATION

BERMUDA'S FAMOUS BEACHES

For many vacationers, it is the chance to bask in the sun on a beautiful pink sand beach that has brought them to Bermuda. There are actually dozens of impressive beaches to enjoy and explore here, especially between May and October when the turquoise sea can reach temperatures of up to 85 degrees Fahrenheit (29 degrees Celsius).

While many hotels and resorts have their own private beaches and swimming areas, many other fine beaches in Bermuda are accessible to the public and are often even more dramatic. Some of these beaches are perfect for socializing while you suntan, while others provide a more secluded and intimate setting. I strongly suggest visiting a few different locations, each with its own unique features.

Some of the more famous beaches (especially along the south shore) offer lifeguard posts, clean bathrooms, changing rooms, showers, snack shops, telephone booths, taxi stands, and snorkeling and beach gear rental shops. Public transportation can take you to most of Bermuda's fine beaches, and a helpful bus schedule and beach location map called *Bermuda's Guide to Beaches and Transportation* is available for free from the Visitors Service Bureaus.

Use common sense when sunbathing or swimming in Bermuda. Take a high SPF waterproof suntan lotion or sun-block with you to avoid a serious sunburn. Read all of the notices posted on the beach so that you can swim in safety. Supervise your children, and consider taking them to one of the more sheltered cove beaches with minimal undertow currents.

Keep in mind that tar will occasionally wash up on the shore, so remove any tar before permanently staining your clothing or footwear. Also keep your valuables in the hotel's safe, as you won't be needing them at the beach. Remember that all beach houses, life guards, and facilities may be closed during the low season.

I've listed my favorite beaches below. Let me know what you think!

Elbow Beach
South Road, Paget

This long stretch of south shore coastline is protected by a series of offshore reefs. The resulting calm waters and small waves are easy to manage, and the water is filled with schools of small friendly sub-tropical fish. Your best best here is to enter the beach from the famous **Elbow Beach Hotel** and pay a $3 charge (free for this hotel's guests) to take advantage of the cabana-style private changing rooms, spotless restrooms, snackshop, and small beach hut that rents snorkeling gear, beach chairs, sun umbrellas, towels, and flotation devices.

This beach is always busy in the warmer months. If you don't need the facilities, you can enter the public part of the beach via Tribe Road # 4 and avoid paying the $3 fee.

Horseshoe Bay Beach
South Shore Park, South Road, Southampton

Horseshoe Bay is perhaps Bermuda's most photographed and famous public beach. The crescent shaped long pink sand beachfront becomes the daytime stomping ground for hundreds of singles and couples during the summer. The water here is deep blue with medium sized waves and a brisk undercurrent.

During the high season there are lifeguards on duty, a beach house with public showers and changing rooms, restrooms, an inexpensive snackshop with a lovely outdoor patio, a telephone booth, a taxi stand, and snorkeling gear rental shop. Admission is always free, and the crowd is rather lively.

Jobson's Cove
South Shore Park, South Road, Warwick

Here you will find a quiet and beautiful small cove beach, sheltered from harsh currents and large waves. Each time I come here I see only a handful of couples swimming and sunbathing on the pristine sandy beach between a series of large shrub-covered cliffs. This is an excellent place to get away from the crowds; admission is free, but there are almost no facilities available here.

Warwick Long Bay Beach
South Road, Warwick

With over a half mile of pink sandy beachfront set against a backdrop of grassy hills, **Warwick Long Bay Beach** is the longest beach in all of Bermuda. The relatively calm waters are sheltered from strong undertows and big waves from the nearby offshore coral reef, a part of which can be seen majestically rising from the sea. Compared to some of the other major beaches in Bermuda, this one is usually half empty.

Facilities here include public restrooms and lots of parking spaces. Admission is free, and the people here are rather down to earth.

Astwood Park Beach

Astwood Park, South Road, Warwick

Set below a wonderful seaside park, this cute little cove style beach offers its visitors a chance to swim and sunbathe in absolute peace and tranquility. The pretty beachfront has soothingly soft pink sand, and the water is fairly calm. You can snorkel a little here, but the beach is more noted as the perfect location to enjoy a wonderfully romantic picnic and catch a few rays. Admission is free; there are almost no facilities.

Tobacco Bay Beach

Coot Pond Road, St. George's

Although a bit out of the way, this cove beach is a fantastic place to enjoy nature's unspoiled beauty. The beachfront here is a bit small, and faces onto sheltered turquoise waters and dramatic sea rock formations which are an easy swim away. A small adjacent beach house offers public restrooms, showers, watersports equipment rentals, changing rooms, and a basic snack shop. Admission is free, but to avoid overcrowded days, come here on summer weekends (when the cruise ships are not in port).

St. Catherine's Beach

Fort St. Catherine, Barry Road, St. George's

This often empty strip of beautiful sand and sea rests just below the massive defensive walls of **Fort St. Catherine** and was once part of the private grounds of the now closed Club Med resort. It's an excellent beach for a good suntan or quick swim, but don't go out too far here, the currents are strong! The old Club Med beach house is now locked up, so bathrooms and other facilities are not available, but admission is free.

Shelly Bay Beach

North Shore Road, Hamilton

Shelly Bay is one of the nicest large beaches on the north shore of Bermuda. It has a great shallow and sandy sea bottom which allows people to walk out way into the sea without even getting your hair wet. Since the calm beach is lined by trees, finding shade is not a problem here.

Located far away from most hotels and resort areas, this beach has become more popular with Bermudians than with tourists. A full service beach house contains public bathrooms, a snackbar, snorkeling gear rental shop, changing rooms, and showers. Admission is free, and weekdays are the best time to visit here.

Church Bay Beach
South Road, Southampton

This is a peaceful secluded cove which has a tiny pink sand beach studded with boulders, calm waters, and a rocky ocean surface that attracts an amazing array of semi-tropical fish species. There are no facilities at this beach; remember to bring your own rafts, snorkeling gear, cold beverages, and towels. Admission to this beach area is free.

Somerset Long Bay Beach
Daniel's Head Road, Sandys

This is a long sandy beach with shallow waters that are perfect for the whole family. Surrounded by a tranquil park and nature preserve, Somerset Long Bay is favored by locals and tourists alike.

As long as you don't mind a constant wind, this is a great place to spend the day getting the perfect tan. Admission is free, but there are no real facilities here except for public restrooms.

BOAT RENTALS & CHARTERS

Renting a sail or motor boat is one of the best ways to enjoy a summer afternoon of exploration. There are several providers of boats in all sizes for all skill levels including sunfish, windsurfing boards, sea kayaks, Boston Whalers, and O'Day Daysailers, as well as more exotic skippered motor yachts and charter schooners. A refundable damage and theft deposit is required for each rental, and gasoline is not included in the price. Not all companies listed operate in the off-season months.

Contact your local branch of the Bermuda Department of Tourism for additional information and other companies.

Boat Rental Companies

- **Dockyard Boat Rentals**, *Royal Naval Dockyard, Sandys. Tel. 441/234-0300.* Sunfish $25/2 hours; Double Kayak $25/2 hours; 16' Skiff $50/2 hours.
- **Mangrove Marina Ltd.**, *Cambridge Road, Sandys. Tel. 441/234-0914.* Sunfish $25/2 hours; 17' Daysailer $35/2 hours; 12' B.Whaler $45/2 hours.
- **Pompano Beach Watersports**, *Pompano Beach Club, Pompano Beach Road, Southampton. Tel. 441/234-0222.* Windsurfers $12/1 hour; Aqua Finns $12/1 hour; Kayak $12/1 hour.

- **South Side Watersports**, *Grotto Beach Hotel, Blue Hole Hill, Hamilton. Tel. 441/293-2915.* Boardsailer $20/1 hour; Sunfish $25/1 hour; Kayak $12/1 hour.
- **Salt Kettle Boat Rentals**, *Salt Kettle, Paget. Tel. 441/236-4863.* Sunfish $40/2 hours; 17' Daysailer $60/2 hours.
- **Rance's Boatyard**, *Crow Lane, Paget. Tel. 441/292-1843.* 16' Gemini $45/2 hours; 13' B.Whaler $50/2 hours.

CHARTERED & SKIPPERED YACHTS

- **Bermuda Caribbean Yacht Co.**, *52' Ketch "Night Wind." Tel. 441/238-8578.* Capacity of 25 people; rates quoted for 6 people: $280 and up (4 hours)
- **Golden Rule Cruise Charters**, *60' Schooner "Golden Rule." Tel. 441/238-1962.* Capacity of 30 people; rates quoted for 8 people: $470 and up (4 hours).
- **Ocean Wind Charters**, *41' Morgan "Ocean Wind." Tel. 441/238-0825.* Capacity of 20 people; rates quoted for 6 people: $270 and up (4 hours).
- **Sand Dollar Cruises**, *40' Sloop "Sand Dollar." Tel. 441/236-1967.* Capacity of 18 people; rates quoted for 8 people: $310 and up (4 hours).

CHARTERED & SKIPPERED MOTOR YACHTS

- **Bermuda Barefoot Cruises**, *32' Cabin Cruiser "Minnow." Tel. 441/236-3498.* Capacity of 20 people; rates quoted for 8 people; $385 and up (4 hours).
- **Salt Kettle Boat Rentals**, *35' motor yacht "Syborata." Tel. 441/236-4863.* Capacity of 18 people; rates quoted for 8 people; $345 and up (4 hours).

BOWLING

There is only one place to go bowling in all of Bermuda: the **Warwick Lane**, *Middle Road in Warwick, Tel. 441/236-5290.* Over 20 lanes are open from 6pm until 12 midnight on Weekdays, and 2pm until 12 midnight on Weekends. The cost per lane is about $3 a game, not including mandatory shoe rental.

The alley is also the host of the yearly WIBC-sanctioned Bermuda Rendezvous Bowling Tournament in February.

CRICKET

This is a serious sport in Bermuda, and can be watched at several locations between April and August including the **St. George's Cricket Club**, *Willington Slip Road, St. George's, Tel. 441/297-0374*, the **Somerset**

Cricket Club *on Broome Street in Sandys, Tel. 441/234-0327,* and the **National Sports Club** *in Devonshire on Middle Road in Devonshire, Tel. 441/ 236-6994.*

The big event in Bermuda's east end versus west end cricket circuit is when as many as 13,000 spectators jam the **Somers Day Cup Match Festival** in late July or early August.

FIELD HOCKEY

Each weekend from September through April, several local hockey teams play at sights around Bermuda including the **National Sports Club** *on Middle Road in Devonshire, Tel. 441/236-6994.* This is also the site of the annual **Bermuda Hockey Festival and Tournament** in August and September.

FISHING

Although some of the world's finest reef, shore, and deep sea fishing takes place off Bermuda year round, the best months to enjoy this sport are from May to November. Since Bermuda is surrounded by plenty of reef lined coast, shallow seafront, and two major offshore fishing banks (known as the **Argus** and **Challenger banks**), over 600 varieties of fish species may be found including blue marlin, greater amberjack, tuna, pompano, shark, wahoo, bonefish, snapper, grouper, mackerel, barracuda, parrotfish, grunt, triggerfish, chub, porgy, blue marlin.

No special license is required to fish off of Bermuda, but there are several regulations that must be adhered to. No spear fishing is permitted within one mile of shore, spear guns and scuba tanks may not be used to go spear fishing. Shore fishing is prohibited at most large public beach areas. Spiny lobsters may only be caught from September through March, and by Bermudian residents only. Protected marine species include whales, turtles, dolphins, porpoises, coral, sea rods, sea fans, conchs, scallops, Atlantic pearl oysters, helmet shells, and others.

If you're interested in participating for prizes in the year-round Department of Tourism sponsored fishing competitions, contact Tom Smith at the **Bermuda Game Fishing Association**, *P.O. Box HM 1306, Hamilton HM FX, Tel. 441/238-0112.* This local organization is affiliated with the International Game Fishing Association, and follows its rules.

For those of you interested in **shore fishing**, you should try your luck at **Spring Benny's Bay**, **Somerset Long Bay**, **Shelly Bay**, **West Whale Bay**, and around the **Great Sound**. Local suppliers will be glad to point out their tips and favorite locations. Expect to spend about $10 per day or $50 per week for rod and reel rentals (plus a $25 refundable deposit), and $4 for a pound of suggested bait (usually squid or fry).

Fishing Gear Rental Companies
- **Four Winds Fishing Tackle**, *2 Woodlands Road, Pembroke Tel. 441/292-7466*
- **Mangrove Marina Ltd.**, *Cambridge Road, Sandys Tel. 441/234-0914*

If you are more interested in **reef and deep sea fishing**, its best to contact one of the many sportfishing and charter boat companies in Bermuda. Most of these licensed boats are fully stocked with tackle, bait, fish locating sonar, fighting chairs, and several comforts including kitchens and bathrooms. Although prices vary, expect to pay about $600 for a half day (4 hour) charter and about $850 for a full day (8 hour) charter, for 4 - 6 passengers depending on the specifics of the boat. Make sure you ask the boat's skipper who gets to keep the catch. On occasion they can arrange a charter share; that way you can join an already existing group for about 20% of the full charter price of the boat. Who knows, maybe you'll break the record of Bill Bundt, an American who landed a 1,190 pound blue marlin!

For more information about charter boat operators, please contact the **Bermuda Charter Fishing Boat Association**, *P.O. Box SB 145, Sandys SB BX, Tel. 441/292-6246*, or the **Bermuda Sport Fishing Association**, *8 Tulo Lane, Pembroke HM 02, Tel. 441/295-2370*. The Bermuda Department of Tourism also prints a free listing of independent charter boats available for hire.

HIKING

Although it is entirely possible to spend your vacation walking down all the country lanes in Bermuda, I have a better suggestion. The **Bermuda Railway Trail** is actually a walking path built upon the former track route of the now defunct Bermuda Railway, circa 1931.

The railroad once ran for some 21 miles starting from the Somerset Bus Depot and crossing the whole country, until winding down all the way over on the outskirts of St. George's on the other side of the country. Although this limestone cliff and hibiscus-laden 1.75 mile-long first section of the trail allows mopeds and scooters as well as pedestrians, all of the other segments are vehicle-free zones. The part of the tracks that once ran through the city of Hamilton has since been replaced by modern roads, thus making the trail only 18 miles or so long these days.

A useful 24-page pamphlet (maps included) entitled *The Bermuda Railway Guide* is available free at any **Visitor's Service Bureau**, and it is the best source for descriptions and directions to the various sights that can be seen from each of the seven sections of the trail. All sections of the trail are always open, but don't walk on its secluded footpaths after dark.

GOLF COURSES

Besides hosting a vast array of professional and amateur golf championships and tournaments, Bermuda offers its visitors a wide range of 9 and 18 hole golf courses to play on. These courses range from beginners level all the way up to world class championship courses created by famous designers. Keep in mind that proper golf attire is requested in most of these locations (shirts must have collars and sleeves, shorts must be Bermuda style, no sneakers, no jeans). Tee off time reservations must be made as far in advance as possible, and at the private clubs you may be limited to specific days of the week as a non-member. Reseeding may take place anywhere between September and November.

Although it is possible to play golf in Bermuda year round, the most popular time is between January and April, when the wind is strong and the temperature is comfortable. Most golf courses will rent clubs and carts, offer private lessons with their Pros, sell golf balls at their Pro shops, and offer refreshments and snacks. Caddies are not commonly available, except at the Mid Ocean Club.

Some of the private high profile courses can be difficult to get a reservation without knowing a member. Let your hotel's social desk or concierge handle these bookings on the day you arrive. If you're interested in joining a tournament, contact any office of the Bermuda Department of Tourism or write the the **Bermuda Golf Association**, *P.O. Box HM-433, Hamilton, Bermuda HM BX, Tel. 441/238-1367.*

Here are some of the better golf courses in Bermuda:

Mid Ocean Club
Tucker's Town, St. George's. Tel. 441/293-0330

This is Bermuda's top golf club, and as you will see from the rates, it maintains a high level of exclusivity. Designed by Charles Blair Macdonald, this 18 hole par 71 championship course of 6547 yards is the site of several PGA tournaments throughout the year. This is a rather private club, and either your hotel's concierge (if they have the right connections) or a club member may be needed to get you a tee off time here.

The non-member price here is about $100 per round, or $50 per guest per round when accompanied by a member, plus cart rental fees. Caddies are available for about $20 per bag, and lessons will cost about $35 per half hour.

Castle Harbour Golf Club
Paynter's Road, Hamilton. Tel. 441/293-2040

This Charles Banks-designed private 18 hole championship par 71 course has 6440 yards of windy oceanview and elevated inland greens.

When they're not hosting a tournament, the course charges $85 per person per round plus cart rental fees, and offers a special sunset rate of $50 per round after 4:30pm, but have your hotel's front desk call well in advance to reserve a round. Lessons are available for $40 per half hour.

Port Royal Golf Course
Middle Road, Southampton. Tel. 441/234-0974

This public 18 hole, par 71 course has 6565 yards of well manicured terrain. Designed by Robert Trent Jones, the course is known primarily for its windy location and elevated tees. The prices here are $50 per round, and only $25 after 4pm, plus cart. Ask your hotel's front desk to arrange tee off times at least a few days in advance.

During the low season, amateur golfers of all levels are may join the club's weekly visitors golf tournament to win special prizes. Lessons can be reserved for about $30 per half hour.

Riddell's Bay Golf & Country Club
Riddell's Bay Road, Warwick. Tel. 441/238-3225

This beautiful private 18 hole par 69 golf course facing the Great Sound has 5588 yards of challenging greens and fairways. First established in 1922, this is the islands' oldest golf course, and manages to keep its links in perfect condition year round. Since the club is so popular with members and visitors alike, you must book tee off times well in advance.

Green fees are about $45 per round on weekdays, and about $55 on weekends and holidays, plus cart rentals. Lessons are $40 per half hour.

Southampton Princess Golf Club
South Road, Southampton. Tel. 441/238-0446

The Princess course is a wonderful place to enjoy a great game of golf, and feel completely welcome by the staff and locals. This par 54 executive 18 hole course has 2684 yards of impeccable greens and fairways. Well maintained and studded with steep hills, this is perhaps the best location to regain your skills before attempting to play on the above (longer) courses.

Each round will cost about $35, or $30 per round if you're staying at this hotel, plus cart rentals. Tee off time reservations can be made at any hotel's concierge desk. Lessons are available for about $30 per half hour.

St. George's Golf Course
Park Road, St. George's. Tel. 441/297-8353.

This beautiful yet windy 18 hole par 62 Robert Trent Jones designed oceanview private course has 4043 yards of small, fast greens. The weekends here are too busy, so try the more relaxing Monday through Friday time slots.

Green fees $35 during the day, and $18 after 4pm, plus cart rentals. Book this one well in advance; it is an unforgettable experience. You can book lessons for about $35 for a half hour.

Belmont Hotel Golf & Country Club
Middle Road, Warwick. Tel. 441/236-1301

Belmont is a nice and easy 18 hole par 70 private golf course of 5777 yards. Since guests of this hotel are offered complimentary green fees, you may find the links to be packed on many days throughout the year. Non-guests will be charged about $53 per round plus cart rentals, and should have their hotel call a few days in advance to make reservations. Lessons are $35 per half hour.

Ocean View Golf Course
North Shore Road, Devonshire. Tel. 441/295-9092

Ocean View is a 9 hole government owned par 35 course with 2956 yards of well manicured fairways and elevated tees. Now going through the final phases of a massive refurbishment, this is becoming a fine place to get in gear for the 18 hole courses.

Rates here are $25 per person during the day for either 9 or 18 holes, and a $12 per round sunset special after 4pm, plus cart rentals. Lessons cost $35 per half hour.

Horizon's Mashie Golf Course
South Road, Paget. Tel. 441/236-0048.

This is a nice 9 hole par 3 private course at the famed Horizon's and Cottages cottage colony on a hilltop overlooking the south shore beaches. This is a good place to come on weekdays when there is almost nobody else on the links.

Open to the public for only $20 per round during the week and $25 per round during weekends and holidays. Just keep in mind that golf carts are not available. Lessons are $40 per half hour.

HORSEBACK RIDING

A variety of trail rides costing from $35 to $45 per person are provided by **Spicelands Riding Center**, *Middle Road in Paget at Tel. 441/238-8212.* For your children, you may wish to contact **Lee Bow Stables**, *Tribe Road in Devonshire, Tel. 441/236-4181* where those under 18 can enjoy trail rides for about $28 per hour. Both of these locations offer English- style instruction.

JET SKIING

These days the safety issues involved with this sport, as well as the local objection to noise pollution, has allowed only one company to continue offering this activity. You can call **Club Wet and Wild**, *Castle Harbour, Tel. 441/293-2543,* or *Tel. 441/234-2426 at the Royal Naval Dockyard.*

Expect to spend about $45 per single and $70 per double each half hour. Reservations are required and children under 16 are not allowed to drive these wave runners.

PARA-SAILING

Weather permitting, para-sailing companies offer exciting flights on powerboat guided para-sails from about March through November. Rates average about $50 per person. You can call **Skyrider**, *the Royal Naval Dockyard, Tel. 441/234-3019;* **South Side Scuba**, *Castle Harbour Resort, Tel. 441/293-2915;* or **Nautilus Diving**, *Southampton Princess Beach Club, Tel. 441/238-2332.*

RUGBY

Bermuda's yearly weekend rugby season is hosted at the **National Sports Club**, *Middle Road in Devonshire, Tel. 441/236-6994.* The season culminates in the fantastic **Easter Rugby Classic**, also held at the same venue, which includes several international teams.

SEA-BASED EXCURSIONS

This is my favorite way to spend a summer afternoon in Bermuda. Since there are so many different companies that offer these services, I am suggesting only the memorable ones. Be careful if you book this through your hotel's front desk or concierge because they make large kickbacks to sell you on the larger and less impressive tours.

Many of these trips are designed as either relaxing sunset sailings, parties on motor yachts, rum swizzle sailing adventures, or various theme cruises. **Snorkeling trips** will usually include visits in a couple of different spots (either the sea gardens, reefs, or ship wrecks) and maybe a stop at a beautiful secluded beach or islet. Lessons and all equipment are included in the cost. Remember to bring a towel, waterproof suntan lotion, and a bathing suit with you. If you want to see shipwrecks and reefs laden with countless varieties of exotic fish, and you don't want to get wet, your best bet is either a **submarine** or a **glass bottom boat ride**. These are the shortest of the sea-based excursions, usually lasting only about two hours or so.

Finally, the most bizarre excursions in Bermuda may very well be the **undersea walk** where adventure-seeking individuals can put on a brass and glass mask (large enough to wear prescription glasses under) and walk along the sea bottom among the fish and coral.

Most of the companies below run during the high season only, and will reschedule excursions if the water visibility or sea conditions are not acceptable. These trips may not depart every day, and credit cards are accepted by only a handful of these companies. Special arrangements can possibly be made to pick you up at a variety of wharf locations other than the listed departure point.

The companies I'd recommend include:

- **Pitman's Snorkeling**, *Tel. 441/234-0700*. Four hour Eco-snorkeling trip; $38 per person; Departs from Somerset Bridge; Morning & Afternoon trips.
- **Hayward's Snorkeling**, *Tel. 441/292-8652*. Four hour snorkeling trip; $38 per person; Departs from Albouy's Point; Morning & Afternoon trips.
- **Hat Trick Trimaran Sailing**, *Tel. 441/234-1434*. Four hour sail - snorkeling trip; $35 per person; Departs from Dockyard; Morning & Afternoon trips.
- **Jessie James Cruises**, *Tel. 441/236-4804*. Four hour snorkeling trip; $40 per person; Departs from Various Points; Morning & Afternoon trips.
- **Sand Dollar Cruises**, *Tel. 441/234-1434*. Four hour dinner - sail; Departs from Castle Harbour; $65 per person; Evening Trips.
- **Enterprise Submarine**, *Tel. 441/234-3547*. Three hour cruise/sub ride; Departs from Dockyard; $65 per person; Morning & Afternoon trips.
- **Underwater Wonderworld**, *Tel. 441/292-4434*. Three hour sea bottom walk trip; Departs from Flatt's Village; $40 per person; Morning & Afternoon trips.
- **Undersea Walk**, *Tel. 441/234-2861*. Three hour sea bottom walk trip; Departs from Somerset; $40 per person; Morning & Afternoon trips.
- **Bermuda Water Tours**, *Tel. 441/295-3727*. Two hour glass bottom cruise; Departs from Front Street; $25 per person; Morning & Afternoon trips.
- **Reef Roamers**, *Tel. 441/292-8652*. Two hour glass bottom cruise; Departs from Front Street; $30 per person; Morning & Afternoon trips.
- **Salt Kettle Boat Co.**, *Tel. 441/236-4863*. Three hour sailing party; $32 per person; Departs from Salt Kettle; Morning & Afternoon trips.
- **Longtail Sailing**, *Tel. 441/292-0282*. Three hour sail - snorkeling trip; $35 per person; Departs from Albouy's Point; Morning & Afternoon trips.

THREE GREAT SEA-BASED EXCURSIONS!

Although there are a seemingly endless array of sea-based excursions to be enjoyed here, these are my picks for three of the best water-based excursions in all of Bermuda.

1) Hat-Trick Catamaran Sailing, Royal Dockyard, Tel. 441/235-5077

For the most relaxing sail of your life, and perhaps a chance to observe Bermuda's marine life up close in true style, reserve a place aboard one of Hat-Trick's unforgettable catamaran snorkel trips or perhaps a shorter tranquil sunset sailing. This amazingly beautiful and rather fast round-the-world racing catamaran departs at 10am, 2pm, and 6pm from either the Watersports Centre at the Royal Naval Dockyard or the pier at Cambridge Beaches. Skipper Keith Ward, the twenty-something son of a respected Bermudian boat builder, expertly navigates his way between the reefs to reach some of the most amazing fish-feeding and observation spots anywhere near the islands. He takes up to a dozen or so fortunate people on one of the most beautiful and relaxing catamaran rides in the world while serving home-made cookies with delicious rum swizzles.

During the ride Keith imparts a good bit of his own superb first hand knowledge of the local marine ecology, Bermudian history, and the unique area culture. If you want to jump in the shallow fish-infested reefs are given wet-suits as well as flotation devises and are then told about which types of exotic fish they may encounter before being led down the steps to the almost unbelievably beautiful undersea world. Those who prefer not to get wet may want to just sit up on the deck and work on their tan while they talk with the exceedingly friendly skipper about whatever comes to mind. Perfect for visitors of all ages and backgrounds, this is certainly the most informative and exhilarating sailing trip of its kind I have ever taken anywhere on the globe. Prices start at a mere $30 per person, and include all gear and refreshments. Private charters and customized sailings can be accommodated with several days advance notice. I strongly suggest calling the folks at Hat-Trick at least a day or two in advance to reserve your space on a trip that you will not soon forget.

2) Bermuda Bell Diving, Flatts Village, Tel. 441/292-4434

Join a team of young, friendly and professional Bermudians that will take you out on a motor launch from Flatts Village and prepare you with instructional videos on what your trip below the surface will be like and what species of marine life you may encounter. Perfect for people of all ages, this trip takes clients under the shallow waters off nearby Harrington Sound. After changing into a wet suit and being fitted with air-tight old world styled brass diving helmets that are pumped full of oxygen (you won't even get you hair wet!), you descend from the boat's sea-ladder and head 20 feet down to the sea floor. You and five other clients will enter a world of colorful coral heads filled with feisty fish that come right up to feed next to your helmet while they surround you in a blaze of color. Using waterproof pens and paper, the skilled, patient staff will point out creatures such as coral, lobsters, fish, and all sorts of marine life while you spend 25 minutes or so in an underwater environment that was formerly seen only by scuba divers. Underwater videos of your trip below are available for sale on board, as well as souvenir T-shirts, cold drinks and snacks. The entire trip lasts about 2 1/2 hours and is offered twice daily when the weather permits. This is a real treat for adults, kids, seniors, and even those who don't like swimming. For less than $50 a person you will definitely have a great time and learn something about the marine enivornment in the process!

3) Robinson's Boston Whalers, Somerset Bridge, Tel. 441/ 234-0914

Rent your own easy-to-operate Boston Whaler motorboat and have the time of your life. These shallow bottomed 40 horsepower boats can fit up to 4 adults comfortably and feature retractable "Bimini" sunroofs. The Whalers can zip even the least experienced landlubber around many of the coast's best fish feeding and observation areas alongside shipwrecks, pristine beaches reachable only by boat, and alongside magnificent Bermudian mansions situated along the coastline as well as many of the small islands that surround Bermuda. Mr. Robinson provides detailed boating instructions, maps, and safety tips, and will have you out to sea and loving every minute of it in no time. Make sure to bring a bottle or two of bottled water, good sun screen, and some old toast or rolls to feed the fish where Mr. Robinson suggests. This is a great thing to do when the weather is nice and should not be missed while staying on this amazing island! A mere $100 will get you a Whaler for 4 hours and is well worth the price for this unique self-guided adventure.

SHALLOW WATER SNORKELING

The south shore of Bermuda has many fine beaches which are perfect for shallow water snorkeling. The best of these is **Church Bay Beach**, but there are fish near almost any beach you find. Resorts and hotels such as **Elbow Beach, Southampton Princess, The Reefs, Pompano Beach Club**, and others have their own snorkeling gear rental facilities.

If you're going off a hotel's property to snorkel, you may want to consider daily or weekly rentals any of the scuba companies above. Expect a mask, snorkel, and fins to rent for about $13 per day or $50 per week, with a mandatory $30 or so refundable loss and damage deposit.

SCUBA DIVING

Bermuda's excellent diving season usually runs from March through November each year. For those of you who are inexperienced in this sport, you can take a resort course and learn the basics on land, practice in a pool, and then go out for a supervised ocean dive.

For those of you with a current PADI certification (bring your card!), there are dozens of wrecks, reefs, and caves to enjoy. One tank, two tank, cave, and night dives can be enjoyed with the assistance of several Bermuda based outfitters, but some necessary equipment will cost an additional fee.

For those who wish to get certified in Bermuda, the cost is about $350 and the process takes about 4 days. Consider the purchase of a PADI diver accident insurance policy, and take all of the proper precautions, as there is only one decompression chamber at **King Edward VII Hospital**.

A well-written pamphlet entitled: *Bermuda – Where to Dive* can be obtained for free from any Bermuda Department of Tourism office. Some of the better places include:

- **Blue Water Divers**, *Tel. 441/234-1034*. Four hour resort course $85; 1 tank dive $40; 2 tank dive $60; Night dive $60; Robinson's Marina, Sandys.
- **Fantasea Diving**, *Tel. 441/236-6339*. Four hour resort course $85; 1 tank dive $40; 2 tank dive $60; Night dive $65; Darrell's Wharf, Paget.
- **South Side Scuba**, *Tel. 441/293-2915*. Four hour resort course $85; 1 tank dive $40; 2 tank dive $60; Night dive $60; Grotto Beach Hotel.
- **Nautilus Diving Ltd.**, *Tel. 441/238-2332*. Four hour resort course $85; 1 tank dive $45; 2 tank dive $65; Night dive $60; Southampton Princess Hotel.

SPAS & RELAXATION

Over the past ten years, a select few hotels in Bermuda have begun to offer a variety of spa services and complete health and beauty programs. These range from the availability of beauty treatments and Swedish massages, to more complex and effective rake, aromatheraphy, and deep tissue sports massages. A handful of the better hotels, such as **Southampton Princess**, **Newstead**, and **Ariel Sands** can arrange massages for their guests on a half and full hour basis, but the treatments may vary greatly in effectiveness depending on the venue and masseuse. While some private "members-only" clubs such as the Coral Beach and Tennis Club also offer good half and full day spa programs, these are not available to the general public and thus will not be discussed here.

These days the most professional and highly regarded operator of spas and beauty salons in Bermuda is a well-established family-owned business known as **BerSalon**, boasting a highly trained staff of English and European-trained massage and beauty therapists. I have personally tried several of their treatments and can attest to the almost immediate reduction in my stress level, the vast improvement of my overall attitude, and an ability to sleep more deeply than ever before. The staff are each specialists in various beauty and relaxation therapies, and utilize the most advanced spa equipment and corresponding sea plant extract products from English and French spa suppliers, such as Guinot of France, as well as custom blended sweet almond based massage oils infused with natural plant extracts from around the world.

BerSalon operates two state of the art spa centers in Bermuda, as well as several hair and beauty salons, all of which provide excellent services. Their opulent new split level Aquarian Baths spa facility at the magnificent **Cambridge Beaches** cottage colony in Sandy's Parish is one of the most relaxing and inviting spas on earth. Complete with a saltwater indoor swimming pool as well as a spa bar serving healthy snacks and fresh juices, this oasis of tranquility and relaxation was recently selected as among the five best spa resorts in the world by the *Conde Naste Traveler* magazine reader survey. The larger BerSalon spa over at the **Sonesta Beach Resort** in Paget parish offers roughly the same treatments, facilities, and services, but can accommodate a greater number of clients at one time in separate ladies and gents sections.

Upon entering the spa you are warmly greeted and offered a warm herbal tea or glass of ice cold water before being shown to your locker. After changing into a plush cotton robe you have plenty of free time to just relax for a while in either a powerful whirlpool bath, a sauna, or Turkish steam bath. Once you have showered off (soaps, shampoos, gels, and even disposable shavers with cream are provided), you can sit back and read one of many chic European magazines about travel and culture in their relaxation lounge. As the hour of your scheduled therapies approaches, one of their superb therapists leads you to a well appointed treatment room complete with relaxing new age music and very comfortable massage tables. Unlike the famous spas that I have visited in Switzerland, France, Germany, and Belgium, the emphasis here is to help the clients relax their bodies and soul without any of the European styled medical testing and clinical procedures that make many North Americans uncomfortable at places like Baden-Baden.

Besides incredibly relaxing Swedish and Hydro massages available for 25 minutes or more, there is a vast array of additional treatments available by the half hour, half day and full day such as Reiki, holistic Reflexology, plant extract Aromatherapy, facial therapies, manicure/pedicure, masks, mud baths, hair styling, and other body beauty beautification therapies for both men and women. I enjoyed several services here and by the time my 120-minute session was finished I was so relaxed and at ease that I just wanted to sit next to the sea and look at the waves for a few hours, something I have never been calm enough to even consider before in my life.

Reservations are essential for any therapy or beauty service, and the prices are well worth the results. Expect to spend about $45 or so for a twenty five minute classic massage, $55 for forty minutes of healing holistic reflexology, $75 for fifty minues of Oriental Reiki, $45 for a French cleansing facial, about $185 for a special men's or women's half day spa sampler package with lunch included, and somewhere around $280 for the best full day complete customized spa & body beautification package. Gratuities are not included in the prices of any spa in Bermuda, and I suggest considering at 15% tip which will be shared by your therapists. BerSalon also offers high-end beauty salons at **Elbow Beach-Bermuda** and **Marriott's Castle Harbour** hotels, as well as along downtown Hamilton's Front Street and in St. George's. For more details, contact the spas and salons directly: *Tel. 441/292-8570, Fax 441/295-2506.*

DOLPHIN ENCOUNTERS

A **dolphin encounter program** is operating in the waters just of Southampton parish's south shore. After their success with similar adventures in both Hawaii and Polynesia, the **Dolphin Quest** company is offering visitors the chance to experience a 30 minute interactive encounter in which they can stand or float in a specially designed three acre manmade lagoon and touch a series of trained Atlantic bottlenose dolphins.

The program is based at the beach club in front of the Southampton Princess and costs around $90 per person. Prior to the actual encounter with the dolphins, participants learn basic information about these friendly creatures and their natural habitat. The experience is available to adults as well as children (at differing times), and is scheduled several times each day of the week all year long (wet suits are both available and required during the off season due to cold sea temperatures) rain or shine.

Also available at extra cost are behind the scenes tours, special young children's 2 1/2 hour long supervised educational activity programs, and more. Due to the often heavy demand for space on these new encounters, it may be necessary to either sign up for a daily lottery given the afternoon before you wish to enjoy this event, or wait on line at Dolphin Quest's offices at the Southampton Princess Hotel's beach area wait on a stand-by-basis if a confirmed participant does not arrive on time.

For further details please contact **Dolphin Quest**, *Tel. 441/239-6957.*

SOCCER

Soccer games are a common sight at school fields and public parks throughout Bermuda. Each April several North American and Caribbean national youth soccer teams compete in the **Diadora Youth Soccer Cup** on assorted fields in Bermuda.

SQUASH

The major squash facility is at the **Bermuda Squash Racquets Club**, *Middle Road, Devonshire, Tel. 441/292-6881.* Here you can play on one of 4 courts for about $6 per hour plus a $5 guest fee. Rental racquets and squash balls are also available.

TENNIS

Since its introduction to Bermuda in the late 19th century, tennis has become a vastly popular sport here. With well over 100 courts available at many large hotels, as well as an assortment of public and private clubs, you will almost never have a problem finding court time if you book it in advance.

Many facilities (including listed resort courts) are open to the public and also offer rental racquets, ball machines, lessons, and may require tennis whites to be worn.

BERMUDA'S LARGEST TENNIS FACILITIES

• *Government Tennis Stadium,* Marsh Folly Road, Pembroke. Tel. 441/292-0105; 8 clay, plexicushion courts-3 lit; Rates from $5 per hour.

• *Southampton Princess Hotel,* South Road, Southampton. Tel. 441/238-1005. 11 plexiplave courts-3 lit; Rates from $10 per hour.

• *Elbow Beach Hotel,* South Road, Paget. Tel. 441/236-3535. 5 laycold courts- 2 lit; Rates from $8 per hour.

• *Castle Harbour Resort,* Tucker's Town, Hamilton. Tel. 441/293-2040. 6 cork courts; Rates from $12 per hour.

• *Port Royal Golf Club,* Middle Road, Southampton. Tel. 441/234-0974. 4 plexiplave courts- 2 lit; Rates from $8 per hour.

• *Sonesta Beach Hotel,* South Road, Southampton. Tel. 441/238-8122. 6 plexiplave courts- 2 lit; Rates from $8 per hour.

WATER SKIING

On warm summer days you can't help but notice several private boats pulling skiers along through the bays, sounds, and harbors of Bermuda. Visitors can join in the fun from March through November, and even take a few lessons.

Expect to pay around $50 per half hour (including lessons) for groups of up to 4 people with all the necessary equipment included.

WATERSKI COMPANIES

• **Bermuda Waterski Centre**, *Robinson's Marina, Somerset Bridge, Sandys. Tel. 441/234-3354*

• **Island Water Skiing**, *Grotto Bay Hotel, Blue Hole Hill, Hamilton. Tel. 441/293-2915*

• **Fantasea Diving**, *Castle Harbour Resort, Harbour Road, Warwick. Tel. 441/293-2543*

• **SouthSideWatersports**, *Hamilton Darrell's Wharf, Tucker's Town, Hamilton. Tel. 441/236-6339*

YACHT RACES

During the year, Bermuda hosts an assortment of international and local races and cup matches between March and November. Please check the Festivals & Special Events section of Chapter 6, *Planning Your Trip,* for more details, or contact the nearest Bermuda Department of Tourism office.

9. SHOPPING

WHAT TO BUY

Bermuda has a great selection of shops and boutiques, mostly centered around the city of Hamilton, the town of St. George, and the Royal Naval Dockyard. The best bargains here tend to be in top quality European designer clothing, jewelry and timepieces, china and crystal, figurines, perfumes, and locally made craft products. Don't expect to be bringing home any Japanese electronic equipment like computers or cameras.

Most shops are open from 9am until 5pm Monday through Friday, but as I have mentioned in each regional chapter, some shops may be open on Sundays (especially at the Clocktower mall at the Dockyard), and during special holiday nights and festivals shops may stay open until at least 8pm. There is no sales tax in Bermuda.

PRODUCTS MADE IN BERMUDA

If you're looking to take home something which has been created in Bermuda, you have several choices. The most famous products that come from here include **Outerbridge's Original Sherry Peppers** sauce (used to spice up such items as Bermuda fish chowder), **Gosling's Black Seal** rum, **Somer's Bermuda Gold loquat** liqueur, **Horton's Original Black Rum Cake**, **Fourways Dark and Stormy** cakes, **Davison's** Bermuda fish chowder, **Lili Perfumes** scents for men women, and a vast amount of locally-produced art, crafts, Bermudian Cedar carvings, and much more.

DUTY-FREE PURCHASES

Several items including antiques, collectibles, and locally-made objects are sold duty free in Bermuda. For liquor products to be sold at duty free prices, you should to purchase them at least 24 hours before you depart Bermuda. After prepaying for the liquor, inform the store of your exact flight information or cruise ship and time of departure, and they will held "In-Bond" at the warehouse and then delivered to you at the airport or ship terminal upon to your departure. All liquor shops offer this service, but there is one hitch: US and Canadian customs allows only about 1 liter of liquor per person to be brought in without paying additional duties, and the minimum "In-Bond" purchase is for two bottles.

I suggest sharing your purchase with your traveling companion. Be careful not to exceed the customs allowances of you own country, our else you may get hit with all sorts of additional taxes. There is no duty free shop at the airport or cruise terminal itself.

WHERE TO SHOP IN BERMUDA

Below is a selection of the best shops and boutiques I have found throughout Bermuda. Whenever possible I have included prices on their best buys, and exclusive lines, which are both subject to change. Most of these establishments accept Visa and Mastercard, some take American Express or Diners Club cards, and they will all gladly take travelers checks or cash (and perhaps offer you a better price).

ANTIQUES

Heritage House, *2 Front Street West , (Hamilton), Pembroke. Tel. 441/ 295-2615.*

Here you will find plenty of high quality British and European antique furnishings and accessories, as well as china, porcelain, glassware, pewter, miniatures of all sorts, cards, old prints (from $15 and up), and a gallery brimming with local and foreign art.

Pegasus Prints & Maps, *Front Street West, (Hamilton), Pembroke. Tel. 441/295-2900.*

This quaint shop sells antique maps from Bermuda, America, and Europe, antique prints, old children's books, original caricatures from Vanity Fair ($35 and up), customized English ceramic house plaques (from $90 and up), and great English greeting cards.

Timeless Antiques, *26 Church Street, (Hamilton), Pembroke. Tel. 441/ 295-5008.*

This is a wonderful shop to browse and shop for antiques including pocket watches, spectacular grandfather clocks, chandeliers, tapestries, and fine English furnishings.

Victoriana, *Royal Naval Dockyard, Sandys. Tel. 441/234-1392.*

Located inside the Clocktower Centre mall, this small store sells affordable Victorian era antiques (and some reproductions) like glass bottles, snuff boxes, silver charms, dolls, and other collectibles.

ART, CRAFTS, & PHOTOGRAPHY

Bermuda Glass Blowing Studio, *16 Blue Hole Hill, Hamilton. Tel. 441/ 293-2234.*

Watch master artisans use steel rods to color and shape molten glass blobs into beautiful plates, cups, statues of fish, and small figurines which sell for between $8 and $225 each. The studio also gives special workshops to the public each month. Admission to the small but lively workshop area is $1 per person.

Bermuda Arts Centre, *Royal Naval Dockyard, Sandys. Tel. 441/234-9809.*

A gallery and workshop which sells and exhibits locally made paintings, sculptures, quilts, dolls, photographs, jewelry, and handicrafts of the highest quality. On occasion you might find a local artist completing a piece while you watch. Admission is about $1.

Bermuda Craft Market, *Royal Naval Dockyard, Sandys. Tel. 441/234-3208.*

Located in the Cooperage Building, this market contains a collection of stalls which sell local hand made cedar wood miniatures, candles, shell art, quilts, dolls, stained glass, perfumes, Bermudian condiments and spices, and all sorts of other gift items. Artists can also occasionally be seen demonstrating their craft in front of visitors.

Island Pottery, *Royal Naval Dockyard, Sandys; branch store on Front Street in the city of Hamilton. Tel. 441/234-3361.*

Situated in a huge airport hangar looking studio, Island Pottery fires up a vast assortment of hand-crafted Bermudian pottery daily. Among the best buys here are the lighthouse style night-light holders ($30 and up), angelfish ashtrays, floral vases ($25 and up), mini moongates ($18 and up), and oval house plaques.

Bridge House Art Gallery, *2 King Street, (St. George), St. George's. Tel. 441/297-8211.*

A cute little craft shop, art gallery, and museum where you can buy prints, watercolors, and hand made gift items by many local artists. There is also an exhibit by the Bermuda National Trust with period furnishings and household goods.

Carole Holding Studio, *Featherbed Alley, (St. George), St. George's; ranch store at King's Square in the town of St. George and at the Clocktower Mall, Royal Naval Dockyard, Sandys. Tel. 441/297-1833.*

These shops and studios operated directly by local watercolor artist Carole Holding and contain a variety of her delightful original scenic watercolors, limited edition collectable prints, regular prints ($12 and up), large matted prints ($35 and up), and local crafts.

Picturesque Gallery, *129 Front Street, (Hamilton), Pembroke Tel. 441/ 292-1452.*

I came here to see some of the finest photography in Bermuda, and I was not disappointed. Matted cibachrome prints from local master photographer Roland Skinner are available from $139 and up.

Queen Street Glass, *Queen Street, (Hamilton), Pembroke. Tel. 441/295-6970.*

This store, located in the Windsor Place Mall, is an outlet for the colorful hand blown glass sculptures and ornaments produced at the Bermuda Glass Blowing Studios. Items include glass bowls, plates, fish figurines (from $25 and up), sailboat sculptures (from $95 and up), and tiny collectibles.

Birdsey Studio, *Stowe Hill Road, Paget. Tel. 441/236-6658.*

This is the best place to find original works and prints by Bermuda's most famous scenic watercolor artist, Alfred Birdsey, and other members of his talented family.

Windjammer Gallery, *87 Reid St, (Hamilton), Pembroke; branch store at Front Street in the city of Hamilton. Tel. 441/292-7861.* The Windjammer galleries offer a huge selection of original Bermudian and imported watercolors, oil paintings, silk screens, limited edition prints, cards, photographs, and a sculpture garden.

Art House Gallery, *80 South Shore Road, Paget. Tel. 441/236-6746.*

This cute shop and gallery offers an assortment of landscape watercolors, hand signed lithographs ($13 and up), unique cards, and screen block prints by Bermudian artist Joan Forbes. She can also be commissioned to create custom works for demanding clients.

The Garden Gallery, *151 North Shore Road, Hamilton. Tel. 441/293-4057.*

A perfect source for inexpensive Bermudian made gifts, original oil paintings, unique cards, local crafts, handmade baby clothing, and all sorts of unusual accessories, starting at under $20 each.

The Gallery, *60 Front Street, (Hamilton), Pembroke. Tel. 441/295-8980.*

The Gallery offers a selection of over 500 original paintings including Haitian primitive pieces, as well as plenty of colorful Bermudian prints (sets of 4 are $25 and up), Murano glass, unique jewelry, African carvings, and other fine hand-crafted items.

BOOKSTORES

The Bermuda Book Store, *Queen Street, (Hamilton), Pembroke. Tel. 441/295-3698.*

This family owned shop offers 2 floors jam-packed with nature guides, travel books, best sellers, and locally published volumes.

The Bookmart, *Phoenix Center, 3 Reid Street, (Hamilton), Pembroke. Tel. 441/295-2640.*
Everything from magazines and children's books to best selling hardcovers and paperbacks at reasonable prices.

Ships Inn Book Gallery, *Royal Naval Dockyard, Sandys. Tel. 441/234-2807.*
They stock thousands of books including historical titles, romance novels, current bestsellers, huge coffee table volumes, and more.

CHINA, CRYSTAL, GLASSWEAR, & PORCELAIN

William Bluck & Co., *4 Front Street, (Hamilton), Pembroke; branch store at Reid Street in the city of Hamilton; branch store at Water Street in the town of St. George; branch store at Southampton Princess Hotel, Southampton; branch store at Sonesta Beach Hotel, Southampton. Tel. 441/295-5367.*
Bluck's has an incredible amount of fine imported crystal, glassware, porcelain, and china from such manufacturers as Royal Copenhagen, Minton, Lalique, Daum, Villeroy and Boch, Royal Crown Derby, Chase, Spode, Ginori, and others. Among the best deals here may be the Orrefors vases ($114 and up), the Kosta Boda wine glasses ($61 and up), and pairs of beautiful Waterford candle holders ($107 and up). They also sell fine English antiques and European silver.

Vera P. Card, *11 Front Street, (Hamilton), Pembroke; branch store at Front Street in the city of Hamilton; branch store at Water Street in the town of St. George; branch store at Sonesta Beach Hotel, Southampton; branch store at Castle Harbour Resort, Hamilton. Tel. 441/295-1729.*
This is the place to go for all sorts of gifts and collectibles including their famous collection of Hummel and Lladro figurines, German and Swiss ship's clocks and watches, Majorica pearls, and other jewelry.

CLOTHING

Archie Brown & Son, *51 Front Street, (Hamilton), Pembroke; branch store at the Clocktower Mall, Royal Naval Dockyard, Sandys; branch store at Duke of York Street in the town of St. George. Tel. 441/295-2928.*
Here you will find 3 floors filled with imported ladies and gents casual and fashion clothing and accessories including Pringle Scottish sweaters, Bermuda shorts made from linen ($40 and up), Kery Hope skirts, ties, Nick Faldo golf shirts ($115 and up) cotton sweaters ($15 and up), docker slacks ($35 and up), knee socks, kilts, cardigans, mohair/wool leisure rugs, and kids stuff.

English Sports Shop, *49 Front Street, (Hamilton), Pembroke; branch store at Somers Wharf in the town of St. George; branch store at Mangrove Bay, Sandys; branch store at Princess Hotel, Pembroke; branch store at Southampton Princess*

Hotel, Southampton; branch store at Sonesta Beach Hotel, Southampton Tel. 441/295-2672.

The incredibly polite and helpful staff of this fine store help you to pick the finest quality English linen jackets ($99 and up), Bermuda logo cotton golf polos ($30 and up), ladies Bermuda logo cotton sweaters ($30 and up), linen blend Bermuda shorts ($42 and up) straw hats, ties, cufflinks, scarves, knee socks ($8 and up) and Shetland sweaters ($40 and up). Upstairs you can find Harris tweed and custom made suits at Alaxandre of England.

Cecile, *15 Front Street, (Hamilton), Pembroke; branch store at Southampton Princess Hotel, Southampton; branch store at Castle Harbour Resort, Hamilton. Tel. 441/295-1311.*

Women looking for the most exclusive European designer ready to wear dresses, gowns, unique sweaters, suits, swimwear, and accessories will sooner or later find themselves in this fashionable establishment. Among the fine labels available here are Louis Feraud, Geiger, Ciaosport, Mondi, Basler, and many more.

Scottish Wool Shop, *7 Queen Street, (Hamilton), Pembroke. Tel. 441/297-0967.*

This tiny and unassuming store is the best place in Bermuda to find deals on high quality woolens for men and women in all sizes such as a great selection of Shetland sweaters starting at only $23 each.

Constable's, *32 Duke of York Street, (St. George), St. Georges. Tel. 441/297-1995.*

Constables of Bermuda sells a unique collection of Icelandic woolen fashions for women. Among the many fine garments here are beautiful natural colored and water repellent jackets and coats, skirts, and sweaters, all fantastically warm and comfortable

Aston & Gunn, *2 Reid Street, (Hamilton), Pembroke. Tel. 441/295-4866.*

Aston & Gunn occupies a corner storefront on Queen and Reid streets where men and women can find fine clothing and accessories such as Arnold Zimmer linen pants ($120 and up), Pierre Balman shirts ($45 and up), sweaters ($55 and up), ties, Bermuda shorts, dresses, jackets, suits, scarves, and other fine imported garments.

Stefanel, *12 Reid Street, (Hamilton), Pembroke. Tel. 441/297-1357.*

As with all other Stefanel boutiques throughout the world, this shop has a small but exciting collection of European men's and women's fashions including Italian sport jackets ($140 and up), woolen skirts, intricate shirts ($45 and up), sweaters, knitwear, trousers, grunge style collections, and all types of accessories. Even the music that the young staff play here is trendy.

Bermuda Railway Co., *27 Reid Street, (Hamilton), Pembroke; branch store at the Clocktower Mall, Royal Naval Dockyard, Sandys; branch store at Water Street, St. George; branch store at Mangrove Bay, (Somerset), Sandys; branch store at North Shore Road, Hamilton; branch store at Crystal Caves, Hamilton; branch store at South Road, Paget. Tel. 441/295-1183.*

This great miniature department store (actually owned by Trimingham's) offers an assortment of affordable men's, women's, and children's casual cotton clothing such as T-shirts ($16.50 and up), Bermuda shorts ($22 and up), polo shirts, hats, gifts, and accessories, many of which display the cute BRCo. logo.

DEPARTMENT STORES

Trimingham's, *37 Front Street, (Hamilton), Pembroke; branch store at Castle Harbour Resort, Hamilton; branch store at Princess Hotel, Pembroke; branch store at Southampton Princess Hotel, Southampton; branch store at Elbow Beach Hotel, Paget; branch store at South Road, Paget; ranch store at Somers Wharf in the town of St. George; branch store at Sonesta Beach Hotel, Southampton; branch store at Mangrove Bay, Sandys; branch store at Mangrove Bay Road, Sandys. Tel. 441/295-1183.*

First established in 1842, this is Bermuda's favorite department store. As you browse around the main store's 3 floors, you'll find perfumes from most major European houses, men's and women's casual garments, swim suits, business attire, and more formal pieces from the world's top designers like Hermes, Karen Kane, Jennifer Reed, Liberty of London, and more including great deals on Ungaro silk scarves ($130 and up), Lamberts wool and cashmere blend ladies classic overcoats ($320 and up), Dak Bermuda shorts ($47.50 and up), and accessories like Coach handbags ($170 and up).

They also stock a full range of English and Bermudian condiments, local handicrafts, and plenty of crystal and china at savings of up to 40% from companies like Mikasa, Lenox, Noritake, Waterford, and others. Make sure to pop into the Botanic Garden Tea Room for a great sandwich or a scone with tea.

H.A. & E Smith's, *35 Front Street, (Hamilton), Pembroke; branch store at Belmont Hotel, Warwick; branch store at Southampton Princess Hotel, Southampton; branch store at Duke of York Street in the town of St. George. Tel. 441/295-2288.*

Smith's is yet another fine department store where you can literally spend hours finding excellent prices on all sort of imported items. Among the highlights here is the impressive perfume room laden with Paris's best brands, a great jewelry room with European gold pendants ($37 and up), miniature Bermudian cottage collectibles, English and Italian handbags ($84 and up), and china and crystal a significant savings from producers like Crown Derby, Baccarat, Swarovski, Queen's, Minton, Rosenthal, Royal Worcester, and others. The store also offers fine men's and women's wear including the fine English made Smith's label, Burberrys of London, Alan Paine, Murry Allan, and special prices on William Locke Scottish lambswool V neck sweaters ($78 and up), and even more seasonal bargains.

A.S. Cooper & Sons, *59 Front Street, (Hamilton), Pembroke; branch store at Princess Hotel, Pembroke; branch store at Southampton Princess Hotel, Southampton; branch store at Elbow Beach Hotel, Paget; branch store at Castle Harbour Resort, Hamilton; branch store at Sonesta Beach Hotel, Southampton; branch store at Somers Wharf in the town of St. George. Tel. 441/295-3961.*

The huge main branch of this fantastic department store offers 4 floors full of surprises. Here you will find porcelain, china, crystal, glassware, and figurines at up to 45% off North American retail prices from Royal Doulton, Wedgewood, Lladro, Orrefors, Kosta Boda, Waterford Crystal, and Aynsley, as well as unique pieces such as Limoges hand painted Easter eggs ($130 and up), and Bermudian cottage music boxes ($70 and up).

The store also has an abundant selection of men's and women's fashions from Ralph Lauren, Polo, Architect, Liz Claiborne, Jones New York, Nipon, and others, European perfumes, scenic prints, children's clothing, and a wonderful outdoor lunch and tea patio called Romancing the Scone.

JEWELRY & TIMEPIECES

H.S. & J.E. Crisson Ltd., *Queen Street (Hamilton). Pembroke, branch stores at Front Street in the city of Hamilton, The Clocktower Mall at Royal Naval Dockyard, Water Street as well as Duke of York Street in the town of St. George, the Elbow Beach Hotel, the Castle Harbour resort, The Hamilton Princess hotel, the Sonesta Beach hotel, and the Southampton Princess hotel. Tel. 441/295-2351.*

Crisson has been Bermuda's leading jewelers since way back in 1922. Visitors and residents alike have always found innovative design, the highest quality merchandise, and substantial savings here. Only at Crisson will you find Rolex, Ebel, Movado, Raymond Weil, Rado, Concord, Tag Heuer, Seiko and Citizen watches- all at savings up to thirty percent below what you would pay at home, as well as similar savings on an exquisite collection of fine jewelry from some of the most famous designers in the world. Crisson's vast selection of over 75,000 different pieces is the largest collection of fine gold and gemstone jewelry in Bermuda, and each and every piece has a lifetime warranty and a certified appraisal upon request.

Fine jewelry names available exclusively at Crisson include Carera Y Carera, Mikimoto, Kabana, Asch Grossbardt, Charles Garnier, Aaron

Basha, Scott Kay, and many more. They are especially proud of their selection of fine European pieces, many of which include exceptional quality diamonds that are hand picked by Andrew and Peter Crisson (expert graduate gemologists). Visitors will also find one of the world's largest collections of earrings, gold and silver chains, sea-life pendants and broaches, and fine writing instruments in their massive glass display cases. With 11 locations to serve Bermuda, Crisson's is the best place to find something special for that someone special in your life. Don't forget to visit Crisson's Gucci boutique at their 71 Front Street location where you will find the complete range of Gucci accessories and shoes at duty-free prices. Highly recommended as the finest and most honest jewelry shop in all of Bermuda.

Astwood Dickinson, *83 Front Street, (Hamilton), Pembroke; branch store at Front Street in the city of Hamilton; branch store at Southampton Princess Hotel, Southampton. Tel. 441/292-5805.*

At this well stocked jewelry store you can find watches from Patek Philippe, Tag Heuer, Omega, Baume & Mercier, Tiffany, Movado, Swiss Army, Tissot, and their own brand of Bermuda flower watches. They also sell a variety of fine gold, silver, and precious stone jewelry, much of which is made at their design studios. Among the unique items here are several unique gemstone gold rings, and a selection of beautiful chains, bracelets, brooches, earrings, pens, necklaces, wedding bands, and accessories on all price levels.

Swiss Timing, *95 Front Street, (Hamilton), Pembroke. Tel. 441/295-1376.*

Even though this small shop is a bit off the main drag of Front Street, it offers a superb collection of lesser known, and thus inexpensive, brands of European and Japanese watches at fantastic prices. They also have a nice but limited selection of gold jewelry.

LINENS

The Irish Linen Shop, *31 Front Street, (Hamilton), Pembroke; branch store at Cambridge Road, Sandys. Tel. 441/295-4089.*

What a fantastic little shop! The pleasant salespeople here can assist you in selecting fine linens and lace from all over Europe including Double Damask and Le Jacquard Francais, and many bargain priced items such as hand embroidered napkins from Madeira ($18 and up), Bermudian made floral pot holders ($3 and up), and some of the most beautiful Irish linen tea towels ($7 and up). The second floor offers a selection of French fabrics by the yard ($27 and up).

Dockyard Linens, *Clocktower Mall, Royal Naval Dockyard, Sandys. Tel. 441/234-3871.*

This shop has a small but affordable selection of imported linen tablecloths, local crafts, handbags, and gift items.

LIQUOR STORES

Gosling's, *33 Front Street, (Hamilton), Pembroke; branch store at Duke of York Street in the town of St. George; branch store at Cambridge Road, Sandys. Tel. 441/295-1123.*

Whether you want a good bottle of wine to drink while on vacation, or need to purchase your duty free in-bond liquor, this store carries almost anything you might want. Retail items include '87 Opus One ($63), '85 Dom Perignon ($83), '83 Chateaux Margaux ($128), '87 Castello Banfi Brunello di Montalchino ($32), and of course their own Black Seal dark rum ($15.50) and less expensive wines and liquors from around the world. Their great duty-free prices on fifths or liters include Goslings 151 rum ($9.50), Jose Cuervo tequila ($9), '82 Sandeman's Vintage port ($28), Kahula ($15), Seagrams Gin ($8), and Chivas Royal Salute 21 yr. Whisky ($67). Prices may drop on duty free items if over (5) fifths are bought.

Burrows Lightbourn, *Front Street, (Hamilton), Pembroke; branch store at East Broadway in the city of Hamilton; branch store at Queen Street in the city of Hamilton; branch store at Water Street in the town of St. George; branch store at Harbour Road, Paget; branch store at Flatts Village, Smith's; branch store at Main Road, Sandys. Tel. 441/295-0176.*

This is another good place to buy beer, liquor, wines, and in-bond duty free packages. For immediate consumption I suggest Piper Heidsieck non vintage Champagne ($32), '84 Chateux Ducru-Beaucaillou Bordeaux ($41), Glenmorangie Single Malt Scotch ($33), and the wonderful Graham 30 year Tawny Port ($57). Duty free prices include fifths and liters of Ameretto Di Saronno ($18), Barcardi 151 ($10), Tanqueray gin ($14), Stolichnaya vodka ($11), Cardhu Malt whisky ($28), and Frangelico ($18). Prices drop on duty free items if over (5) fifths are bought.

LEATHER GOODS & LUGGAGE SHOPS

Harbourmaster, *Reid Street, (Hamilton), Pembroke. Tel. 441/295-5333.*
If you have bought too many gifts to fit inside your luggage, or you intend to travel again soon, this is the perfect place to shop for luggage. This great shop has beautiful imported leather and nylon luggage, wallets, handbags, and briefcases.

PERFUME & COLOGNE

Peniston Brown, *23 Front Street, (Hamilton), Pembroke; branch store at Queen Street in the city of Hamilton; branch store at Front Street in the city of Hamilton; branch store at King's Square in the town of St. George.*

Peniston Brown is perhaps the leading perfume store in Bermuda. Among the many European scents available here at discounted prices are Jean Patou, Guerlain, Lauren, Yves St. Laurent, and Calvin Klein.

Bermuda Perfumery, *North Shore Road, Hamilton. Tel. 441/293-0627.*

At the Lili of Bermuda factory and gardens you will first be guided on a tour through the perfume making process, and then finish up sampling their fragrances with names like Oleander, Frangipanni, Easter Lily, Passion Flower, Bermudiana, Cedarwood, Bravo, Bambu, and Navy Lime.

T-SHIRT & SOUVENIR SHOPS

Riihiluoma's Flying Colors, *5 Queen Street, (Hamilton), Pembroke. Tel. 441/295-0890.*

Here you will find 2 floors full of T-shirts and unusual gift items which start at under $10 each. Most of the time they offer a buy 3 get two free T-shirt sales. A great place to find something special.

Bananas, *7 Front Street, (Hamilton), Pembroke; branch store at Front Street in the city of Hamilton; branch store at Queen Street in the city of Hamilton; branch store at King's Square in the town of St. George; branch store at Water Street in the town of St. George; branch store at Sonesta Beach Hotel, Southampton. Tel. 441/295-1106.*

Bananas is another great source for cotton T-shirts and a variety of gift items like umbrellas, towels, and sweatshirts. Here you can either buy 6 and get 6 for free, or if you're on a cruise ship, look for the lucky cabin number on display here and maybe win something.

Treasure Chest, *3 Queen Street, (Hamilton), Pembroke; branch store on Front Street in the city of Hamilton. Tel. 441/295-2288.*

If you need to find reasonably priced memento, this may be the place for you. Here you can buy typical tourist items like silver pendants, lapel pins, perfume, coral and pearl jewelry, post cards, prints, and cute gifts.

Luger Bits & Pieces, *Royal Naval Dockyard, Sandys. Tel. 441/234-3794.*

This diverse souvenir shop offers nautically minded gifts, cards, prints, paperweights, silver jewelry, cedar crafts, and odd ball items.

Crackerbox, *Duke of York Street, (St. George), St. George's. Tel. 441/297-1205*.

Here you can buy inexpensive souvenirs like nice T-shirts, shells of all sorts, pendants, post cards, sunglasses, calenders, hats, Bermudian condiments, cedar figurines, and other knic-knacks.

Hodge Podge, *3 Point Pleasant Road, (Hamilton), Pembroke. Tel. 441/295-0674*.

This is yet another little souvenir shop that sell straw bags, pendants, local condiments, cover ups, suglasses, T-shirts, posters, postcards, chimes, cedar carvings, and film.

10. BERMUDA'S BEST PLACES TO STAY

COTTAGE COLONY CATEGORY

POMPANO BEACH CLUB, *36 Pompano Beach Road, Southampton. Tel. 441/234-0222, Fax 441/234-1694. Toll Free Reservations (Hotel's US Offices) at 800/343-4155 US & Canada. Internet: www.pompano.bm. Low season rack rates from $200 per double room per night (B.P.). High season rack rates from $330 per double room per night (B.P.). Dine-Around M.A.P. meal plan available from $20 per person per day. 56 ocean-view rooms and suites with air conditioning and private bathrooms. Two restaurants with two outdoor dining terraces, and two bars. Cash, Traveler's Checks, and all major credit cards accepted. Member of "The Bermuda Collection" of fine hotels.*

This delightful, friendly seaside cottage colony is located on a cliff above the sea next to Southampton Parish's famed Port Royal Golf Course. Pompano has become my favorite place to stay anywhere in Bermuda and is where I choose to go for my vacations.

This wonderful medium-sized property offers nine charming pink and white low-rise cottages and a central clubhouse on or near the edge of a bluff which rises up to expose dramatic views of the turquoise colored waters of the Atlantic. Each cottage contains several spacious and comfortable double rooms and stunning suites (many of which can be made to adjoin for family usage) that feature individually controlled reverse cycle air conditioners, large deluxe private bathrooms, Mexican tiled balconies with patio furnishings and panoramic views out to sea, beautiful selection of hardwood and tropical rattan furnishings, king and twin sized Simmons bedding, hair dryers, direct dial telephones, 50 channel satellite-cable televisions, electronic mini-safe systems, either wet bars or mini-refrigerators, hair dryers, am-fm clock radios, steam irons with collapsible ironing boards, comfortable waffled cotton bathrobes, optional VCR units, and large picture windows or sliding French doors that open up unforgettable views or the sea.

Tom and Larry Lamb of Boston are the friendly owners & managers and have done a wonderful job in converting their father's quaint little fishing lodge into one of the world's most relaxing and laid back beach-side resorts. The recent elongation of their tranquil private pink beach has made Pompano even more desirable for those who love the sand and sea. While I personally start my visits here by hopping on a Suncat motorized floating lounge chair and gliding along their 250 yard long sandbar to reach a beautiful coral reef full of semi-tropical fish, there are a wide variety of other superb facilities to occupy even the most active visitors.

The Pompano Beach Club offers a large heated outdoor fresh-water swimming pool, several seaside sun-decks with complimentary lounge chair and sun umbrella service, two piping hot open air sea-view hot tubs, a new oceanfront wading pool, free usage of four all weather and one har-tru tennis courts, a fully equipped health club complete with Lifecycle and Stairmaster computerized exercise gear and a variable incline treadmill, temporary membership privileges at all of Bermuda's world class golf clubs including the adjacent Robert Trent Jones designed Port Royal Golf Course, a fantastic water-sports center where you can rent all sorts of water-craft and snorkeling gear during the high season, on-site scooter and bicycle rental, free use of professional fishing tackle (the chefs here will be glad to cook up your very own catch of the day), express laundry and dry cleaning, available baby-sitters, breakfast in bed, and much, much more. If there is anything at all that you need to arrange excursions or day-trips, just feel free to ask for advice from either assistant manager David Block or any of the hotel's other cheerful staff members.

Dining here is fantastic. Even breakfast is a gastronomic delight, with huge cooked to order American breakfasts served in the clubhouse, or a light healthy continental breakfast sent to your room. Superb evening meals may be enjoyed at the lovely ocean-view Cedar Room restaurant (ties are always optional, even on the three nights per week when jackets are required), while hearty lunches are served either al fresco at the seaside terrace or inside the cozy atrium area.

Evenings are also a delight with the added bonus of scheduled live entertainment by talented Bermudian musicians and local art shows. The Foc's'le bar and pool-side terrace serve Bermuda's either Velda's or Mervyn's infamous frozen top shelf cocktails at prices that are hard to beat. Guests may also take advantage of the Carousel dine around program that allows them to enjoy gourmet dinners at four other fine "Bermuda Collection" hotel restaurants. Those here on romantic escapes will be delighted by the incredible sunsets that can be viewed from almost anywhere on the property, including your own room.

CAMBRIDGE BEACHES, *30 Kings Point Road, Sandy's. Tel. 441/234-0331, Fax 441/234-3352. Toll Free Reservations (Hotel's Direct) at 800/468-7300 US & Canada. Internet: cambeach@ibl.bm Low season rack rates from $205 per double room per night (B.P.). High season rack rates from $400 per double room per night (M.A.P.). 81 rooms, suites, and private one & two bedroom villa style cottages with air conditioning and private bathrooms. Three restaurants with two outdoor dining terraces and a bar. Low season M.A.P. meal plan also available for $30 per person per day upon request. Cash, Checks, Traveler's Checks, Visa and Mastercard accepted. Children under five years old must be accompanied by an au pair. Member of "The Bermuda Collection" of fine hotels.*

Cambridge Beaches is Bermuda's most refined, exclusive and secluded luxury vacation hideaway. This breathtaking 25 acre private luxury cottage colony resort & spa is ideally situated on a beautiful narrow peninsula surrounded by a string of five crescent shaped pink sand beaches. Located just a few short kilometers away from the historic Royal Naval Dockyard and its fine shopping, dining, cultural and entertainment possibilities, this peaceful resort consists of several traditionally styled pink Bermudian cottages, each with one or more superbly appointed oversized accommodations.

Each room, suite, and self-standing villa features powerful reverse cycle air conditioning systems, giant marble tiled private bathrooms (most also have a great Jacuzzi), tranquil sea or garden views, private terraces, a carefully selected collection of English country style hardwood furnishings, imported designer fabrics, large mini-safes, direct dial telephones with voice mail and data ports, available remote control cable televisions, irons with ironing boards, adjacent peaceful gardens, and plenty of windows that let in both the sounds of nearby crashing waves as well as an occasional refreshing sea breeze.

Recently voted in as one of the world's top best spa resorts by the prestigious *Traveler* magazine readers' poll, Cambridge Beaches easily lives up to its international reputation as offering its guests spacious accommodations, superb gourmet cuisine prepared by one of France's top master chefs, Bermuda's only true world class health and beauty spa, an almost unending array of in-house facilities, and an outstanding level of 5 star service provided by a superb staff. Whether you decide to reserve a private self-standing villa, or instead choose a luxury suite, you will find yourself in a state of total comfort and relaxation within seconds of your arrival.

Many guests now arriving here from North American and European flights (during both high and low season) decide to take full advantage of custom tailored beauty and relaxation treatments offered at their lavish new Aquarian Baths spa center. The twin level spa structure is covered by a retractable sun roof and boasts facilities such as six specialized treatment rooms where both ladies and gents can enjoy an outstanding array of European style health and beauty treatments ranging from Swedish massages to various forms of natural hydra and aromatherapies. The spa also has fully equipped exercise and workout rooms, a 30 foot long heated indoor swimming pool, new sauna and Turkish steam bath areas, whirlpool jet baths, a natural juice bar that offers light snacks, and a full range of special "Spa-Holiday" programs for those concerned with improving their appearance or reducing stress, weight, or the side effects of aging.

Additional in-house facilities include a large outdoor saltwater swimming pool with sun desk, a complete marina with water-sports equipment and boat rentals, customized deep sea or reef fishing and scuba diving excursions, complimentary use of three professionally surfaced tennis courts (one can be lit at night), private summertime motor launch service to and from downtown Hamilton, temporary privileges at all major Bermudian golf courses, a putting green and a croquet lawn, on-sight scooter and bicycle rentals, a wonderful lending library with countless novels and historical texts, a fully equipped business center with regally appointed private meeting rooms, a new late checkout facility, an extensive gourmet room service menu (with the island's best cooked to order breakfast in bed), complimentary afternoon tea served with finger sandwiches and sweets in the Clubhouse, nearby public bus and ferry stops, a daily schedule of exciting activities, a Monday evening manager's swizzle party, and stunning grounds embellished by magnificently landscaped semi-tropical gardens with charming foot paths that also run along the coast. During the warmer months there is also live evening entertainment, sumptuous outdoor Barbecue buffets, and much more.

Executive chef Jean Claude Garzia (a recent winner of Europe's prestigious "Meilleurs Ouvriers de France" gold medal for gastronomy) and his international kitchen staff serve up sinfully delicious American and Continental breakfasts, casual luncheons, and five course gourmet dinners (with a special spa cuisine menu also available) every day of the week. Elegant evening meals are presented by candle light in the opulent Tamarisk dining room while more casual meals may be enjoyed at the al fresco Terrace restaurant when weather permits. In addition you will also find a list containing a collection of fine vintage wines by either the glass or bottle from France, Italy, Australia, California, Portugal, and South Africa. Cambridge Beaches also participates in the "Carousel Dine Around" program so that those on the meal plans may reserve dinner at four other fine Bermuda Collection restaurants at no extra charge.

HORIZON'S & COTTAGES, *33 South Shore Road, Paget. Tel. 441/ 236-0048, Fax 441/236-1981. Toll Free Reservations (Relais & Chateaux) at 800/468-4100 US & Canada. Low season rack rates from $230 per double room* *per night (M.A.P.). High season rack rates from $310 per double room per night (M.A.P.). 48 rooms, suites, and private cottages with air conditioning and private bathrooms. One restaurant with an outdoor terrace, and one bar. Cash, Checks, and Traveler's Checks only, No Credit cards accepted. Member of the "Relais & Chateaux" group of hotels.*

Situated on a peaceful 25 acre hilltop sea-view garden teeming with colorful hibiscus and bougainvillea, Horizon's & Cottages is Bermuda's oldest and most venerable cottage colony. Frequented by wealthy older English, European, and American vacationers for several decades now, this somewhat formal old world style property has the refined ambiance of a regal English colonial country inn. The hotel centers around a Colonial mansion originally built in 1710 and has been painstakingly converted into the main clubhouse. The clubhouse is now home to the reception area, an opulent dining room, nice cozy guest rooms, and some of the most charming antique fireside parlors anywhere in the country. Dotting the tranquil gardens that surround the clubhouse are thirteen one- and two-story pink and white cottages that in most cases feature common lounges with televisions, working, fireplaces, lending libraries, and corridors which lead to several independent guest accommodations.

All of Horizon's 48 spacious rooms and suites feature air condition-ing, private bathrooms, electronic trouser press, ceiling fan, direct dial telephones, private terraces, heated towel racks, mini-safe, hair dryers, and large comfortable beds. Several of these units have working fire-places, while others can be made adjoin for family use. Typically the guests staying in each of the cottages will meet and socialize with each other in their shared lounges. There is also a deluxe one bedroom private villa available for those seeking complete privacy.

Horizon's dining room is well known as being one of Bermuda's best places to dine, and features both indoor and outdoor seating areas serving French influenced gourmet cuisine and fine imported wines complete with silver and crystal service. Guests can also chose to have their breakfast cooked to order and delivered directly to their rooms. Each afternoon the staff prepare a refined afternoon tea followed by complimentary hot and cold hors d'erves.

Among the facilities offered here are a nine hole par three pitch and putt golf course, three outdoor tennis courts, a putting green, a tranquil heated outdoor swimming pool and sun-deck, on-sight scooter and bicycle rentals, complete temporary membership privileges at the exclu-sive Coral Beach & Tennis Club, discounted green fees at major are golf courses, several acres of semi-tropical garden paths to wander upon, and a great Bermudian cedar wood pub.

ARIEL SANDS BEACH CLUB, *South Shore Road, Devonshire. Tel. 441/236-1010, Fax 441/236-0087, Toll Free Reservations (Hotel Direct) at 800/468-6610 US & Canada. Internet:www.arielsands.com. Low season rack rates from $220 per double room per night (B.P.). High season rack rates from $340 per double room per night (B.P.). 47 ocean-view rooms, suites, and private cottages with air conditioning, private terraces or balconies, and private bathrooms. One restaurant, one outdoor dining terrace, and two bars. Cash, Traveler's Checks, and all major credit cards accepted. M.A.P. meal plan available for $40 per person per day. Member of "The Bermuda Collection" of fine hotels.*

Situated in Devonshire Parish on Bermuda's peaceful south shore, Ariel Sands has recently emerged as one of Bermuda's best values. This laid back beach-side getaway has been family-owned and operated since 1954, but it wasn't until recently that family member (and Hollywood actor) Michael Douglas helped to fund a multimillion dollar facelift which has completely transformed this property into a superb full small luxury hotel and spa center.

Ariel Sands rests on a picturesque 14 acre estate in charming Devonshire, just an eight minute ride from Hamilton. The property consists of several traditional one- and two-story coral colored Bermudian cottageswith a variety of spacious accommodations. There are a total of 40 deluxe rooms, 3 one bedroom suites, and 2 two bedroom self-standing cottages that all offer fine sea views, air conditioners, private bathrooms, terraces or patios, bleached pine furnishings, executive style desks, remote control cable television, direct dial telephone, mini-safe, walk-in closets, Mexican tile flooring, coffee machines, am-fm clock radios, irons, mini-refrigerators, cotton bath robes, hair dryers, locally created works of art, and comfortable king or dual twin bedding. There are also two lavish two bedroom private cottages with full kitchens and working fireplaces that can also be rented for long stays during the low season.

As part of an intensive enhancement and expansion of their facilities, Ariel Sands now offers its guests a complete Nirvana Day Spa pavilion with customized hydra-therapies and European body treatments, a 24 hour private fitness center with plenty of free weights and Lifecycle equipment, a new unisex beauty salon, two of the world's most inviting ocean fed salt water swimming pools, an outdoor freshwater heated swimming pool, a charming fireside lounge with a well stocked lending library, a large business meeting and conference center with a full range of audio/video equipment, three all weather tennis courts (two are night-lit), a putting green, in-room or beach-side massages, room service, discounts to area golf courses, scenic walking trails, and of course a wide sandy beach complete with lounge chairs and woven palm umbrellas.

Both guests and visitors arrive each day to dine at the casual Caliban's restaurant, which serves up tasty lunches and dinners of Bermudian-influenced Mediterranean dishes in its candle-lit dining room or near the beach along a palm-lined outdoor dining terrace when the weather is nice. Guests on the M.A.P. meal plan may also choose to participate in the Bermuda Collection's "Carousel" dine around program to experience fine dinners at a half a dozen other fine restaurants. The clubhouse is also home to a vintage cedar paneled bar that serves ice cold beer, Port wines, and Cuban cigars.

FOURWAYS INN & COTTAGE COLONY, *Middle Road, Paget. Tel. 441/236-6517, Fax 441/236-5528, Toll Free Reservations (Hotel Direct) at 800/962-7654 US. Low season rack rates from $150 per double room per night (C.P.). High season rack rates from $230 per double room per night (C.P.). 11 rooms and suites with air conditioning, balconies, and private bathrooms. Two restaurants, and one bar. Cash, Traveler's Checks, and most major credit cards accepted. M.A.P. meal plan is also available for $42.50 per person per day upon request.*

This peaceful little deluxe cottage colony rests on a private harbor-view estate in the heart of Paget Parish. Fourways Inn and Cottage Colony consists of several adjacent two-story pastel colored cottages, each with a deluxe double room and a lavish one bedroom suite that can be adjoined to create a two bed/two bath private cottages.

Each accommodation here has a deluxe private bathroom with dual basins and gold trimmed fixtures, giant garden or harbor view balconies, remote control large screen cable color televisions, marble tile flooring, direct dial telephones, a collection of antique and reproduction hardwood furnishings including executive style desks, individually controlled air conditioning systems, overhead fans, original Bermudian artwork, both wet bars and mini-bars, small hideaway kitchenettes stocked with cooking utensils, mini-safes, plenty of closet space, an assortment of high quality English hair and skin care products, dual hair dryers, retractable make up mirrors, plush bathrobes and slippers, irons with boards, and in some cases even exposed beam chapel ceilings.

Fourways is an exceptionally quiet and secluded cottage colony with the services and facilities one would ordinarily expect to find in much larger four star hotels. Among the many facilities are a large heated outdoor freshwater swimming pool and sun deck, full access to the nearby Stonington hotel's beach club, temporary membership privileges to many of Bermuda's best golf and tennis clubs, a complimentary in-room continental breakfast featuring freshly baked gourmet pastries, a complete range of special valet and concierge services, express laundry and dry cleaning, available secretarial and baby sitting services, and of course direct access to the incredible Fourways restaurant and equally impressive Peg Leg Bar and luncheon room.

SMALL LUXURY HOTEL CATEGORY

THE REEFS, *56 South Shore Road, Southampton. Tel. 441/238-0222, Fax 441/238-1214. Toll Free Reservations (Hotel Direct) at 800/742-2008 US & Canada. Internet: www.The Reefs.com. Low season rack rates from $244 per double room per night (M.A.P.). High season rack rates from $376 per double room per night (M.A.P.). 67 rooms, suites, and private cottages with air conditioning and private bathrooms. Two restaurants with outdoor terraces, and two bars. Cash, Traveler's Checks, and all major credit cards accepted. Member of "The Bermuda Collection" of fine hotels.*

If I was asked to close my eyes and imagine a perfectly deluxe and romantic beach-front hotel, The Reefs is exactly what would come to mind, This little resort is one of the finest small luxury hotels anywhere on earth. Perched just above a sun-drenched bluff that rises up from one of the country's most beautiful pink sand beaches, this gem of a hideaway has always been the highlight of my many trips to Bermuda.

The property contains 67 spacious and well appointed (yet under-stated) rooms, suites, and cottages that all offer individually controlled air conditioners, private bathrooms complete with a selection of fine English perfumed soaps and shampoos, tropical rattan furnishings, ceiling fans, direct dial telephones with unlimited free local calls, wet bars with mini-refrigerators, Mexican tile flooring, mini-safes, plush sofas, original Bermudian paintings, large closets, remote control cable televisions (available upon request), hair dryers, irons with ironing boards, a tray of complementary beverages upon check-in, and in many cases there are even private furnished sea-view balconies with unforgettable vistas out onto a superb beach area. The accommodations range from nice double rooms to massive one bedroom suites with Jacuzzis, or nearby independent villa style sea-side and garden-side cottages with one or two bedrooms.

Guests may choose to relax on one of the beach's complimentary sun lounges before utilizing a fully equipped fitness center with free weights and state of the art Cybex exercise gear, a freeform outdoor heated swimming pool with sun deck, two professionally surfaced outdoor tennis courts, shuffle board and croquet areas, and much more. There are also membership privileges and discounts on Bermuda's best golf courses, dozens of optional excursions, private guide services, scooter and bicycle rentals, both breakfast in bed and complete room service menus, weekly manager's cocktail parties, opulent lounges and fireside sitting rooms, a well-stocked lending library, walking paths through lush semi-tropical gardens, and a host of world class sports and water-sports programs available upon request.

Dining at The Reefs is an equally impressive experience starting at 8:00am each day with one of Bermuda's best breakfasts featuring both a fresh fruit and cheese buffet as well as many made to order items such as omelets or fruit filled pancakes. In the afternoons and evenings guests can visit either the Clubhouse dining room or the superb (and more casual) Coconuts sea-front terrace (open only in high season), which both offer some of the county's most innovative gourmet cuisine and vintage wines by the bottle and glass. You may also wish to indulge yourself at the beach-side snack bar, sip refreshing drinks at one of two delightful bars, or just socialize during each afternoon's complimentary tea service. You can take advantage of the complimentary Carousel dine around program that allows them to enjoy gourmet dinners at half a dozen other fine "Bermuda Collection" properties.

WATERLOO HOUSE, *Pitts Bay Road, (City of Hamilton), Pembroke. Tel. 441/295-4480, Fax 441/295-2585, Toll Free Reservations (Relais & Chateaux) at 800/468-4100 US & Canada. Internet: www.bermudasbest.com. Low season rack rates from $190 per double room per night (B.P.). High season rack rates from $260 per double room per night (B.P.). 30 rooms and suites with air conditioning and private bathrooms. One restaurant, one luncheon terrace, and one bar. M.A.P. meal plan is available from $40 per person per day. Cash, Traveler's Checks, and all major credit cards accepted. Member of "Relais & Chateaux" hotels.*

Waterloo House hotel is a superb little luxury hotel located alongside Hamilton's picturesque harbor. As one of Bermuda's most refined yet relaxing places to both overnight and dine, this delightful 30 room inn is a favorite among visiting executives as well as vacationers who wish to have cozy Auberge-style accommodations just a three minute walk to the boutiques and attractions of downtown Hamilton. This welcoming bastion of tranquillity consists of several adjoining 19th century townhouses surrounded by beautifully groomed gardens, patios, waterside terraces, and inner courtyards.

Guests are offered one of thirty spacious rooms and suites featuring air conditioners, oversized private bathrooms stocked with fine European soaps and shampoos, a selection of beautiful hardwood furnishings, electric trouser press, direct dial telephones with data ports and optional Internet access, remote control color cable television, a fine collection of old Bermudian prints and lithographs, mini-refrigerator, mini-safe, large picture windows with stunning views, and in many cases either harbor or garden view patios and large Jacuzzis. All of the property's lovingly decorated country style accommodations and exquisite public spaces help reinforce a relaxed yet elegant ambiance.

The inn is also home to the simply fantastic Waterloo House dining room, a romantic gourmet restaurant that presents French-influenced gourmet Bermudian cuisine of the highest standards each afternoon and evening. Waterloo House's many additional features include a daily complimentary full English or American breakfast (served in the restaurant or, if preferred, in your room at no additional charge), a traditional afternoon tea service complete with dozens of freshly made finger sandwiches and mouth watering pastries, a romantic harbor-front al fresco luncheon patio (open when weather permits), fireside sitting rooms and regal lending libraries, a charming little outdoor freshwater swimming pool and sun deck, tranquil inner courtyards and harbor-front terraces, my favorite lounge in town, and a snooker room with board games.

In addition, you are given temporary guest membership privileges at the beach, spa, and sporting facilities of the private Coral Beach & Tennis Club and several famous Bermudian golf courses, available dine-around programs in conjunction with Horizon's & Cottages and Coral Beach Club, a weekly manager's cocktail party, scheduled concerts and cultural events, and an array of tranquil sitting rooms full of antiques and priceless works of art. The service here is simply outstanding, with a small friendly staff that remember their guests' names and special requests.

NEWSTEAD, *Harbour Road, Paget. Tel. 441/236-6060, Fax 441/236-7454, Toll Free Reservations (Hotel Direct) at 800/468-4111 US, 800/236-2451 Canada. High season rack rates from $315 per double room per night (B.P.). Low season rack rates from $246 per double room per night (B.P.). 42 air conditioned rooms and suites with air conditioning and private bathrooms. One restaurant, one luncheon terrace, and one bar. M.A.P. meal plan available for $40 per person per day upon request. Cash, Traveler's Checks, and all major credit cards accepted.*

After the recent change of ownership as well as the completion of a major renovation project, and a change of managers, Newstead has once again become a delightful full service inn. Located at the edge of a scenic harbor, this property consists of a former manor house filled with antiques and surrounded by several adjacent cottage style wings each with delightful views of the city of Hamilton.

There are 42 harbor and garden view rooms and suites that all feature air conditioning, private bathrooms, beautiful furnishings, direct dial telephones, mini-safes, remote control cable television, irons with boards, electronic trouser press, heated towel racks, fresh cut flowers, and in many cases private terraces and gardens with some of the nicest views imaginable. All room rates come complete with a full American breakfast, daily afternoon tea with finger sandwiches and desserts, reduced rate access to the facilities of the nearby Coral Beach & Tennis Club, and much more.

Newstead's impressive range of facilities include two tennis courts, a putting green, a nice outdoor swimming pool with sun-deck, on-site ferry service to downtown Hamilton, a wonderful selection of opulent sitting rooms and lounges, and a large semi-tropical garden. Dining here is a real treat with Mediterranean-styled menus offered in both their water-view indoor dining room and the popular Noah's outdoor restaurant.

MAJOR RESORT HOTEL CATEGORY

ELBOW BEACH - BERMUDA, *South Shore Road, Paget. Tel. 441/236-3535, Fax 441/236-8043. Toll Free Reservations (Hotel Direct) at 800/344-3526 US; 800/447-7462 (Prima Hotels) Canada. Low season rack rates from $205 per double room per night (E.P.). High season rack rates from $415 per double room per night (E.P.). No meal plan available. 244 deluxe rooms, suites, and private cottages with air conditioning and private bathrooms. Four restaurants with two outdoor dining terraces, and two bars. Cash, Traveler's Checks, and all major credit cards accepted. Member of "Prima Hotels".*

Once again, the magnificent Elbow Beach hotel has proven itself to be the most opulent and luxurious large seaside resort in Bermuda. This regal island getaway has been welcoming the rich and famous with unsurpassed style and grace ever since it was first opened its doors back in 1908. Now operated by the prestigious Rafael Group of Hoteliers from Monaco, the property has just completed the final phase of an extensive $40 million renovation and enhancement project that has assured its unique position as one of the world's most memorable four star resorts.

Located about 32 miles away from the city of Hamilton on Bermuda's famous south shore, this posh and truly luxurious deluxe hotel is surrounded by over 50 acres of beautifully landscaped gardens that face directly onto a superb mil- long stretch of pink sand beach. The centerpiece of the hotel is a pastel colored five story main hotel wing with a lavish marble tiled main lobby area as well as two restaurants, a tranquil bar, and several plush sitting rooms and terraces. There are 138 well-appointed rooms and suites. Scattered throughout the rest of the garden-lined estate are an outstanding array of world class sporting facilities, a private beach club, tranquil walking trails, an additional 20 cottages each with several super-deluxe accommodations, as well as a few super-deluxe independent one and two bedroom villas for those seeking additional space and privacy.

The majority of Elbow Beach's beautifully decorated rooms and suites have sliding glass doors that open up onto sea-view balconies or garden-side terraces, individually controlled air conditioners, marble embellished private bathrooms stocked with English milled soaps and shampoos, fine antique reproduction furnishings, Spanish tile or ornate carpeted flooring, European designer fabrics, mini-bars, direct dial telephones with data ports, executive style desks, electronic mini-safes, 44 channel remote control color large screen cable televisions, am-fm clock radios, comfortable king or double bedding, large closets with irons and boards, plush cotton bathrobes and slippers, hair dryers, additional pull out sofa beds, and much more. The private villas also feature giant living rooms, wet bars, remote control audio/video systems, wood burning fireplaces, exposed wood beam ceilings, overhead fans, and their own delightful gardens complete with hammocks and deluxe patio furnishings.

Elbow Beach Hotel offers an Olympic sized heated outdoor swimming pool with a new open air hot tub, giant sun decks with complimentary beach chair and sun umbrella service, a health club, a Bersalon health spa and beauty center, five professionally surfaced plexipave outdoor tennis courts (two are lit at night) with a great pro shop, a full compliment of daily guest activities, half day supervised children's activity programs during the high season, over half a dozen different fully equipped business meeting or convention rooms with private reception areas, a couple of wheelchair accessible rooms for the physically challenged, on-sight scooter and bicycle rental, several boutiques and newsstands, daily afternoon high tea service, a Thursday evening manager's cocktail reception, optional baby sitting by the hour, an excursion desk, a putting green, temporary membership privileges at most Bermudian golf courses, a nearby public bus stop and taxi rank, Bermuda's best 24 hour gourmet room service, and the only real concierge service on the entire island.

The resort's amazing pink sand beach is home to a private beach club where you can enjoy complimentary use of Riviera-styled private cabanas, or for a small fee sail or snorkel out 125 yards or so to reach an incredible protected natural reef area filled with colorful semi-tropical fish, learn how to scuba dive, just lay back and relax on a comfortable sun chair to work on your tan, enjoy refreshing snacks and beverages over at Mickeys' bistro and sand bar, or perhaps even kayak along the turquoise seashore. During the warmest months of the year several attendants will deliver freezing cold towels and cocktails to you.

Dining here is a delightful experience with four completely unique restaurants presided over by award winning Executive Chef Neville King and a team of highly skilled sous-chefs. The open kitchen of the resort's new Seahorse Grill creates an impressive evening menu of Bermudian based European/Asian/West Indian fusion cuisine, in an inspiring contemporary setting complete with post-modern architectural elements. The sophisticated yet relaxing Verandah Bar and terrace offers its own unique blend of delicate Mediterranean-inspired international cuisine served in a stunning old world setting with live piano music nightly. Over at the beach-front's Café Lido guests and visitors can enjoy hearty classic Northern Italian dishes in the sea-view dining room and terrace. And last, but certainly not least, is the hotel's brand new Surf Club micro-brewery and sushi bar along downtown Hamilton's harbor-front .

CANADIAN PACIFIC SOUTHAMPTON PRINCESS HOTEL, *South Road, Southampton. Tel. 441/238-8000, Fax 441/238-8245. Toll Free Reservations (Canadian Pacific Hotels) at 800/441-1414 US & Canada. Internet: www.cphotels.com. Low season rack rates from $169 per double room per night (E.P.). High season rack rates from $439 per double room per night (E.P.). Special golf getaways and low season packages usually available. 597 air conditioned rooms with terraces and private bathrooms. Six restaurants, three bars, and one showroom. Dine Around (M.A.P.) meal plan is also available from $45 per person per day upon request. Cash, Traveler's Checks, and all major credit cards accepted.*

The Southampton Princess is one of Bermuda's top golf, tennis, and beach resort hotels. Perfect for anyone, this excellent full service resort rises six floors above a superb championship golf course with views over a picturesque harbor and a spectacular beach-front. Winner of multiple A.A.A. "Four Diamond" awards for excellence in providing extremely comfortable accommodations and outstanding culinary delights, this 597-room luxury resort offers more services and facilities than any other hotel on the island.

The Southampton Princess began life in 1972 when famed billionaire industrialist Daniel K. Ludwig decided to spend a good part of his fortune building an opulent modern-Colonial styled deluxe resort on Bermuda's beautiful south shore. Recently purchased by Canadian Pacific Hotels, who are planning to add even more features and facilities, the hotel rests amidst some 100 acres of plush rolling lawns and semi-tropical gardens that are also home to a large variety of the Southampton Princess's world class leisure and sporting facilities.

Besides offering guests discounted rates and preferred tee-off times at their own wonderfully landscaped 18 hole par three golf course, the hotel also features 11 professionally surfaced tennis courts, both indoor and outdoor swimming pools with sun-decks, a fully equipped health club with sauna, optional spa and beauty therapies, and of course a beautiful stretch of pink sandy beach with its own private beach club and seaside food and beverage venues. Other facilities and special services here include a wonderful "Dolphin Quest" dolphin encounter program for kids and adults alike, an on-site scuba and water-sports center, guest services and excursion desks, a team of patient golf and tennis pros, round-trip private ferry service to the Hamilton Princess, over a dozen designer boutiques and logo shops, free shuttle service to all points on the property, a superb high season supervised children's activity program, a giant state of the art multimedia amphitheater, several opulent meeting and convention rooms, and complete schedule of free daily guest activities for the whole family ranging from exciting guided hikes down the Railway Trail to gourmet cooking classes.

All of the nearly 600 peach-colored rooms and suites here are surprisingly spacious and contain individually controlled air conditioning systems, custom built tropical rattan and hardwood furnishings, large panoramic balconies with patio furnishings, private bathrooms, remote control televisions with some 30 channels of international cable stations, king or double beds, walk in closets with mini-safes, irons with ironing boards, executive style desks with direct dial phones and computer modem plugs, and lots of natural sunlight. The structure's top floor is reserved (during high season) as a special executive/VIP floor known as the Newport Club and for a surcharge over regular rates it offers private check-in and concierge services as well as complimentary continental breakfast, afternoon tea and evening cocktails.

Among the best of the seven dining establishments are the luxurious gourmet Newport Room and the equally impressive Waterlot Inn. Those desiring more casual dining may choose between the Windows on the Sound, the Rib Room steak and seafood grill-room, the beach-front Whaler Inn, Wickets Brasserie, or the beach Cabana bar. The evenings here are also quite fun at the Neptune Room show lounge featuring live entertainment nightly.

CANADIAN PACIFIC HAMILTON PRINCESS HOTEL, *Pitts Bay Road, Hamilton, Pembroke. Tel. 441/295-3000, Fax 441/295-1914. Toll Free Reservations (Canadian Pacific Hotels) at 800/441-1414 US & Canada. Internet: www.cphotels.com. Low season rack rates from $119 per double room per night (E.P.). High season rack rates from $289 per double room per night (E.P.). 413 air conditioned rooms and suites with private bathrooms. Three restaurants, one bar, and one showroom. Royal Dine Around (M.A.P.) meal plan is also available from $45 per person per day upon request. Cash, Traveler's Checks, and all major credit cards accepted.*

Every time I stay at the beautiful Hamilton Princess hotel it seems to be even more enjoyable than the last time. This delightful 4 star waterfront leisure resort and executive class hotel is the only truly full service large deluxe property in Hamilton. Situated on a beautifully landscaped stretch of prime real estate and surrounded by the sea, a picturesque inlet, and lush semi-tropical gardens, this has become the favored home away from home for many international businessmen and quality minded vacationers.

Built back in 1884, the Hamilton Princess has recently been purchased by Toronto-based Canadian Pacific Hotels who will add even more high end facilities and services to an already great hotel. There are 413 beautifully decorated rooms and suites featuringcontain antique reproduction hardwood furnishings, fully stocked private bathrooms, comfortable king or double twin bedding, direct dial telephones with data ports and optional dial-up local Internet access, 26 channel remote control color television, huge closets, delightful earth-tone carpets and fabrics, huge picture windows with either garden or water views, electronically controlled irons with boards, fire detectors, coffee makers, and in many cases there are also sofa-beds, mini-bars, sitting rooms, and amazing private patios with outdoor furniture. Corperate guests have access to a special recently renovated Princess Club floor with their own private check-in, concierge, and complimentary continental breakfast, daily international newspaper, afternoon tea with cakes, and evening wine and cheese hour.

The fortunate guests of the Hamilton Princess have access to a full range of service and facilities including complimentary use of a well equipped health club complete with sauna, a pair of newly resurfaced salt and freshwater outdoor swimming pools with sun-decks, a putting green, an amazing Japanese garden with tranquil walking paths, several lounge areas, and of course their famous scheduled private ferry service to the full range of golf, tennis, dolphin encounter, and beach facilities (as well as restaurants) at their sister hotel in Southampton. Additionally there are several designer boutiques, a tobacconist & newsstand, a beauty salon, optional massage, a full service excursion desk, a full service business center, in-house scooter and bicycle rentals, express laundry and dry cleaning services, and much more. For business meetings and receptions there are several conference rooms and regal reception halls capable of hosting almost any special event conceivable.

The main wing of the hotel is home to three wonderful restaurants, including the lavish Tiara Room where buffet breakfasts and sumptuous semi-formal al la carte Continental dinners are available several nights a week. Those who desire Mediterranean cuisine should check out their delicious offering at the more relaxed Harley's bistro, while delicious casual pub fare and live entertainment can be enjoyed over at the wonderful little Colony Pub piano bar and steakhouse. Throughout the year there are plays and comedy skits presented by a talented local troupe at the Gazebo Lounge showroom.

SMALL INNS & GUESTHOUSES

ROYAL PALMS HOTEL, *Rosemont Ave., Hamilton, Pembroke. Tel. 441/292-1854, Fax 441/292-1946. Toll Free Reservations (Hotel Direct) at 800/ 678-0783 US: 800/ 799-0824 Canada. Low season rack rates from $143 per double room per night (C.P.). High season rack rates from $180 per double room per night (C.P.). M.A.P. meal plan available for $43 per person per night. 9 rooms, 11 mini-suites, 4 deluxe one bedroom suites, and one deluxe self standing cottage, all with garden views, air conditioning and private bathrooms. One restaurant with an outdoor dining terrace, and one bar. Cash, Traveler's Checks, and all major credit cards accepted.*

Situated on a peaceful estate just a short eight minute walk away from downtown Hamilton, this pair of adjacent turn of the century converted traditional Bermudian mansions feature several spacious English country style rooms, mini-suites and one bedroom deluxe suites. Each room is decorated with a wonderful selection of both antique and reproduction hardwood furnishings, oriental rugs, fresh flowers, spacious bathrooms with either marble or hand painted ceramic trim, comfortable bedding, remote control cable color television, individually controlled air conditioning, hardwood furnishings, direct dial telephones with voice mail and data ports, available mini-refrigerators, quaint French picture windows with stunning garden views, and complimentary coffee and tea stations. The suites have been especially designed for visiting international executives and in some cases also contain small modern kitchens with microwave ovens and mini-refrigerator, as well as computer fax modem adapters.

Guests here may choose to enjoy a delicious home-cooked continental breakfast, as well as superb gourmet dinners at the opulent Ascots restaurant. Additional facilities include an outdoor swimming pool with sun-deck, several tranquil reading rooms, an intimate cedar wood paneled bar area, and optional scooter and bicycle rentals. The inn's accommodations were so delightful that I wanted to cancel my next series of scheduled hotel inspections and just stay here to relax for a week or two. Royal Palms is a truly warm and friendly place, where guests are offered a level of individualized hospitality that no other hotel or large resort could ever even come close to. In fact, the one time that I managed to pull myself out of bed at the crack of dawn, I was pleasantly surprised that the inn's charming housekeeper (Lorna) was already on the property ready to offer me a hot coffee and a friendly smile.

SALT KETTLE HOUSE, *Salt Kettle Road, Paget. Tel. 441/236-0407, Fax 441/236-8639. Low season rack rates from $90 per double room per night (B.P.). Low season rack rates from $110 per double room per night (B.P.). Eight rooms and cottage apartments with air conditioning and private bathrooms. No* *restaurant, but the inn has a breakfast room. Cash, Checks, and Traveler's Checks only, No credit cards accepted.*

This delightfully casual (and affordable) little bed and breakfastguest-house on the edge of the harbor is a real gem. The Salt Kettle House is comprised of a main house and several smaller Bermudian cottages located on water's edge just an eight minute bus, ferry, taxi, or scooter ride from downtown Hamilton.

Inside the inn's main house there are four beautifully furnished rooms each with air conditioning, private full bathrooms, comfortable beds, nice collections of antiques, large picture windows, and plenty of sun. There are also four extremely spacious one and two bedroom air conditioned cottage apartments complete with fully stocked kitchens, private bathrooms, and even wood burning fireplaces in some cases. Every unit is uniquely decorated with bright French style soft furnishings, adorable collectibles, and is stocked with good novels to read at night. There is also a TV room and lounge area in the main house.

Although there is no restaurant on the premises, all guests are served a fantastic complimentary full breakfast complete with homemade pancakes, muffins, fresh fruit, eggs, French toast, bacon, cereals, juices, coffee, tea, and marmalade. All cottage units also have their own kitchenettes, while guests in the main house rooms can use the ground level common kitchen throughout the day and evening.

Other special features of the Salt Kettle House include ferry service to downtown Hamilton and other points, nearby swimming and boating facilities, lots of harbor-front lounge chairs, and more charm than I could possibly describe. The wonderful woman that owns this guest-house (Hazel Lowe) is a remarkable source for all sorts of local information, and her manager (Margie Smith) will be sure to make your stay an unforgettable one.

AUNT NEA'S INN, *1 Nea's Alley, St. George's, St. George's. Tel. 441/297-1630, Fax 441/297-1908. Internet: www.auntneas.com. Low season rack rates from $110 per double room per night (C.P.). High season rack rates from $135 per double room per night (C.P.). 11 deluxe non-smoking rooms and suites with air conditioning and private bathrooms. One breakfast room. Cash, Traveler's Checks, and most major credit cards accepted.*

This charming family-owned and operated small deluxe inn is a truly special place to stay while visiting Bermuda. Located in a beautifully converted 18th century mansion on a peaceful historic lane a couple of minutes walk from the center of St. George's town, Aunt Nea's is in a league by itself. Originally operated as a simple cozy guesthouse for shipwrecked sailors by the late Mrs. E. Trew Robinson, Aunt Nea's is now run by her son Delaey and his wife Andrea. Together they have worked incredibly hard to transform the once simple guesthouse into what has become one of the most beautiful and welcoming small bed & breakfast inns anywhere.

Aunt Nea's features 11 imaginatively decorated rooms and lavish suites which feature Andrea's amazing hand stenciled cabinetry, individually control air conditioning and/or ceiling fans, twin or romantic four poster and canopy bed in iron and rare woods, the nicest hand woven rattan furnishings I have ever seen, stunning granite tile-lined private bathrooms (which in some cases have glassed-in shower areas as well as scallop shell sinks and whirlpool baths), Spanish tile flooring, a beautiful collection of Bermudian watercolors and photography, mini-refrigerators, hair dryers, am-fm clock radios. Some units also have original exposed beams extending through the ceiling and offer tranquil garden views.

Besides several cozy sitting rooms, lending libraries, a hand made local gift shop, and a television lounge filled with plush sofas and plenty of local charm, Aunt Nea's has a wonderful garden-view terrace that is the perfect place to glance out over their limestone Moongate and sip a warm afternoon tea. With its close proximately to fine golf, shopping possibilities, good local restaurants, fine sandy beaches, and historic sights, Aunt Nea's is the best place to stay anywhere near St. George's.

11. SANDYS PARISH

Bermuda's northwesternmost parish of **Sandys**, named after Sir Edwin Sandys, is one of the most relaxing parts of this country to explore by foot, taxi, bus, or scooter. The parish is comprised of various small and large islands, including **Ireland Island North**, **Ireland Island South**, **Boaz Island**, **Watford Island**, **Somerset Island**, and a sliver of the western portion of **Great Bermuda Island** – all connected by a series of bridges.

Sandys is a fairly tranquil residential and commercial parish, boasting plenty of coastline with small but beautiful pink sand beaches, prominent historical sights, great museums, shopping (even on Sundays) multiple embarkation points for all types of sea excursions, fine and casual dining possibilities, and a handful of great places to stay. A new and unexpected adventure seems to await every visitor at the turn of each corner.

ARRIVALS & DEPARTURES

The best way to be transported between the hotels in Sandys Parish and the **Kindley Field International Airport** is to take a taxi ride for about $32.50 each way. Depending on where exactly you are staying, the drive is about 25 kilometers (16 miles) long and usually takes about 45 minutes.

ORIENTATION

Since Sandys Parish is actually a series of beautiful windswept islands that are attached to each other by bridges, the seashore itself is the most obvious landmark. It is fairly difficult to get lost here, but bring along a copy of the free *Bermuda Handy Reference Map*, available at any Visitor's Service Bureau office including the one at the Royal Naval Dockyard.

GETTING AROUND

Getting around this part of Bermuda is a rather easy task. To begin with, this parish is divided by a series of wide roads that are all connected together from end to end to form a major intra-parish thoroughfare. Public bus routes #7 and #8 run the length of Sandys and head all the way into Hamilton. Additional ferry services connect various points throughout Sandys to both each other as well as to Hamilton.

Taxis are always available around here, and **Sandys Taxi Co.** runs a frequent **West End Mini Bus Service**, *Tel. 441/234-2344*, that can shuttle people from the Somerset Bridge to the Royal Naval Dockyard. For those walking, you will soon see that you are in for a pleasant surprise via the **Railway Trail** and many fine side roads that wind through the suburban sectors of this nice area.

WHERE TO STAY

CAMBRIDGE BEACHES, *30 Kings Point Road, Sandy's. Tel. 441/234-0331, Fax 441/234-3352. Toll Free Reservations (Hotel's Direct) at 800/468-7300 US & Canada. Internet: cambeach@ibl.bm Low season rack rates from $205 per double room per night (B.P.). High season rack rates from $400 per double room per night (M.A.P.). 81 rooms, suites, and private one & two bedroom villa style cottages with air conditioning and private bathrooms. Three restaurants with two outdoor dining terraces and a bar. Low season M.A.P. meal plan also available for $30 per person per day upon request. Cash, Checks, Traveler's Checks, Visa and Mastercard accepted. Children under five years old must be accompanied by an au pair. Member of "The Bermuda Collection" of fine hotels.*

Cambridge Beaches is a luxurious and exclusive cottage colony located on a peaceful 25 acre beach lined peninsula just a few minutes walk away from Somerset Village. This superb property has long been favored by wealthy European and American vacationers seeking some of Bermuda's finest ocean-view accommodations and gourmet cuisine.

This property's 82 lavishly appointed rooms, suites, and private villas feature large private beach or garden view terraces, individually controlled air conditioning, direct dial telephones, ceiling fans, imported hair and skin care products, large picture windows or sliding French doors, regal hardwood furnishings, and in most cases, exposed beam ceilings, fireplaces and marble bathrooms complete with Jacuzzis.

Facilities here include a fully equipped Spa where you pamper yourself with European body treatments such as Swedish massage and hydrotherapy (special personalized spa packages complete with gourmet spa cuisine meals are available upon request), indoor and outdoor swimming pools, a tranquil main clubhouse with several reading rooms and lounges, a full service private marina, snorkeling and scuba excursions, sail boat and motorboat rentals, deep sea and reef fishing trips, three outdoor tennis courts, a putting green, guest membership privileges at many fine golf courses, bicycle and scooter rentals, weekly manager's rum swizzle receptions, room service, live high season evening entertainment, and direct access to five of the country's prettiest sandy beaches. Dining here is also a real pleasure with two gourmet restaurants, an outdoor dining terrace, and a luncheon patio serving classic and nouveau Bermudian influenced Continental cuisine prepared by master chef Jean-Claude Garzia. Guests who take the hotel's great M.A.P. meal plan may also choose to enjoy a few dinners in any of five other fine Bermuda Collection restaurants at no additional charge.

This peaceful and refined cottage colony has an abundance of charm and a unique sense of privacy that makes it a perfect deluxe hideaway for those that just want to get away from it all. Management and staff make sure that you thoroughly enjoy your stay here. Cambridge Beaches earns my highest recommendation.

Selected as one of my *Best Places to Stay* – see Chapter 10.

WILLOWBANK, *Somerset Road, Sandys, Tel. 441/234-1616 Fax 441/234-3373; Toll Free (Direct) at Tel. 800/752-8493 US; Tel. 800/463-8444 Canada. High season rack rate from $176 per double room per night M.A.P. Low season rack rate from $138 per double room per night M.A.P. 62 air conditioned rooms with private bathroom. One restaurant with and no bar. Cash, Checks, and Traveler's Checks only, no credit cards accepted.*

Willowbank is a non-denominational Christian hotel only a minute away from the Somerset Bridge. This basic resort hotel is situated on six acres of gardens that look out over both the sea and some tranquil gardens. The cottage style rooms (some are seaview) are nice and comfortable, but tend to be a bit on the basic side. The guests here are almost all middle age to elderly clients who prefer the ambiance of a medium sized full service Christian guest center. Although religion is a prominent part of the resort, it is not overly imposed except during grace before meals.

Facilities include a medium sized freshwater pool, 2 private beaches, 2 tennis courts, a great pier for fish feeding, guest laundry room, and big old cedar beam public spaces in the main manor. An excellent value for those who know what to expect.

WHERE TO EAT

TAMARISK DINING ROOM *at Cambridge Beaches, Kings Point Road, Sandys. Tel: 441/234-0331. Open 7:00pm until 9:30pm nightly. Dress Code ranges from Smart Casual to Jacket and Tie depending on the specific night. Reservations Required. Cash, Travelers Checks, Visa and Mastercard accepted.*

The beautiful Tamarisk dining room inside Cambridge Beaches main clubhouse is a wonderful place to enjoy superb French influenced gourmet cuisine. Master chef Jean-Claude Garzia of France (winner of the 1996/7 "Meilleurs Ouvriers de France" gold medal for culinary excellence) and his team select and expertly prepare delicious five course dinners every night. Besides offering seating under a exquisite exposed wood beam ceiling embellished with fine imported chandeliers, on most nights there is also live classical piano or guitar music to help get you in the right mood for a special evening out.

On my latest visit to this fine establishment I was presented with an extensive menu that changed daily and included so many exotic treats that I had a tough time choosing what to order. Among my favorite dishes here are the tart of rock shrimp ragout in lemon wine sauce, potato gnocchi topped with Roquefort cream, French goat cheese profiteroles in a fresh thyme and rosemary vinaigrette, Bermuda pumpkin soup, roasted rack of lamb encrusted in honey, local sea bass sauteed in an anise root infused olive oil, Black Angus sirloin steak topped with black truffle sauce, grilled breast of chicken atop a bed of wild mushroom polenta, and many other surprises. The kitchen also creates a half dozen or so sumptuous desserts including a piping hot soufflé of the day.

If you want a low fat meal, their delicious five course Spa Menu averages about 600 calories and features tasty dishes such as asparagus with balsamic vinegar dressing, fresh mushrooms stuffed with cheese, garden vegetable soups, locally grown onion and tomato salad, grilled chicken breast, broiled fresh fish with lemon, lamb chops with wild rice, filet mignon, strawberry crepes, and fresh fruit salad. The wine stewards may also have a surprise in store for you as the wine list here is reasonably priced and full of surprises. There are great wines from France, Italy, Portugal, Spain, California, South Africa, Chile, and Australia that in many cases can be ordered by the glass, half or full bottle. The overall service here is impeccable. Expect dinner for two to average around $120 plus wine.

IL PALIO, *Middle Road, Sandys. Tel. 441/234-1049. Open 6:00pm until 10:15pm nightly. Dress Code is Casual. Reservations Suggested. Cash, Travelers Checks, and all major Credit Cards accepted.*

I really love dining at this tiny two-floor Northern Italian regional cuisine restaurant on the outskirts of Somerset. Owner and restaurant mogul Mr. Fosco Nannini (originally from Sienna, Italy) has created a charming and unusually inviting little restaurant where you will be impressed with both the food and the friendly ambiance. At times you can almost swear that your neighbor's Italian grandmother must be hard at work in the kitchen. After enjoying a fine cocktail at the downstairs bar you will be escorted to the upper floor dining room that is designed to seat just a few dozen in extreme comfort. Service here is a true delight, with plenty of attention and hospitality evident from your first step through the front door.

Among my top picks here are the fantastic baked mussels in white wine and tomato sauce, tomato and mozzarella salad with garden picked basil, the best Caesar salad in all of Bermuda, jumbo shrimp sautéed in an Elba island styled garlic and butter sauce, penne pasta with pesto and shrimp, home-made linguini with seafood, spinach and meat cannelloni, veal scaloppini, chicken with red peppers and tomatoes, broiled sirloin steak, lamb chops, and delicious homemade cakes. They also offer an extensive list of moderately priced Italian wines and gourmet coffees. Expect dinner to cost around $83.50 a couple plus wine. They also offer a superb 3-course early bird dinner during much of the year and it only costs about $19 per person. Highly Recommended.

THE FROG AND ONION PUB, *Cooperage Building, Dockyard, Sandys, Tel. 441/234-2900. Open 12noon to 12midnight; Closed on Mondays during low season. Dress code is Informal. Reservations are suggested, but not always necessary. Cash, Traveler's Checks, Visa and MasterCard accepted.*

This is my favorite spot for lunch in the Royal Naval Dockyard. The unique medieval-looking castle atmosphere and decor are upstaged only by the best pub fare outside of the Cotswolds. For lunch you can enjoy great sandwiches, excellent cheeseburgers, hearty chowders, superb pub pies (including a vegetarian version), ploughman's lunches, authentic fish and chips, and typical English desserts like bread and butter pudding. The dinner menu might include grilled sirloin with stilton sauce, lamb chops, and an amazing house special of baked fish, scallops, and shrimp in a tomato basil sauce.

Meals here are served in one of the candelabra-laden dining rooms, at the long pub bar, or on one of the small outdoor tables. A vast selection of British and other imported beers are available on tap and in bottles.

A great place for couples, families, and exhausted tourists looking for a casual but delicious and down to earth eating establishment. Dinner for two should set couples back about $59 while a great lunch for two should cost somewhere around $23.50 or so, not including wine or drinks.

WATERSIDE INN, *Dockyard, Sandys, Tel. 441/234-0112. Open 12noon until 11:30pm daily. Dress Code ranges from Smart Casual to Jacket and Tie. Reservations are suggested. Cash, Traveler's Checks, and most major credit cards accepted.*

This enchanting waterfront restaurant doesn't seem to get the credit it really deserves for offering rather good meals at relatively low prices by Bermudian standards. The restaurant is situated at the edge of the dockyard area near the Maritime Museum, and offers an intimate indoor dining room seating about 48 people, and a fantastic sun-drenched patio for 90 guests. The international cuisine served here includes unique items such as gazpacho Andaluz, Scottish smoked salmon, burgers with shrimp and cheese, grilled chicken, seafood pasta, and a fine nightly *table d' hote* offering. Dinner here should cost about $63 per couple before adding drinks.

THE SOMERSET COUNTRY SQUIRE, *Mangrove Bay, Sandys, Tel. 441/234-0105. Open 11:30am until 10:30pm daily. Dress Code ranges from Informal to Smart Casual. Reservations Suggested. Cash, Traveler's Checks, and most major credit cards accepted.*

This bayside restaurant and pub is mostly known for its informal outdoor dining area that overlooks the boats of Mangrove Bay, although it also has a traditional wood-panelled interior dining room as well. This establishment offers good food served in large portions at reasonable prices, with a younger and more lively clientele. Among the house specialties are Caesar salads, Bermudian fish chowder, steak and kidney pie, assorted pasta dishes, huge burgers, fresh seafood meals, and great home made apple pie. Dinner should set a couple back for about $53 and lunch for two about $27, without drinks.

SOMERSET PHARMACY SNACK SHOP, *Mangrove Bay, Sandys, Tel. 441/238-9414. Open 8am until 2pm Monday through Saturday. Dress Code is Informal. Reservations are not necessary. Cash and Traveler's Checks only, no credit cards accepted.*

Remember the days when you could go into a neighborhood drug store and order a sandwich from its luncheonette counter? Well, this is the real thing, without any tourist trap prices and synthetic ambiance. This vintage soda shop is the best place around to sit down and order huge egg breakfasts, burgers, tuna sandwiches, BLTs, curried chicken pies, chili, frozen yogurt, and bagels with cream cheese at low, low prices.

There are only enough counter seats for 9 people and 2 small tables, but I am sure you will always find an empty seat. A great find for those looking for the real Bermuda experience. Lunch for two will cost only about $9.75.

PIRATE'S LANDING, *Dockyard Terrace, Sandys. Tel: (441) 234-5151. Open 11:30am until 10:00pm nightly. Dress Code is Casual. Reservations not Necessary. Cash, Travelers Checks, and most major Credit Cards accepted.*

Located just a short walk from the Clocktower Centre and the cruise ship port at the Royal Naval Dockyard, this cute restaurant and luncheon terrace is the best choice for reasonably priced dining in the entire Dockyard area. Pirate's Landing offers extensive lunch and dinner menus featuring a wide array of family-style dishes (and many vegetarian selections), including shrimp cocktails, lightly fried calamari, fresh tomato and mozzarella salad with basil, Bermuda fish chowder, chicken tikka patiala marinated in Indian spices, fettuccine Alfredo, an amazing Caesar salad, fresh daily locally caught fish on a sesame bun with fries, huge burgers with assorted toppings, shrimp baked with lemon butter, tenderloin of beef with porcini mushroom sauce, boneless chicken caccatiatore, and much more.

Their wine list is a real treat with 20 different old and new world selections at reasonable prices. For only $19.50 a person, a special 3-course early bird dinner is available from 6pm until 7pm daily. Expect a great lunch for two to set you back about $29, while dinner may cost you about $68 per couple plus wine

FOUR STAR PIZZA, *Somerset Road, Sandys, Tel. 441/234-2626. Open 11am to 12midnight daily. Dress Code is Informal. Reservations are not necessary. Cash and Traveler's Checks Only, no credit cards accepted.*

This is one in a chain of new pizza take out and delivery restaurants that make decent pizzas in several sizes that can feed up to 4 people. While the pizzas here can't compete with their North American counterparts, they are better than I had expected. A variety of different toppings are available at an additional surcharge. A pizza for 2 with a few toppings (for eat in, free local delivery, or take out) should cost around $14.50 or so. A good choice when you need a break from formal gourmet dining.

SEEING THE SIGHTS

The Royal Naval Dockyard

To begin your tour of this part of Bermuda, consider taking a taxi, scooter, public ferry, the not so direct west end mini-bus shuttle, or the public bus (line #7 or #8) all the way to the end of the line at the **Royal Naval Dockyard** area on the tip of **Ireland Island North**. This fortified and once heavily armed port zone was formerly used as Britain's major western Atlantic naval base of operations between the early 1800's until 1951 when it was officially decommissioned.

Constructed primarily by English convicts and local slaves laboring under the direction of Royal Engineers, the Dockyard was designed to replace several important colonial naval ports on the eastern coast of what is now the United States which Britain lost use of after being defeated in the war of the American Revolution. The Dockyard was also used to launch English warships dispatched to attack and destroy Washington, DC, during the War of 1812.

These days about the only continuing sign of the Dockyard's maritime usage can be seen from the massive cruise ship terminal, several sea excursion embarkation slips, a few dozen moored yachts, and an occasional visit from the huge Cable and Wireless overseas telephone line repair vessel. After several years of neglect, the Dockyard area was finally redeveloped by the **West End Development Corporation** (**Wedco**) and has become a pleasant seaside complex of boutiques, restaurants, pubs, art centers, entertainment venues, and an excellent maritime museum. They're all housed in a series of the naval base's original 19th century stone block buildings. This area also features great promenades, public parks, walking trails, and comfortable benches facing the sea.

THE BERMUDA TRAIN CO. TROLLEY TOURS OF DOCKYARD

A recent addition to the high season attractions of the Royal Naval Dockyard is the Bermuda Train Co.'s train-like trolley that runs daily from 9:00am until 5:00pm in the summer months. The trolley will take passengers between the cruise ship terminal and the Clocktower mall for a mere $2.50 or so round trip. Optional long-range tours may be offered during high season depending on demand.

To start off your self-guided tour of the Dockyard area, I suggest beginning at the entrance to the famed **Bermuda Maritime Museum** complex off of Maritime Lane, just a short walk away from either the public bus stop or ferry landing. This wonderful tribute to Bermuda's naval history is a must-see for all visitors. The museum is located on some ten acres of walled seaside property and is housed within a small grouping of beautifully restored stone block buildings with four foot thick walls that were originally built to house, supply, and protect British sailors that were stationed at the Dockyard.

When you first arrive at the museum you will be handed a small pamphlet entitled *Your Guide to the Bermuda Maritime Museum*. A self-guided walking tour of about 45 minutes will bring you through exhibits including displays of Bermudian history, British Royal Navy history, antique navigational instruments, unusual treasures discovered beneath the sea by famous local treasure hunter Teddy Tucker, whaling artifacts, antique currency, old maps, scale models of famous English sailing vessels including both the *Sea Venture* and *Deliverance,* restored full-size Bermuda fitted dingys, old cannons, and lots more.

Besides these main buildings, visitors can also view the **Commissioner's House**, which historians believe to be the western hemisphere's first prefabricated structure (shipped over piece by piece from England in the 1820's). Another attraction on the museum's property is its series of memorable walking trials and wall walks that rise up between the bastions. If you have any specific questions about the museum, try to find either Mr. Ivor Grant or any of the other helpful wardens who will be happy to tell you all kinds of colorful stories and lesser known facts. *The museum currently costs $7.50 per adult, $6 per senior citizen, $3 per child under 12 years of age, and is free for kids under five years old. A special Family Pass may be purchased for $15 which will admit two adults with two children. The museum's opening hours are between 9:30am and 4:30pm every day of the week.*

For those with kids, just a few feet away on the opposite side of Maritime Lane is a small **children's playground area** designed to resemble a ship, while just a minute's walk behind the playground is the entrance to a high season only **snorkel park** with gear rentals that has just opened.

From the main exit door of the arts center, make a right turn to continue down Maritime Lane for a few steps until passing the arched entrance to the old **Cooperage Building**. This beautiful building was once the sight of a factory that manufactured wooden barrels which were used for storing food on 19th century sea journeys. The majority of the Cooperage Building has now been converted to house the **Bermuda Craft Market**. This large market is actually a collection of individual stalls which offer many items for sale including hand made Bermudian crafts, candles, quilts, stained glass, cedar wood gift items, perfumes, dolls, condiments, and other unusual items. *Admission to the craft market is free and it is open from 10:00am until 5:00pm every day of the week.*

Also in the Cooperage Building is the delightful **Frog and Onion Pub** bar and restaurant which serves up some of the finest English-style pub style fare in all of Bermuda. The pub's dramatic interior is embellished with stone block walls, cast iron candelabras, a massive fireplace, old billiard tables, old English public phone booths, antique portraits of sailors, and even amusing rest rooms that are known as The Poop Deck. Besides great hearty meals, the pub's long wooden and brass bar also offers a superb array of English and Bermudian beers at reasonable prices. Just across the courtyard from the pub is the main entrance to the **Neptune Cinema** where first run Hollywood movies are shown several times a day. There are also a several public bathrooms located in the Cooperage Building. *The pub's dining room is open from 11:00am until at least 9:30pm every day of the week (except during low season when it is closed on Mondays). The pub's long bar is open from 11:00am until at least 1:00am.*

After departing the Cooperage Building, make a right turn to continue heading down Maritime Lane. At the next corner you will turn

FESTIVAL DAYS AT DOCKYARD

Special events such as the April through October Family Days on many Sunday afternoons resemble small festivals with free live music, inexpensive food kiosks, and kid's entertainment. May's Bermuda Taster's Day offers visitors and locals alike to sample great affordable Bermudian food and enjoy live Calypso music. Mid-October is the time for the Dockyard's great Jazz Festival when international headliners perform live on the first Friday and Saturday after Columbus Day (admission to Jazz Festival is about $45 per ticket). For more information, please contact the Bermuda Department of Tourism.

right in front of the **Pirate's Landing Restaurant** and walk along a street named the **Dockyard Terrace**. A few steps later you will pass by a few shops and offices including the extremely helpful **Visitor's Service Bureau** tourist information office where a staff of friendly local women will be pleased to hand out free maps and give some great advice on what to see and do around the Dockyard or elsewhere on Bermuda. *The tourist information center is open from 10:00am until 5:00pm every day of the week.*

As you continue walking up the Dockyard Terrace you will pass by the **Dockyard Marina Co.**, where nautical gear and great poster sized navigation charts may be purchased, the **Dockyard Convenience Store** selling ice cold beverages and snacks. The next important sight on this short street is the **Victualling Yard**, a fortified yard that was once the primary storage area for provisions which were salted and packed into wooden barrels for use during long voyages on the open sea.

After exiting the Victualling Yard you will continue along the Dockyard Terrace, and a the next corner bear left to wander along Camber Road. This long wide road is lined on the right hand side by several business including a branch of **Oleander Cycles** scooter rentals, the offices of the **Department of Marine Ports and Navigation**, the new **Bermuda Clay Works** pottery shop where artisans work their clay magic by hand, and a few other shops in converted old Naval buildings.

At the next corner, keep walking straight to pass alongside the **Clocktower Centre** shopping mall. This impressive structure dates back to 1857 and was originally part of the British naval station. Set within one of the structure's two 100 foot high towers is a beautiful four faced antique clock from London, while the other tower houses a high tide indication gauge.

You will also notice a huge sculpture in front of the main building consisting of three large anchors which have been leaned up against each other. The main building and its adjacent west wing are surrounded by plenty of lawns and benches that allow visitors to sit back and ponder what the old days must have been like for 19th century British sailors arriving in Bermuda for the first time. The West End Development Corporation (WEDCO) was responsible for developing these historic buildings into the shopping attraction that it has become today, winning an award from the Bermuda National Trust for the tasteful conversion and restoration.

The lower floor of these two adjacent structures contain a variety of great boutiques, artist's studios, dining venues, and gift shops such as **Crisson's Jewelers**, **Trimminghams' little Trim's** shop, the **Dockyard Humidor** with Cuban and Dominican cigars, the **Dockyard Wine & Spirit** shop, a **Makin' Waves** T-shirt shop, an **Uncommon Scents** perfume boutique, the **Ripples** kids clothing shop, **Michael Swan's** art gallery, a **Calypso** designer women's wear store, **Beethoven's** café and lunch spot,

A.S. Cooper & Sons glass & porcelain emporium, **Smith's** department store, **Nannini's Hagen Dazs** ice cream parlor, the **Bermuda Railway Co.** clothing shop, **Davison's** department store, and the **Seaside Health Corner** pharmacy, as well as a few phone booths, public self service fax machines, clean rest rooms, and ATM bank machines.

The Clocktower mall's hours of operation are normally from 10:00am until 5:00pm From Monday through Saturday, 11:00am to 5:00pm on Sundays and Holidays, and during Summer they extend on Tuesday through Thursday from 9:30am until 6:00pm. As one of the only places that stores are open on Sundays, this place gets quite crowded with families arriving from church that are looking for a fun afternoon out.

Also in the Clocktower Centre are pay phones, a self-service fax machine, the affordable **La Brioche** pastry shop and tea room, and several other retail shops, banquet rooms, and a few small exhibits (located on the top floor). Hours of operation for most of the Clocktower shops is from 10am until 5pm Monday through Friday and 12noon until 5pm on weekends. This is one of the only places to shop for gifts in all of Bermuda on Sundays, and I can assure you that the prices in several of these shops tend to match their downtown Hamilton counterparts.

TAKE A GUIDED WALK!

During the low season, a series of suberb free guided walks depart the Dockyard area. A one and a half hour nature tour departs Sundays at 11am from the front of the Clocktower Centre, while 45 minute history walks depart Thursdays at 2:15pm from the Clocktower Centre and on Sundays at 2:15pm from the Bermuda Crafts Market at the Cooperage building.

After finishing with the Clocktower Centre, you can either walk next door for a home cooked meal at the down to earth **New Freeport Restaurant & Bar,** or you can take a peek above the bluff to see the now closed **Casemates Prison.** This eerie old jail (lovingly referred to by locals as the Harbourview Hotel) was once one of the most feared maximum security prisons in this part of the world, and has now become the sight of possible future development by WEDCO. Although I would like to see this structure transformed into Bermuda's newest theme hotel, of course called the Harbourside (complete with iron bars and jail doors), plans are being discussed to turn Casemates into either an aquarium or an another shopping mall.

In an effort to humanize the reputation of Bermuda's jail system, the government has just completed a multimillion dollar campus style jail called the **Westgate Corrections Facility** just next door. In an act of what many locals call overcompensation, this new jail has facilities that rival some of the larger resorts on the island, and is fully air conditioned. These are the least expensive seaview accommodations in all of Bermuda, and meals are also included. Unfortunately, you may find your vacation to be a bit extended if incarcerated here.

For the more adventurous souls who are looking for a bit of excitement, try one of the many interesting high season only dockyard-based excursions. There are half-day snorkel cruises offered on the beautiful **Hat Trick** trimaran for $35 per person, bungee jumping off the 140 foot tall **Adrenaline Extreme** platform, summer parasailing with the unforgettable **Sky Rider** team for about $50 per person, the memorable **Enterprise Submarine** undersea sub ride which offers a great 3 hour trip of which over 40 minutes is spent submerged within a shipwreck and reef area for $65 per person, the **Dockyard Boat Rentals** at the dockyark marina offers Sunfish for $25 for two hours, kayaks for $20 per hour, Carolina Skiffs for $50 for 2 hours, and **Dive Bermuda** which has 3 hour reef and wreck dives for PADI certified divers starting at $40 per person plus equipment rentals.

After a full day at the dockyard, I am sure that you will return to your hotel quite satisfied and a bit exhausted.

West from Dockyard to Somerset

To depart **Ireland Island North**, just take a taxi, scooter, mini bus shuttle, or public bus out onto Pender Road and pass under the archway below Casemates prison. Soon you will find yourself crossing the **Cut Bridge**, which leads onto Cockburne Road on **Ireland Island South**. This route now passes by the entrance to the swimming and picnic areas, nature trails, tranquil mangroves, various species of birds, and tiny jetties of **Lagoon Park** in the island's interior. Admission is free to the park and it is always open.

After exiting the park you have two choices of routes to take towards the next island in the chain. About half a kilometer (500 yards) or so past the top (north end) of the park, Cockburne Road continues straight down the island's north shore passing by **Black Bay** and onto the old naval cemetery. The somewhat parallel Graddock Road forks off to the left (south) and winds down the island's eastern shore merging with Lagoon Road as it slips by a calm and photogenic inlet known as **The Crawl**, moves past a great little beach area at **Parson's Bay**, continues to and reconnects with the main road just before reaching **Grey's Bridge**. After crossing this bridge onto **Boaz Island**, you will be traveling down **Malabar Road** that will take you next to some nice seaside views before you transverse yet another bridge leading onto **Watford Island**.

Boaz Island and **Watford Island** offer little of interest to tourists. The real fun begins when crossing over the **Watford Bridge** and onto **Somerset Island**, the largest landmass in Sandys parish.

Somerset Village & Environs

Beautiful **Somerset Island** is loaded with superb beaches, interesting attractions, nature preserves, historical sights, walking trails, cute boutiques, excellent dining possibilities in all price ranges, exciting sea-based excursions, and some of Bermuda's most intimate resorts and inns. I love almost every part of Somerset Island, and although most tourists don't seem to spend much time here, I strongly recommend this somewhat off the beaten path destination.

Just as you cross over the **Watford Bridge**, which is only about a 9 minute ride if coming from the dockyard, you can see the peaceful **Mangrove Bay** on your right side. When you start walking around this bay, filled with boats and featuring a fairly nice beach area, you will see the edge of **Somerset Village** with its quaint assortment of shops and restaurants.

In order of location on the main road at Mangrove Bay, you can stop by and have seafood lunch or dinner at the fantastic **Loyalty Inn** restaurant with its bayview terrace and live music on most weekend nights, shop till you drop at the **Bermuda Railway Co.** and **Trimingham's** department stores, and order a good burger and fries at the casual **Maritime Cafe** and sit upstairs on its rooftop panoramic dining section.

If you need some cash, stop in at the Bank of Bermuda's ATM machine. Continue around town by looking for unique bargains at the **Old Market** ladies clothing shop, browse at imported sportswear at the **English Sports Shop**, check out the **W.J. Boyle & Son** shoe store, enjoy great inexpensive sandwich at the **Somerset Pharmacy** lunch counter, stock up on sundries at the **Village Corner**. Across the road you can also pop into the **Let's Party** greeting card and party supply shop, pick up a bottle of fine spirits at **Frith's Liquor**, or walk under the moongate and relax at the bayside patio for lunch or dinner at the rather casual and moderately priced **Somerset Country Squire** restaurant and bar.

LEARN ABOUT AREA ATTRACTIONS!

During the low season, a free guided tour and slide presentation about the area's history, architecture, and plantlife departs on Thursdays at 10am from the **Somerset Country Squire** *restaurant.*

After walking, eating, and shopping your way through this part of Somerset, you have several additional possibilities for excursions, hikes, and sightseeing. A unique undersea adventure awaits all those who desire a wonderful walk on the bottom of the sea with Greg and Lynda Hartley's **Undersea Walk**. This exciting $40 high season-only excursion puts glass diving helmets (big enough to wear glasses in) on both children and adults and then guides them on a spectacular walk on the shallow fish and coral dotted sea bottom. Departures for this undersea walk take place by appointment only and leave from the backyard dock at the rustic Village Inn restaurant at the foot of the Watford Bridge.

For a nice change of pace, continue down along the main road from the Mangrove Bay area and make a right turn when you reach the area's new post office. As you wander down this small side road a small beach area will soon come into view on your right hand side. A short distance later you may also choose to turn right and follow the signs into the Mangrove Bay Wharf. This wharf is home to the **Mangrove Marina Ltd.** excursion slip which in high season rents out Boston Whaler motor boats for $55 (two hours), wind-surfing boards for $15 per hour, sunfish sail boats for $15 per hour, sea kayaks for $12 per hour, and sailing lessons at $50 a person. Special sail and snorkel cruises may also be reserved with advance notice.

From the wharf you can walk or ride straight (to the west) onto Cambridge Road and then turn right (north) onto King's Point Road to reach **Cambridge Beaches**, one of Bermuda's finest and most private resorts. Although Cambridge's five secluded pink sand beaches, full service spa, and gourmet restaurant are typically utilized only by guests, call ahead and try to book a fine dinner or excellent spa treatment. As you exit the resort and turn right (to the west) back onto Cambridge Road you can price some wonderful handmade European table cloths, tea towels, and napkins at the charming **Irish Linen Shop** which is housed in a memorable 18th century Bermudian estate house.

A bit further down Cambridge Road (to the west), this street forks to both Middle Road and Daniel's Head Road. Bear right onto Daniel's Head Road for a couple of minutes until reaching the entrance for the **Somerset Long Bay Park** with its enchanting **Bermuda Audubon Society Nature Reserve** and wonderful shallow beach.

This fine sandy beach gets plenty of high intensity afternoon sun and is a great place to swim. The adjacent park is typically deserted except for spirited weekend family picnics where visitors are often invited to sample grandma's delicious cod fish cakes or perhaps join in a family ball game. The park is free to all visitors and is open all the time.

If you head back to the last intersection at Cambridge Road and Main Road, follow Main Road down (south) for a few minutes, you can stop in the romantic little **Il Palio Restaurant** for a delicious authentic Italian dinner. After a good sun bath, ocean swim, and perhaps a fine meal, you may wish to return to the Mangrove Bay area. If you want to see a real old-style Bermudian neighborhood, turn left (east) onto East Shore Road and follow the signs to **Carvello Bay**. This is a cute little seaside residential area where time just seems to have stood still.

Those of you who have had enough running around can either take a ferry from the **Carvello Bay Dock** or **Watford Bridge Dock**, hop on a bus at the **Somerset Bus Depot** around the corner at Beacon Hill Road, call a taxi, or ride a scooter back to your hotel and save this next part of Sandys parish for another day.

Somerset Village to the Somerset Bridge & Beyond

Below Somerset Village, this residential island takes on a more inactive tone. **Somerset Road** winds its way down the rest of this parish with the famous **Bermuda Railway Trail** running almost parallel and just about a quarter of a mile east from both this main road and most of the area's remaining attractions. Visitors to this part of Sandys and its sights can substitute the scenic Railway Trail for the more commercial Somerset Road and veer off on side streets to get to the following attractions.

The first stop on this route will be the less than impressive **Springfield & Gilbert Nature Reserve** off Somerset Road. This antique farm house with slave quarters is open to the public, although a few rooms inside this historic home now contain a branch of the Public Library system.

Surrounding the main house is a 5 acre estate with a series of nature walks called the **Anita Wingate Trails** that have become a bit overgrown and less than navigable these days. Although the property, managed by the **Bermuda National Trust**, is supposed to be an architectural masterpiece, it is in desperate need of some serious work but still has the potential of regaining its former elegance. Admission is free and the estate is open daily from sunrise to sunset.

Continue south on Somerset Road for a few blocks before reaching the **Somerset Visitors Service Bureau** office to get a few detailed maps and local brochures. The bureau is only open from 10am until about 4pm Monday through Saturdays in high season. Just steps further down Somerset Road you will see the dramatic facade and restored massive spire of the late 18th century **St. James Anglican Church**, worth a brief glimpse. As you will soon begin to notice, each parish in Bermuda has at least one Anglican (Church of England) parish church. This pretty house of worship is open from sunrise to sunset and admission is free.

From St. James Church, continue down Somerset Road until you reach the 43-acre **Heydon Trust Estate**. The estate offers several walking paths that wind their way past fruit trees and water views. A tiny and understated 17th century chapel can still be visited on the estate grounds. Admission is free to the estate, and it is open to the public daily. As you return to Somerset Road, keep going down (south) and you'll pass by the entrance to **Willowbank**, Bermuda's only Christian-oriented resort hotel, with its cozy inexpensive seaview rooms just steps from the beach.

As you continue down the road you will shortly find the signposted approach road to the **Scaur Hill Fort Park**. As you wander or ride up the long uphill blacktop road to the fort, the park's 22 acres of beautifully manicured grounds are a pleasant surprise. At the top of the hill visitors can tour **Fort Scaur** which was a polygonal shaped moated fortress built by British Royal Engineers on the top of Somerset Island's tallest hill between 1868 and 1880 to protect the rear flank of the Royal Naval Dockyard. A self-guided tour will reveal several underground bunkers, cannons, ditches, and walls with gun slots which where used by garrisoned British troops up to World War 1 and further occupied by US artillery units during World War II. The park area contains many seaview benches that provide fine panoramic views, and with the addition of public bathrooms has become one of the best spots in Bermuda for a romantic picnic. Admission to the fort and park is free and it is open from 9am until 4:30pm daily.

After once again returning to Somerset Road and heading south to the end of the parish, you may notice two stone pillar gateposts with a brass plate announcing the access road to the opulent **Lantana** cottage colony resort. This secluded complex of suites and cottages rests at water's edge on the lovely **Great Sound**. If you know you are passing by this area during lunch time, check to see if they can fit you in on their fantastic outdoor **La Plage** restaurant.

A few hundred meters further south on Somerset Road will take you past **Robinson's Marina** where you have several high season excursion departures. At the marina you can rent a Boston Whaler for $45 for 2 hours, and Winner Bowriders at $65 for 2 hours from **Robinson's Charter Boats**, utilize the **Bermuda Waterski Centre** for lessons at $50 per half hour and 30 to 60 minute rides, or **Blue Water Divers** scuba facilities to take $85 beginners resort and wreck dives, $365 for a complete PADI certification course, $40 for a single tank dive, rent or purchase dive equipment and underwater cameras, and arrange all types of specialty dives and charter adventures.

This marina is also the departure area for the incomparable **Pitman's Snorkeling** trips. The proprietor, Joffre Pitman, offers the finest and most educationally advanced snorkeling adventure (on a glass bottom motor yacht) in all of Bermuda for about $40 per person. Be advised that a trip with Mr. Pitman is well worth the hassle of occasional trip cancellations and rescheduling due to poor undersea visibility and conditions.

Finally, just a few steps past the marina, we come to the end of Somerset Island, at the foot of the world famous 17th century **Somerset Bridge**. Touted as the world's smallest draw bridge, the bridge does not in fact open and close like a typical draw bridge. A 32 inch wide split wooden plank can be raised from the middle of the bridge to allow the masts of Bermuda rigged sailing vessels to pass under without damage. The **Somerset Bridge Ferry Dock** at the far side of the bridge offers daily service to Hamilton.

After passing over the Somerset Bridge, the street changes its name to **Middle Road** and you will finally reach the last segment of Sandys parish. The strip of land between here and the border of Southampton parish contains mostly middle class homes, schools, a couple of private beaches, and a few moderately priced eating establishments including a local hang out with good Bermudian food called **Traditions Restaurant**, a new **Four Star Pizza** takeout shop, a fantastic little Filipino takeout restaurant, and several grocery shops and small businesses.

NIGHTLIFE & ENTERTAINMENT

If you haven't figured out by now that Sandys is a quiet residential area, you will soon find out when looking for a place to go out at night for drinks. The only real nightclub in the whole parish is the **Club 21** jazz bar, located at the dockyard. This huge and dimly lit club only gets jumping when a cruise ship drops anchor at the nearby dockyard terminal.

Other than that, your best bet is the weekend live band nights local pubs and restaurants (especially at the **Loyalty Inn**). Most of the hotels and cottage colonies also offer occasional live music during the evenings in their own bars (the music is best over at **Cambridge Beaches** and **Lantana**). Most high energy night crawlers will find themselves heading out by taxi to Hamilton for nocturnal adventures and excitement.

12. SOUTHAMPTON PARISH

Southampton Parish, originally named after the 3rd Earl of Southampton, is a beautiful wide tract of pink sand beaches, craggy coastlines, and rural interior lands located on much of the western portion of **Great Bermuda Island**. You'll find plenty of distractions here, including an historic lighthouse, fine waterside restaurants, beachfront accommodations in all price ranges, and a great inexpensive golf course. It may take up to two days to see most of the fine attractions and natural wonders in this part of Bermuda, so I have included different segments for both the north shore route and also the south shore route, which can be followed on different days.

This parish is first bisected by **Middle Road**, which is crisscrossed by Section 2 of the **Railway Trail** as it heads in an easterly direction down the parish's north shore, while the dramatic **South Road** splits off towards the famed beaches of the south shore.

ARRIVALS & DEPARTURES

The best way to travel between the superb resorts and inns along Southampton Parish and Bermuda's **Kindley Field International Airport** is to take a taxi for about $26 each way. Depending on what property you are staying in, the ride should average about 19 kilometers (12 miles) long and usually takes about 35 minutes or so.

ORIENTATION

Southampton Parish, one of the most famous sections of Bermuda, is a long wide strip of hilly land which is surrounded by the Atlantic Ocean to the south and a peaceful boat-filled sound to the north. There are only two major roads that cross through this parish, and the best landmark to use as a point of reference here is the towering white **Gibbs Hill**

Lighthouse, which sits atop the highest elevation in the country and can be seen for miles around.

GETTING AROUND

Getting around most of Southampton is an easy task, with lots of available taxis and wide roads for walking and scooter riding. Or you can take public bus route #8 that heads down the length of Middle Road, and public bus route #7 that eventually travels on scenic South Road.

WHERE TO STAY

POMPANO BEACH CLUB, *36 Pompano Beach Road, Southampton. Tel. 441/234-0222. Fax 441/234-1694. Toll Free Reservations (Hotel's US Offices) at 800/343-4155 US & Canada. Internet: www.pompano.bm. . Low season rack rates from $240 per double room per night (M.A.P.). High season rack rates from $385 per double room per night (M.A.P.). A $20 per person per day deduction can be requested if you prefer Breakfast Plan only. 56 ocean-view rooms and suites with air conditioning, terraces, and private bathrooms. Two restaurants with two outdoor dining terraces, and two bars. Cash, Traveler's Checks, and all major Credit Cards accepted. Member of "The Bermuda Collection" of fine hotels.*

Simply stated, the Pompano Beach Club is my favorite hotel in all of Bermuda. While there are several other superb hotels and inns on the island, no other place has made me feel quite so relaxed, at home, and comfortable. Owned and operated by the charming Boston based Lamb family since its inception a few decades ago, this delightful seaside cottage colony resort rests atop a stunningly landscaped cliff which in turn rises above a beautiful private pink sand beach. Ideally situated next to the fabulous Port Royal Golf Course, about 12 1/2 miles west of downtown Hamilton, Pompano is the perfect place to relax and enjoy what may very well be Bermuda's best value in both accommodations and gourmet cuisine.

Each of Pompano's 56 large, understated, and beautifully decorated sea-view rooms & suites contain individually controlled remote control air conditioner/heaters, deluxe private bathrooms stocked with a full range of fine imported soaps and shampoos, romantic private ocean-view terraces or patios, remote control cable television, VCR units (upon request), a great selection of charming hardwood and tropical rattan furnishings, mini-refrigerators, irons with boards, hair dryers, mini-safes, waffled cotton bathrobes, and windows or French doors that look directly out onto panoramic views of the turquoise seas.

This casual oasis of hospitality is the perfect place to go and enjoy a wide array of on-site facilities such as world class golf, tennis, sandbar fishing, windsurfing, outstanding snorkeling, and a superb pink sand beach, as well as a health club, a beautiful heated outdoor freshwater swimming pool, a new oceanfront wading pool, two California-style open air hot tubs, and serene sun decks located both beside the pool as well as along picturesque cliff ledges near the sea. Nearby other activities such as horseback riding along the beach, sunset cruises, guided nature & historical hikes, shopping excursions, scuba diving and yes...even jet skiing can be arranged by the front desk staff with just one phone call and a half day's notice.

The Pompano Beach Club offers an outstanding cooked to order full American breakfast each day in the main Clubhouse, but those wishing a bit more privacy or perhaps a more romantic beginning to the day may instead choose a delightful continental breakfast with fresh juices, fruits, and hot pastries be placed at their doorstep each morning at no extra charge. The hotel's sea-view luncheon atrium and terrace serve up hearty lunches such as fresh tuna melts with imported aged cheddar on toasted English muffins as well as massive cheeseburgers with crispy fries and garden fresh salads. Dinner is a more elaborate affair, with four nights each week that are casual in nature, and just three nights per week when men are expected to wear jackets (but not necessarily ties). Whether during their immense weekly gourmet buffet, served on the terrace when weather permits, or their daily menu featuring some fresh Bermuda fish and imported prime cuts of meat and game, the food here is worthy of the trip in and of itself.

Owner/managers Larry & Tom Lamb have somehow managed to hire the nicest and friendliest staff imaginable, and have encouraged them to treat visitors with a special blend of true Bermudian charm, hospitality, and personalized service that can be found nowhere else.

Selected as one of my *Best Places To Stay* – see Chapter 10.

THE REEFS, *56 South Shore Road, Southampton. Tel. 441/238-0222, Fax 441/238-1214. Toll Free Reservations (Hotel Direct) at 800/742-2008 US & Canada. Internet: www.The Reefs.com. Low season rack rates from $244 per double room per night (M.A.P.). High season rack rates from $376 per double room per night (M.A.P.). 67 rooms, suites, and private cottages with air conditioning and private bathrooms. Two restaurants with outdoor terraces, and two bars. Cash, Traveler's Checks, and all major Credit Cards accepted. Member of "The Bermuda Collection" of fine hotels.*

The Reefs is a deluxe beachfront luxury resort hotel within walking distance to Horseshoe Bay and several other south shore attractions. This incredible small hotel has luxurious rooms, suites, and cottages, most of which have romantic sunset views. All of the accommodations are beautifully furnished and contain fine artwork, telephones, refrigerators, mini-safes, marble basins, and deluxe amenities.

The Reefs also offers fine gourmet dining inside its clubhouse as well as more relaxed open air dining at the Coconut's sea terrace, and afternoon snacks and drinks from the Sand Bar. Additional facilities include a great health club, large private cove beach, two well-maintained tennis courts, scenic seaside walking trails, a large freshwater pool and sundeck, and the welcoming clubhouse which hosts afternoon tea and live music on most evenings.

Neal Stephens, the hotel's ever-present manager, greets each guest personally, and has selected one of the most professional staffs at any resort in Bermuda. The Reefs is the perfect place to experience the highest standards of quality and comfort without any attitude whatsoever and I highly recommend it.

Selected as one of my *Best Places to Stay* – see Chapter 10.

CANADIAN PACIFIC SOUTHAMPTON PRINCESS HOTEL, *South Road, Southampton. Tel. 441/238-8000, Fax 441/238-8245. Toll Free Reservations (Canadian Pacific Hotels) at 800/441-1414 US & Canada. Internet: www.cphotels.com. Low season rack rates from $169 per double room per night (E.P.). High season rack rates from $439 per double room per night (E.P.). Special golf getaways and low season packages usually available. 597 air conditioned rooms with terraces and private bathrooms. Seven restaurants, three bars, and one showroom. Royal Dine Around (M.A.P.) meal plan is also available from $45 per person per day upon request. Cash, Traveler's Checks, and all major credit cards accepted.*

This is the largest and most deluxe of Bermuda's big seaside resort hotels. The Southampton Princess offers an endless supply of facilities including both indoor and outdoor pools, an executive 18 hole golf course, 11 tennis courts, a great private beach and beach club with scuba and watersport excursions, over a hundred acres of beautifully maintained grounds, direct ferry shuttle service to the capital city of Hamilton, special non-smoking and concierge floors, a high season full day children's activity program, free property wide shuttle service, a helpful social desk, over a dozen boutiques, a full service spa and health club (additional charge), a state of the art 450 person multimedia conference room, and a complete room service menu.

All of the rooms are beautifully decorated, and feature huge sea or garden view balconies, lavish tropical inspired furnishings, deluxe bathrooms, walk-in closets with mini-safes, remote control cable television with 25 international channels, direct dial phones with computer modem jacks, writing desks, irons with ironing boards, hair dryers, plush bathrobes, and lots of sunlight. Guests have the option of dining at seven great restaurants that range from opulent gourmet dining rooms to casual bistros and beach-side snack pavilions.

With the new addition of the Dolphin Quest dolphin encounter program, the Southampton Princess has become an impressive full service large resort.

Selected as one of my *Best Places to Stay* – see Chapter 10.

WHALE BAY INN, *Whale Bay Road, Southampton Tel. 441/238-0469, Fax. 441/238-1224. Low season rack rates from $90 per double room per night (E.P.). High season rack rates from $120 per double room per night (E.P.). Special long term rates available in the low season upon request. 5 air conditioned one bedroom apartments with kitchenettes and private bathrooms. No restaurants. Cash, Checks, and Traveler's Checks only, no credit cards accepted.*

Beautifully situated near the sea on the 14th hole of the Port Royal golf course, this converted mansion contains five spacious and nicely decorated one bedroom apartments. Owned and managed by Phillippa Metschnabel, this small friendly inn is one of Bermuda's best values in vacation apartment rentals. Whale Bay offers a peaceful location and nice units with private bathrooms, fully stocked kitchenettes, ceiling fans, cable television, am-fm clock radios, telephones, and maid service.

Located just a few minutes walk away from the picturesque West Whale Bay Park and its old fortress and sandy beachhead, the owner and her staff will be more than happy to point out the best area sights and attractions. This is an all but unknown little gem, well worth the money if you prefer some privacy and want to do some light cooking during your vacation. Children are welcome, and pets are also accepted with advance notice.

MUNRO BEACH COTTAGES, *Whitney Bay, Southampton. Tel. 441/234-1175; Fax 441/234-3528. High season rack rate from $160 per double room per night E.P. Low season rack rate from $99 per double room per night E.P. 16 air conditioned one bedroom apartments with private bathroom. No restaurants, but all units have full kitchens. Cash, Checks, and Traveler's Checks only, no credit cards accepted.*

Munro Beach is a small grouping of 8 nice oceanview cottages on the edge of the famed Port Royal golf course in Southampton parish. Each cottage contains 2 one-bedroom apartments, although some can adjoin to form a private independent two bedroom villa. All of these units contain television, radio, telephone, ceiling fans, large modern kitchens with both standard and microwave ovens, and an additional sofa bed that can accommodate another two people. The property faces a small private beach which is a good spot for bone fishing and snorkeling.

Besides having daily maid service and access to outdoor barbecue areas, guests can arrange deliveries of scooters, groceries, and liquor directly to their apartment. The ambiance here is casual and most clients seem to be rather relaxed as they lounge in their lawn chairs while the dramatic sunsets takes hold. Nearby golf and tennis facilities are available within a few minutes walk. Perfect for budget minded couples or families who prefer to cook most of their own meals.

SONESTA BEACH HOTEL, *South Shore Road, Southampton. Tel. 441/ 238-8122, Fax 441/238-8463, Toll Free Reservations (Sonesta Hotels) at 800/ 766-3782 US & Canada. Low season rack rates from $130 per double room per night (E.P.). High season rack rates from $280 per double room per night (B.P.). 400 rooms and suites with air conditioning and private bathrooms. Five restaurants with two bars. Cash, Traveler's Checks, and all major Credit Cards accepted. M.A.P. meal plan is also available from $55 per person per day upon request.*

Beautifully situated steps away from the sea, and lined by a series of three crescent pink sand beaches, the modern 4 star Sonesta Beach Hotel is a nice deluxe resort hotel on Bermuda's spectacular south shore. Besides offering its guests a vast array of world class services and facilities, the property boasts 400 beautifully decorated rooms, junior suites, and suites on six different floors that in many cases look right out onto some of the most picturesque sea views imaginable. All of the resort's spacious and recently renovated accommodations are nicely decorated and offer individually controlled air conditioning systems, extremely comfortable king or double bedding, remote control cable-satellite television with over 30 channels, full size deluxe private bathrooms, am-fm clock radios, direct dial telephones, and nice private terraces or tranquil patios.

Facilities include three private beach areas lined with comfortable lounge chairs and sun umbrellas, seaside snack and beverage bars, both indoor and outdoor freshwater heated swimming pools, a large beauty salon, a newly redesigned exercise room, six wonderful seaside tennis courts (two can be lit at night) with a pro shop, a superb high season half or full day supervised children's activities program, an opulent grand ballroom and well over a dozen business meeting/reception rooms of all sizes, a fully equipped on-site scuba and water-sports excursion center with boat rentals, half a dozen fine boutiques, a croquet lawn, off shore fishing areas, shuffleboard, a full range of daily activities, a nearby public bus stop, a taxi rank, free car and scooter parking, and both temporary membership privileges and easy nearby access to some of Bermuda's best golf courses.

The Sonesta also offers a wide variety of restaurants to choose from, including a delightful weekly Bermudian Barbecue as well as special international theme nights hosted at Seagrapes, featuring seafood and steak specialties at the Boat Bay Club, and more elegant continental fare served in a posh yet relaxed setting over at Lillian's. Hearty American buffet breakfasts here are a true delight and are presented daily at several venues. Room service can be ordered as well.

CHANCE IT COTTAGE, *Granaway Heights Road, Southampton. Tel. 441/238-0372; Fax 441/238-8888. High season rack rate from $110 per double room per night E.P. Low season rack rate from $75 per double room per night E.P. 6 air conditioned one and two bedroom units with private bathroom. No restaurants, but each apartment has a full kitchen. Cash, Traveler's Checks, and most major credit cards accepted.*

Chance It is located up a long winding road above the sea halfway between West Whale Bay and Church Bay on the south shore. This nice converted house contains five self-catering one bedroom apartments, and a 2 bedroom penthouse suite with panoramic terrace. This is the perfect getaway for casual budget minded visitors who desire pretty seaviews and prefer to cook for themselves.

Each apartment has a full kitchen, spacious private bathroom, and daily maid service. Guests are free to utilize the exercise room, sun deck, outdoor pool, TV lounge, and lovely patio. Since the location is a bit remote, I strongly advise that you consider renting a scooter. Beaches, golf, and tennis are all less than a 15 minute ride away.

ROYAL HEIGHTS, *Lighthouse Road, Southampton. Tel. 441/238-0043; Fax 441/238-8445. High season rack rate from $125 per double room per night B.P. Low season rack rate from $100 per double room per night B.P. 5 air conditioned rooms and one suite with private bathroom. No restaurants, but breakfast is served in the dining room. Cash, Traveler's Checks, and most major credit cards accepted.*

Perched on a hillside behind the Southampton Princess golf course and overlooking the sea, most of this lovely private house has been converted into a cozy 6 room bed and breakfast inn with a nice saltwater pool and terrace. In all of the five well decorated rooms (and 1 suite) there's a patio, television, refrigerator, microwave, coffee machine, and windows that look out onto either the Gibbs Hill Lighthouse or the sea.

This property has the ambiance of a good home-style bed and breakfast inn and contains a large sofa filled living room for guests to meet, relax, and feel as if they were at their own summer home. The secret to the welcoming and tranquil ambiance is the inn's owner, Jane Richardson, who enjoys offering insider's tips to visiting guests from all over the world. A nice continental breakfast is served to guests each morning, and several fine restaurants in all price ranges are just a few minutes walk or ride away. Children are quite welcome here, and the suite with its adjoining bedroom are perfect for families.

SOUND VIEW COTTAGE, *Bowe Lane, Southampton. Tel. 441/238-0064; Fax: None. High season rack rate from $50 per double room per night E.P. Closed during most of the Low season. 3 air conditioned studio units with private bathroom. No restaurants, but each apartment has a full kitchen. Cash, Check, and Traveler's Checks Only, no credit cards accepted.*

Sound View is the least expensive place to stay in all of Bermuda, and it is surprisingly pleasant. Each of the three studio apartments contain kitchenettes with microwave ovens, private bathrooms, and have daily maid service. The sweet and amazingly helpful owners, Barbara and Eldon Raynor, are great sources of local information and will even lend guests their own appliances if asked. The studios are a bit small, but contain all of the necessary elements to assure satisfaction. The house is located on a hill up a winding road which looks out over both the south and the north coastlines. Facilities include a nice pool and panoramic sundeck, outdoor barbecue area, and seaview patios.

Although the inn is close to all major south shore beaches and sights, I suggest renting a scooter to get around with. A good choice for budget minded vacationers looking for accommodations with a touch of typical Bermudian life.

WHERE TO EAT

THE NEWPORT ROOM *at the Southampton Princess Hotel, South Road, Southampton. Tel. 441/238-8000. Open 7:00pm until 10:00pm daily. Dress code is jacket and tie. Reservations required. Cash, Traveler's Checks, and all major credit cards accepted.*

The Newport Room is an unusually inviting gourmet dining room located just off the lobby of the famous Southampton Princess Hotel. This intimate restaurant is adorned with model ships, antique compasses, brass yachting implements, and a rich dark wood paneling that conjures up images of the grand salon of a royal yacht. Frequented mainly by beautifully dressed local businessmen and visiting couples seeking a bit of elegant romance along with their dinner, the Newport Room is one of the best classical French-oriented restaurants in any major hotel on the island.

Executive chef Thomas Frost works his special blend of culinary magic at this bastion of gastronomical delights. He is a master at creating Bermudian-influenced Continental cuisine with subtle new world touches, and the menu here (which changes seasonally) is packed with wonderful game, seafood, steak, fowl based ingredients flown in fresh from exotic locations around the globe. You might be treated to an amazing Armagnac flamed lobster and Bermuda fennel bisque with caviar and mascapone, Beluga caviar, jack rabbit meat with wild mushrooms served with flaming cognac, truffle juice injected tenderlion of beef with a rich stilton and Port wince sauce, mint glazed rack of lamb atop croquettes of potato and goat cheese, traditional filet of lemon sole meuniere, or a local lobster on the half shell which has been stuffed with a superb salmon mousse. Desserts are a true art form here with several choices each evening including Gran Marnier soufflé, crepes Suzette prepared at your table, and a drop dead delicious parfait of roasted hazelnut and almond ice cream.

The impeccable wait-staff here always offers superb service, and the wine steward can help you to select the perfect wine to accompany a fine meal from a 14 page list that included $35 to $850 bottles of selections such as Cakebread Chardonnay, Opus One, Chateaux Lafite and Chateaux D'Yquem. If you appreciate the finer things in life and want to experience a meal you will never forget, don't miss at least one evening here.

THE WATERLOT INN, *Middle Road, Southampton. Tel. 441/238-0510. Open 6:30pm until 9:30pm daily. Closed January 2 until March 4. Sunday Brunch Buffet from 12noon until 2pm. Dress Code ranges from Smart Casual to Jacket and Tie. Reservations are required. Cash, Traveler's Checks, and most major credit cards accepted.*

The Waterlot is a fine gourmet restaurant, serving fine continental and Bermudian cuisine in the setting of a 325 year-old converted warehouse and inn at water's edge. Each of the restaurant's intimate dining rooms is adorned with period furnishings, antique cedar trimmings, old paintings of seagoing vessels, silver and crystal service, and lots of charm. On Sundays, the outdoor waterside terrace hosts a wonderful Sunday brunch (the best brunch in Bermuda!) with a live Dixieland jazz quintet. As one of the best upscale restaurants in Bermuda, the Waterlot's impressive French executive chef, Regis Neaud, creates superb a la carte menus with such mouth watering choices as salmon tartar, mussels Catalon with safron and garlic, excellent Bermuda fish chowder, fresh Caesar salads prepared at your table side, pan fried Bermuda fish on a bed of mushrooms and arugula, perfectly grilled rack of lamb, and an incredible assortment of rich desserts such as marscapone cheesecake with cappuccino sauce.

On most nights there is live piano music which perfectly accompanies the fine meals, aperitifs, and vintage wines that the Waterlot has become renowned for. Expect a full dinner without wine to cost each couple about $110, and brunch to set couples back some $60. Highly Recommended.

CEDAR ROOM, *at the Pompano Beach Club, 36 Pompano Beach Road, Southampton. Tel. 441/234-0222. Open 7:00pm until 9:00pm nightly. Dress Code is Smart Casual except Tuesday, Thursday, and Saturday nights when Jackets are required. Reservations required. Cash, Traveler's Checks, and all major Credit Cards accepted.*

This superb seaside restaurant is a large part of the magic over at the Pompano Beach Club. The Cedar Room has become one of the island's best places to dine and is filled to the brim with the kind of welcoming, warm, and subtle ambiance that I rarely, if ever, see in Bermuda's more famous gourmet establishments – embellished by picture windows with beautiful sunset views over the sea, exposed beams of Bermuda cedar, and beautifully set tables.

The Cedar Room and its adjacent outdoor terrace offer a wonderful array of gourmet dinners that all show the talents of recently appointed Executive chef Paul Proverbs. The excellent new chef here displays a bold style of incorporating the freshest possible locally harvested produce and a selection of top quality imported ingredients into typical Bermudian dishes as well as both innovative New World and classic European recipes.

The Cedar Room's fabulous five course dinner menu, which changes each day, may consist of such mouth-watering items as char grilled Thai chicken with ginger sauce served atop smoked vegetable ratatouille, yellowfin tuna carpaccio, smoked Scottish salmon wrapped around herb-walnut cream cheese, asparagus risotto, escargots in garlic butter, grilled portobello mushrooms with goat cheese, Bermuda codfish cakes, chilled pear and Bleu cheese soup, broccoli & stilton cheese soup, Bermudian lobster stuffed with shrimp and mushrooms, spinach or garden salads with your choice of superb dressings, roast prime rib, Jamaican styled jerk chicken, sesame encrusted rack of lamb, classic filet mignon, penne pesto, grilled Mahi Mahi, shrimp and scallop kebabs, vegetarian ravioli with wild mushrooms, and many other treats.

The restaurant's dress code here is usually smart casual with the exception of Tuesday, Thursday, and Saturday nights when jackets are required. On Monday nights, following the Manager's complimentary Rum Swizzle party, there is an outstanding casual evening BBQ buffet (during the warmer months) featuring a huge salad bar, cooked to order black Angus steaks, barbecued ribs, grilled local sport fish, curried mussel pie, teriyaki chicken, and dozens of other unique selections.

Desserts here are a serious matter, with a great selection of Swiss pastry chef Jorg Rudolf's freshly made masterpieces such as peach mousse, Linzer tort, black rum pineapple cream tart, chocolate Grand Marnier mousse, brownie cheese cake, strawberry almond pillows, frozen peach passion fruit parfait, sun-dried apricot dumplings with vanilla brandy sauce, and an unforgettable banana royale. Expect an extraordinary dinner for two to cost about $84 plus wine.

CLUBHOUSE DINING ROOM, *The Reefs, South Road, Southampton. Tel. 441/238-0222. Open 12:30pm until 2:30pm during low season. Open 7pm until 8:45pm daily. Dress Code ranges from Smart Casual to Jacket and Tie. Reservations are required. Cash, and Traveler's Checks only, no credit cards accepted.*

The tranquil main dining room of this seaside resort offers fine European influenced cuisine served by an attentive wait staff in an opulent yet inviting atmosphere. The dining room's five course table d'hôte menu features the freshest local and imported ingredients which have been perfectly blended so as not to overpower or mask each other.

During my most recent series of meals here I sampled such delicious items from chef Kevin Kapalka's kitchen as steamed mussels with leek, cream of mushroom soup, Bermuda fish chowder, crab cakes with homemade mayonnaise sauce, scallops in mushroom cream, ravioli stuffed with smoked mozzarella cheese and eggplant, sesame beef kebabs in a sweet cucumber sauce, vegetarian risotto with fresh basil and Asiago cheese, seared sand lobster tails in a ginger fondue, chicken parmesan with herbed pasta and sun-dried tomatoes, grilled double bone lamb chops, broiled roughy fish in tomato basil linguini, and many other daily or seasonal specials.

The wine list here is also a real pleasure to order from, and features a great selection of moderately priced French, Californian, Italian, Spanish, South African, Australian, and Chilean wines by the glass and bottle. The restaurant's superb Maitre d' (Mr. David Lambert) can easily accommodate most special meal requests if he is called in at least a day in advance. While the dress code usually requires that men wear a jacket, there are smart casual evenings on both Monday and Thursday. Expect a wonderful meal for two to cost about $100 not including wine. Highly Recommended.

COCONUTS, *The Reefs, South Road, Southampton. Tel. 441/238-0222. Open 12:30pm until 2:30pm and 7pm until 9pm daily. Closed in Low Season. Dress Code is Smart Casual. Reservations are required. Cash and Traveler's Checks only, no credit cards accepted.*

This is, without the slightest doubt, the most romantic place in the world to have an open air sunset dinner. This pleasant windswept cliffside dining terrace faces out past the beach onto an unforgettable panoramic view of the ocean, and is booked solid almost every evening. Whether you call a few weeks in advance for dinner or just show up for lunch, you will be treated very well by the delightful wait staff.

The fairly priced lunch menu consists of unusual chilled and hot soups, fresh fruit plates, tasty tuna salads, grilled locally caught fish sandwiches, veggie pitas, BBQ beef sandwiches, huge sirloin burgers, fries, onion rings, and refreshing ice cream desserts and cakes. At dinner time, the food is a more eclectic blend of exotic dishes from around the globe including imported goat cheese with onions and tomatoes, fantastic cod fish cakes (the best in Bermuda!), Thai curried beef, calamari antipasto, daily soup selections, Caesar salads, grilled Bermuda Wahoo, rosemary marinated leg of lamb, an impressive pasta with fennel pesto and vegetables, seafood with ginger and coconut on black rice, thick veal sirloin steaks, and much, much more.

The wine list here contains an excellent selection of 18 or so moderately priced international vintages. Make sure to save some room for some of the fine desserts included with your meal, including the devilish chocolate Pot de Creme custard. Expect lunch to set you back somewhere around $23 per couple, and dinner to cost just about $100 per couple without wine.

SEA GRAPE BAYSIDE GRILL, *Sonesta Beach Hotel, Southampton. Tel. 441/238-8122. Open 11:30am until 2:30pm on Weekdays and from 6:30pm until 10pm daily. Dress code is Smart Casual. Reservations Suggested. Cash, Traveler's Checks, and all major credit cards accepted.*

This well-established bayside al fresco restaurant has recently been converted into a delightful new international open-grill dining establishment. Simple round and square tables for between two and twelve people surround an open grill where chefs from around the world are busy grilling very tasty steaks and fish filets. Situated at the confluence of the hotel's main outdoor pool and one of its three crescent shaped beaches, the Sea Grape now offers a truly superb menu and great service, two things it was never known for in the past.

The new executive chef has created a wonderful selection of tasty international grilled dishes the likes of which are found nowhere else in Bermuda. Among my favorite picks here (all served with a huge Caesar salad bar) are the spicy Jamaican styled jerk chicken, fresh conch fritters served with roasted yams and topped by a wonderful tomato-lime salsa, Spanish influenced tapas including both fried corn tortillas rolled with fresh wahoo and raw tuna carpaccio, as well as a vast selection of fresh fish filets, Filet Mignon, and several other meat and seafood dishes with a choice of delicious sauces like the sopicy mango-habenero salsa or a cool black rum and banana yogurt sauce. They also have vegetarian dishes, great fruit-based desserts, a nice wine list with many vintages by the glass, and huge side orders of potatoes and veggies. The service here was truly top notch during my last two visits here, and the casual seaside ambiance is really something special for clients of all ages. Dinner here will cost somewhere around $90 per couple.

HENRY VII RESTAURANT & PUB, *South Road, Southampton. Tel. 441/238-1977. Open 12 noon until 3pm and 6pm until 10:30pm daily. Dress Code is Smart Casual. Reservations suggested. Cash, Traveler's Checks, and all major credit cards accepted.*

This large Old English Tudor style restaurant across from the Sonesta Beach hotel features a huge menu of English-inspired Bermudian, American, and European dishes. Filled almost every night with tourists and local residents, this restaurant serves an assortment of pretty good meals such as hearty pub pies, an excellent English mixed grill, chicken kiev, delicious pan fried mahi-mahi, mussel pie, prime rib, Yorkshire pudding, black rum cake a la mode, and lot of other filling dishes.

The restaurant also is home to a Wednesday night *Royal Feast buffet* and theme party eating orgy that includes wine and beer, and a large

Sunday afternoon brunch, both of which are complimented by live music and lots of fun. Each night there are two shows featuring comedy and musical acts that can be enjoyed either with or without dinner.

The more affordable lunch menu ranges from simple salads, sandwiches, and burgers, to more elaborate choices. The pub is open fairly late for those of you who prefer just to indulge in strong ales and cocktails. Expect lunch to cost about $24 per couple, and dinner to go for around $85 per couple. The show's minimum is $35 per person, and the Royal Feast costs about $105 per couple with drinks included.

OCEANFRONT LUNCHEON TERRACE, *Pompano Beach Club, Pompano Beach Road, Southampton. Tel. 441/234-0222. Open 12:00noon until 2:30pm daily with light snacks available until 5:00pm. Dress Code is Casual. Reservations are not necessary. Cash, Traveler's Checks, and all major credit cards accepted.*

While touring around Bermuda's tranquil West End, you may find yourself wanting to stop somewhere special for lunch. The Pompano Beach Club's Oceanfront Luncheon Terrace offers an awesome array of lunch items every day of the week. Their extensive lunch menu features some of the country's best Bermuda fish chowder, jumbo shrimp cocktails, spicy nachos, garden salads, chef's salads, Greek salads, Chinese chicken salads, tropical fresh fruit salads, turkey and bacon club sandwiches, grilled Ruebens, B.L.T.'s, fresh tuna melts, cheeseburger platters, and hot dogs which can be accompanied by either crispy French fries or onion strings.

They also serve up refreshing frozen cocktails, wines by the glass, local and imported beers, and soft drinks. During the low season, or when it rains, the indoor Foc's'le bar is utilized instead. No other area restaurant offers such huge portions for the money, and the unforgettable sea views here will really make your day. This is also the best place to stop off for a relaxing snack or full meal on the way to, or from, the Royal Naval Dockyard area. Expect a giant and delicious lunch for two to set you back around $25-30 plus drinks. Highly Recommended.

TIO PEPE, *South Road, Southampton. Tel. 441/238-1897. Open from 2pm until 10pm daily. Dress Code is Informal. Reservations are suggested, but not always necessary. Cash, Traveler's Checks, and most major credit cards accepted.*

This clean and basic Italian restaurant and outdoor patio is situated on South Road, just across from Horseshoe Bay. Tio Pepe is a great place to enjoy a casual dinner after a long day of getting sunburnt at the beach.

The simple and inexpensive (by Bermudian standards) menu is filled with basic but tasty choices such as cold antipasto, fresh mozzarella with marinated mushrooms and oil, fried calamari, eggplant parmigiana, fresh salads, soups, a vast array of good pizzas and pastas, veal piccata, chicken breast sauteed in light cream and champagne sauce, reasonably good desserts, and a small selection of affordable wines. Expect dinner for two to start at around $46 without wine.

LIGHTHOUSE TEA ROOM, *Lighthouse Road, Southampton*. *Tel. 441/238-8679. Open from 9am until 5pm daily. Dress Code is casual. Reservations are not necessary. Cash, Checks, and Traveler's Checks only, no credit cards accepted.*

After finishing a long walk up and down the lighthouse above, there is no better way to finish your visit than popping in this cute English style restaurant for a nice small snack. The traditional English menu features croissants, scones, crumpets, teacakes, quiche, ploughman's platters, pot pies, sausage rolls, Cornish pastries, afternoon teas, finger sandwiches, desserts, cold beverages, and hot chocolate.

The interior is much like an English country cottage, and the service is unrushed. Expect a filling in-between meal snack to cost somewhere around $22 per couple.

SEEING THE SIGHTS
The Middle Road Route

Once you have crossed over from Sandys parish into Southampton parish from its border at the Somerset bridge, you soon pass an entrance on your left (east) to the now closed yet still off-limits **US Naval Air Station** on Tucker's Island which was shut down after the American military left Bermuda in 1996. Continue heading south along **Middle Road** for 3/4 of a kilometer (1/2 a mile) or so before turning right (west) down Pompano Beach Road. Proceed down this long winding road along a golf course (or use the free Pompano courtesy phone to request a complimentary shuttle ride) until coming to the entrance of the beautiful **Pompano Beach Club**, one of Bermuda's best and deluxe cottage colonies. This welcoming seaside hotel at the edge of the Port Royal Golf Course is so nice that many visitors to Bermuda (including me) have decided to check out of the resort they are already staying in and check in here for the duration of their vacation.

Another great reason for visiting Pompano is to take advantage of their outstanding lunches (a perfect way to unwind after a long ride to, or from, the Royal Naval Dockyard) served in the casual Oceanfront Lunch Terrace, as well as gourmet dinners available in the delightful Cedar Room restaurant with its own spectacular seaside terrace. Be forewarned that the fresh Bermudian tuna melts in your mouth and delicious frozen ice cream cocktails are highly addictive. The hotel also is home to the high season only Pompano Beach Club Watersports Center which rents O'Brien windsurf boards for $12 per hour, sea kayaks at $10 per hour,

Aqua Finn sailboats for $12 per hour, and paddle boats at $10 per hour, as well as offering snorkeling on one of the country's finest coral reef sandbars full of colorful semi-tropical fish.

After visiting Pompano, return to Middle Road and turn right to follow it for another 1/4 kilometer (250 yards) or so before passing the famed public **Port Royal Golf Course**. This dramatically landscaped 18 hole par 71 course features 6565 yards of stunning greens and fairways and was designed by Robert Trent Jones. Known for its challenging terrain and memorable views of the sea, Port Royal is one of Bermuda's most popular places to play golf. A round here will cost around $50 per person plus cart rentals; tee times can be booked by any hotel on the island.

Another 1/2 kilometer down along Middle Road is a small lane called Whale Bay Road that passes along the far edge of the golf course and leads to **West Whale Bay Park**. This small park area is highlighted by the 19th century **Whale Bay Battery**, an old British fortress that was originally built with massive long range cannons that were used to help defend the nearby Royal Naval Dockyard. While not much remains of the old fort itself, the park offers an exhilarating cliff-side walking trail that can be followed to reach a fantastic deserted beach area and panoramic lookout points.

This general area is also home to two other nice (and almost unknown) moderately priced places to stay: the cozy sea-view Whale Bay Inn and the private Munro Beach Cottages, which both offer nicely furnished apartments with fully equipped kitchens and impressive views of nearby Whale Bay. The park, fort, and beach are all open to the public from sunrise to sunset daily with no entrance fee of any kind.

Now continue south along Middle Road for about another 3/4 of a kilometer (1/2 mile) until bearing right (west) onto **Industrial Park Road**. Lined by the S.A.L. limestone quarries and examples of light industry, this busy road is home to the **Bermuda Golf Academy**, home to the island's only all-weather driving range. They offer a 320 yard driving area (lit at night) with 40 (mostly covered) practice bays, an 18 hole practice green, professional instruction, rental clubs, a kids playground, a nice little bar and restaurant, and a great mini-golf course for kids and adults alike. *The golf academy is open daily from 9:00am until 10:30pm rain or shine and charges $7 for mini-golf, $4 for a driving basket of golf balls during the day, and $5 during the evening. For more details call them at Tel. 441/238-8800.*

A tiny bit further down Industrial Road you will find the **Bermuda Triangle Beer Micro-brewery**. This full working brewery uses fine imported European hops and malts to brew limited quantities of outstanding Wild Hogge Amber Ale, Spinnaker pilsener, Full Moon pale ale, and powerful Hammerhead stout, all of which can be purchased in gift-packed containers at the brewery itself or enjoyed on tap at many leading

Bermudian bars and restaurants. Visitors will be given an explanation of the beer making process and will then be taken on a tour of the fermentation tanks and bottling line before being handed glasses in which they can consume free samples of several Triangle products. The brewery's retail shop sells great triangle shaped sampler cartons with several different bottles, and great tee shirts at reasonable prices.

The Triangle brewery offers visitors free tours and beer tasting every Saturday year round at 4:00pm, and on Wednesdays (between March and October only) at 4:00pm, with no admission charge.

Turnoff onto the South Shore Route

After leaving the brewery and returning to Middle Road, continue south for about 3/4 of a kilometer (1/2 mile) until reaching a turnoff on the right hand side that has a sign indicating "To Hamilton via South Road and the Beaches." Make this right turn onto the famous **South Road** and soon you will see the first in a string of pretty pink sand beaches beginning over by **Church Bay**. Church Bay Beach itself is a great little spot to relax and enjoy superb snorkeling. If you happen to be hiking along the **Railway Trail** you must depart the trail at this point to find most of the sights listed below.

A GREAT PLACE TO SNORKEL!

*The first of several beaches with seaside parks along South Road in this beautiful parish is the great little **Church Bay Beach**. This is one of Bermuda's best coastal snorkeling areas and consists of a small beach with a rocky ocean floor that attracts an amazing array of semi-tropical fish. Since there are no real facilities here, remember to bring your own rafts, snorkeling gear, cold beverages, towels, and perhaps a few pieces of bread to feed the marine life. Admission to this beach and the surrounding park is always free.*

When you're done hanging out with the fish over at Church Bay, return to South Road and follow the coastline for another 1000 yards or so until you pass next to the entrance to **The Reefs**. This romantic and lavishly appointed small luxury hotel not only offers what may be the finest sea-front accommodations in Bermuda, but also allows non-guests (if space is available) to enjoy snacks, lunches, and dinners in either its awesome **Coconuts** high season ocean-side terrace (with the best sunset views on earth) or the more refined **Clubhouse Dining Room**. Even if you're not in the mood to eat, I strongly suggest popping inside the property to see its wonderful private cove beach, limestone moon-gate, and rock-lined walking paths.

Just a few hundred yards further along South Road from The Reefs is the massive, modern **Sonesta Beach Hotel**. This extended beachfront is also home to the **South Side Scuba** excursion company, offering beginners resort scuba classes with a shallow sea dive for $85 a person as well as night dives for certified divers at $60 a person, and full P.A.D.I. certification classes for around $375 a person.

Continue along South Road for a minute or so before turning right (north) onto Lighthouse Road where you can't help but notice the towering **Gibbs Hill Lighthouse**, first constructed in England and then shipped over and reassembled on this sight in 1846. Typically jam packed with bus and taxi excursion passengers struggling to climb its 185 narrow steps to the top, this huge cast iron lighthouse stretches out atop the tallest hill in Bermuda to reach its peak at over 362 feet above sea level. A self-guided walk brings visitors up to a narrow panoramic lookout platform (not for those with weak knees) with unsurpassed views out over the entire country. A small cottage at the base of the lighthouse is home to the quaint **Lighthouse Tea Room** which serves fresh tea, quiche, scones, salads, sandwiches, and desserts throughout the morning and afternoon. The lighthouse is open from 9:00am until 4:30pm daily and costs $2 per adult to enter.

Once you have had your fair share of vertigo, return yet again to South Road and keep following this scenic coastal road. The next interesting sight around here is the **Henry VIII Restaurant & Bar** where you can have a good dinner, or enjoy a massive Wednesday night eating orgy known as the Royal Feast which is presided over by a man dressed as King Henry VIII.

A bit further along the road is the estate that belongs to the famous **Southampton Princess Hotel**. On the right side of the road you will see the **Southampton Princess Beach and Tennis Club**, which is also the site of the **Whaler Inn** seafood restaurant. The same area is home to a manmade lagoon that now hosts the **Dolphin Quest** dolphin encounter program, and the **Nautilus Diving Ltd.** snorkeling and scuba excursion company. Just opposite on the right hand side of the road you will see the stunning 18 hole par 54 executive Princess Golf Course which can be enjoyed with advance reservations for around $40 a person plus golf cart rental. Just behind the golf area is the towering facade of the deluxe Southampton Princess Hotel with a host of world class facilities including the superb **Newport Room** gourmet restaurant.

From the Southampton Princess you will keep following South Road until passing the first in a series of amazing pink sand beaches that are known all over the world. Most of the following local beaches are part of a wonderful seaside recreation area known as **South Shore Park**. The park has various walking paths that connect an enchanting chain of adjacent beach areas to one another. The most famous of these great beaches is the long and sandy crescent shaped **Horseshoe Bay Beach**, often seen gracing the covers of many travel guides and magazines. The beach is well equipped to deal with the hundreds of sunbathers that flock here on hot summer days and boasts dramatic cliffs, enchanting sea-rock formations, public changing rooms and showers, bathrooms, beach chair rental kiosks, and lifeguards during the summer months.

Be careful while enjoying the sea here, because of the unexpectedly strong undertow and the occasional visit by some unfriendly Portuguese Man of War. Also on the beach is the great little Horseshoe Bay Beach House where you can enjoy moderately priced sandwiches and snack foods or ice cream at one of many indoor or outdoor tables from about 10:00am until around 7:00pm in the warmer months. The nearby cliff-top trails lead out towards a selection of equally impressive but less busy secluded cove beaches to the east with names like **Peel Rock Cove**, **Butts Beach**, **Middle Beach**, **Wafer Rocks Beach**, **Angle Beach** and **Chaplin Bay**. These spots are good places for romantic evening walks. All of the beaches in South Shore Park are open all the time and have no admission fees.

CRABS ON PARADE!

*Although small **red land crabs** (Gecarcinus Lateralis) may occasionally try to steal your lunch while enjoying a picnic or outdoor meal along the south shore beaches, these crabs put on a much more dramatic yearly demonstration of mother nature's powers. A swarm consisting of tens of thousands of spawning crabs converge across South Road for a handful of nights after each full moon during July and August in order to reproduce near the beach-front. Even though countless hundreds of these small crunchy animals get squashed to death by passing cars, scooters, and hungry seabirds (producing plenty of free roadkill crab cakes for everyone) more than enough of them make it to the beach in one piece to ensure the species' future survival.*

The Alternative Route via the North Shore

If you prefer to travel along Southampton parish's tranquil north shore after exiting Sandy's parish, all you have do is to continue straight ahead along Middle Road (or the adjacent Railway Trail) after passing Whale Bay. This route will take you past the tranquil **Little Sound** area and further eastward. Among the many lesser visited sights along the way are the large sand dunes, public wharves, and various fishing harbors that may be found around **Black Bay** and **Jews Bay**.

A few hundred yards later is one of Bermuda's better restaurants known as the **Waterlot Inn** (owned by Princess Hotels) which serves up steak, seafood, and international fusion cuisine in the romantic setting of a 300 year old converted warehouse filled with antiques. Just next to the restaurant is a pier where you can board Thursday evening starlight glass bottom boat cruises. Reef Roamers offers these cruises during the high season for about $35 a person.

NIGHTLIFE & ENTERTAINMENT

Most of the evening action in this part of Bermuda takes place at the Oak Room pub and the dinner shows at **Henry VII.** Show lounges at the major resorts such as the **Southampton Princess**, or the lounges and bars at the **Reefs** and **Sonesta Beach** also offer some form of diversion.

Once again, if you are a true party animal, I suggest a short cab ride into Hamilton where you can find a vast assortment of like-minded people.

13. WARWICK PARISH

The parish of **Warwick**, originally named after the second Earl of Warwick, is known primarily for its long sandy beaches. Situated in the center of **Great Bermuda Island**, this parish offers a wide variety of natural attractions, beautiful beaches, seaside parklands, winding country roads, golf courses, sporting activities, moderately priced seaside resorts, inexpensive guesthouses, and rental apartments. Since this is a rather small parish, it may only take a few hours to see most of its major sights. There are however, enough great beaches and sporting activities to keep some people here for days.

The heart of this parish is crisscrossed by **Middle Road**, while **South Road** follows close to the the parish's southern boundary, and **Harbour Road** branches off towards the parish's northern coastline. Parts of section 3 and 4 of the **Railway Trail** also dissect the middle of Warwick while passing through some of the more rustic parts of this area.

ARRIVALS & DEPARTURES

There are two ways to travel between the hotels in Warwick Parish and the **Kindley Field International Airport**. Either you can take a taxi ride for about $22.50 each way, or you contact Bee Line Transportation or Bermuda Hosts Ltd. a day or two in advance and pay around $24.50 per person round trip. Depending on where you're staying, the ride should be about 16 kilometers (10 miles) long and takes about 20-25 minutes.

ORIENTATION

Warwick Parish is a small section of central Bermuda with a variety of parks and undeveloped interior lands. The topography varies greatly and includes rugged cliffs, pristine beach zones, quaint villages, and dramatic rural country roads that cross over lush hills. There are three major roads cutting through this parish which are easy to follow, and several small lesser used lanes (and sections of the Railway Trail) that are a bit more difficult to navigate.

If you intend to divert away from the South, Middle, or Harbour Roads, bring along a copy of the free *Bermuda Handy Reference Map,* available at any Visitor's Service Bureau office.

GETTING AROUND

Getting around Warwick is no problem, with plenty of taxis roaming the major roads, nice rural lanes for peaceful hikes, and good blacktop streets for scooter riding. You can take bus route #8 that continues across Middle Road, and bus route #7 that stays near the coast on South Road.

Since there are several major attractions located off each of the three major roads running through this parish, I have included different segments for each of these routes.

WHERE TO STAY

THE BELMONT HOTEL, *Middle Road, Warwick. Tel. 441/236-1301, Fax 441/236-0184, Toll Free Reservations (Forte Hotels) at 800/225-5843 US & Canada. Low season rack rates from $147.50 per double room per night (E.P.). High season rack rates from $185 per double room per night (E.P.). 151 rooms and suites with air conditioning and private bathrooms. Two restaurants, and two bars. Cash, Traveler's Checks, and all major credit cards accepted. M.A.P. meal plan is also available for $50 per person per day upon request.*

Belmont is a good, moderately priced full service resort hotel centrally located in Warwick parish. The property is surrounded by 114 acres, including the well maintained 18-hole par 70 golf course, 3 nightlit tennis courts, and tranquil gardens overlooking the Great Sound. Most of the guests tend to be either retired or semi-retired and usually come here to take advantage of the low room rates and complimentary green fees and tennis facilities. The 151 guestrooms here are all the same size (except for the one suite) and each room comes with cable television, telephones, Queen Anne furnishings, and large picture windows.

Other facilities include a large outdoor pool and sundeck, on-site moped rental, room service, tour desk, poolside snack bar, and the Harboursights lounge which has live entertainment during high season. Guests are also given free taxi transfers to and from Horseshoe Bay Beach, while the ferry to Hamilton is just a couple of minutes walk away. Guests can enjoy meals at either the Tree Frog restaurant with its casual breakfast as well as smart casual sit down and buffet dinners on an alternating schedule, and Kiskadee's restaurant that serves informal lunches and dinners. Take advantage of the Forte 30 program which offers a 30 day advance reservation discount of an additional 30% off.

MARLEY BEACH COTTAGES, *South Road, Warwick. Tel. 441/236-1143; Fax 441/236-1984; Toll Free (Bermuda's Small Prop.) at Tel. 800/ 637-4116 US & Canada. High season rack rate from $172 per double room per night E.P. Low season rack rate from $132 per double room per night E.P. 14 air conditioned apartments with private bathroom. No restaurants, but each unit has a full kitchen. Cash, Checks, and Traveler's Checks, call to ask about credit cards.*

A great pair of beautiful cottages with a fine collection studio and one bedroom apartments (some with fireplaces) located on a panoramic bluff above the sea. The property is conveniently situated in a quiet exclusive residential area near almost everything a guest would want to see and do. All of units have impressive sea views, televisions, full kitchens, telephones, waterview patios, nice furnishings, and maid service daily. The cottages are just a couple of minutes walk from the secluded Marley Beach with its excellent snorkeling, fishing, and nearby Longtail nesting sites.

The property also has a rather nice solar powered heated pool, whirlpool, sundeck, and large lawn area with lots of garden furniture. The property's great resident manager, Ronnie Sloper, will be happy to answer any questions about local activities and excursions. This is a great place to stay for couples and families alike. Highly Recommended.

VIENNA GUEST APARTMENTS, *Cedar Hill Road, Warwick. Tel. 441/236-3300; Fax 441/236-6100; Toll Free (Bermuda's Small Prop.) at Tel. 800/ 637-4116 US & Canada. High season rack rate from $90 per double room per night E.P. Low season rack rate from $65 per double room per night E.P. 6 air conditioned studios and apartments with private bathroom. No restaurants, but all units have kitchenettes. Cash, Traveler's Checks, and most major credit cards accepted.*

Vienna Guest Apartments is one of the nicest and newest rental apartment groupings in the country. Located in a peaceful tree-lined area between the Riddell's Bay and Belmont golf courses, this mansion-style complex contains beautiful units priced well below their market value. All of the large and airy studio and one bedroom apartments have brand new kitchens with microwave ovens, coffee machines, digital clock radios, huge closets, telephones, TV, new wooden furnishings, and patios.

All guests can also use the complex's fine facilities, including an outdoor pool, barbecue area, and coin-operated laundry machines. Leopold Kuchler, the friendly European owner/manager will be quite happy to assist his clients in finding great local activities, excursions, restaurants, and scooter rentals. This is a great place for couples, families, and all those who are looking for high quality accommodations at inexpensive prices. Highly Recommended.

ASTWOOD COVE APARTMENT RESORT, *South Road, Warwick. Tel. 441/236-0984, Fax 441/236-1164, Toll Free Reservations (IRS) at 800/ 441-7087 US & Canada. Low season rack rates from $76 per double studio apartment per night (E.P.). High season rack rates from $114 per double studio apartment per night (E.P.). 20 studio units and one bedroom suite apartments with kitchenettes, air conditioning, and private bathrooms. No restaurant or bar. Cash, Checks, and Traveler's Checks only, no credit cards accepted.*

Astwood Cove is a nice little grouping of affordable studio and 1 bedroom apartments located across from Astwood Park within walking distance of the south shore beaches. Each of the spacious units are well maintained and include kitchenettes, telephones with free local calls, clock radios, patios, and simple but comfortable furnishings. All guests have access to on-site facilities including a wonderful rooftop patio, barbecue area, TV lounge, coin operated laundry machines, sauna ($8 surcharge), pool, and sundeck. Scooter, liquor, and grocery deliveries can be arranged with no problem.

The clientele is from all age groups (although the place gets a lot of younger European and American guests) who tend to be as friendly, casual, and down to earth as Nicky Lewin, the ever-present manager.

SYL-DEN GUEST APARTMENTS, *Warwickshire Road, Southampton. Tel. 441/238-1834; Fax 441/238-3205. High season rack rate from $90 per double room per night E.P. Low season rack rate from $80 per double room per night E.P. 5 air conditioned apartments with private bathroom. No restaurants, but each unit has a full kitchen. Cash, Traveler's Checks, and most major credit cards accepted.*

This small apartment grouping is situated just a few minutes ride away to the south shore beaches. Each of the 5 huge apartments have modern kitchens, telephones, private bathrooms, clock radios, security locked windows, and ceiling fans. The complex also has a nice pool and sundeck. Syl-Den is priced well below what one might expect for this size and quality of accommodations. A good place for both families and couples who prefer to cook for themselves, and have either rented scooters or don't mind taking taxis.

SOUTH VIEW GUEST APARTMENTS, *Kings Lane South, Warwick. Tel. 441/236-5257; Fax 441/236-3382; Toll Free (Rep.) at Tel. 800/ 441-7087 USA. High season rack rate from $80 per double room per night E.P. Low season rack rate from $60 per double room per night E.P. 3 air conditioned apartments with private bathroom. No restaurants, but all units have kitchenettes. Cash, Traveler's Checks, Visa, and MasterCard accepted.*

These two relaxing little houses at the end of a quiet (but hard to locate) residential street offer two 1-bedroom and one studio apartments, all with nice views out over the ocean. Each of these basic apartments has telephone, television, ceiling fan, clock radio, and simple pine and formica furnishings. The units are well maintained by Mr. Raymond Lauder, the polite and insightful owner. Additional features include solar powered hot water systems, adjacent gardens, a nice rooftop sundeck, and lots of lawn furniture. Dozens of beaches and south shore attractions are just a few minutes walk or scooter ride away.

LONGTAIL CLIFFS APARTMENTS, *South Road, Warwick. Tel. 441/ 236-2864, Fax 441/236-5178, Toll Free Reservations (Bermuda Reservation Services) at 800/637-4116 US & Canada. Low season rack rates from $130 per double apartment per night (E.P.). High season rack rates from $215 per double apartment per night (E.P.). 13 apartments with kitchenettes, air conditioning, and private bathrooms. No restaurant or bar. Cash, Traveler's Checks, and most major credit cards accepted.*

Longtail Cliffs is a moderately priced apartment complex is located off Mermaid Beach on Bermuda's south shore. Each of the dozen oceanview two-bedroom units come with basic furnishings, telephone, television, clock radio, two private bathrooms, full kitchenettes with microwaves, irons and ironing boards, wall to wall carpeting or tiled floors, a coffee machine, and big seaview patios.

An additional 1-bedroom unit (no view) might also be available. The apartments are housed in one long cement block building that looks out past the pool onto the sea.

WHERE TO EAT

PAW PAWS, *South Road, Warwick. Tel. 441/236-7459. Open 11am until 5pm and 7pm until 10pm daily. Dress Code is Informal. Reservations are suggested, but not always necessary. Cash, Traveler's Checks, Visa, and MasterCard accepted.*

This warm, friendly family style restaurant and outdoor patio is located on South Road, not far from Astwood Park. With a vast selection of soups and sandwiches during lunch, and affordable European and locally inspired dishes served at dinner hours (except for some Tuesdays during high season when they may be closed), this great little unpretentious spot is a true delight.

Try some of the house specialties such as their full-bodied Bermuda fish chowder, paw paw and beef casserole, lobster ravioli, locally caught fish, grilled chicken, and other fine entrees that can be ordered along with tasty desserts. Expect lunch to cost as little as $21 per couple, and a more complete dinner for two to cost around $68 without wine.

SEEING THE SIGHTS

The South Road Route

As you cross over from Southampton into Warwick on the scenic South Road, you'll see the continuation of **South Shore Park**, with its great beaches. This part of the enchanting seaside park contains some of the prettiest beaches imaginable, including (from west to east) the cute grottos of **Stonehole Bay**, the calm sheltered waters at **Jobson's Cove**, and the shrub and grassy hills that stretch the full length of fantastic **Warwick Long Bay** beach.

Area Beaches

As its name suggests, the windy pink sand beach at Warwick Long Bay is rather long (perhaps the longest stretch of beach in Bermuda), and contains public restrooms and lots of parking – although lifeguards are not on duty here since the undertow is not particularly strong. These are all great places to enjoy the sun and sand in relative isolation. The park and its fine beaches are always open, and admission is free.

After reaching the end of the park, you will once again end up on South Road, which continues eastward passing by the moderately priced seaview rooms and apartments at both the **Mermaid Beach Club** and the **Longtail Cliffs Apartments**. A few hundred yards further east, you will run into the entrance way of the beautiful **Astwood Park**. This park is one of my favorite picnic and hiking areas, which also has the added benefit of the small secluded **Astwood Park Beach** surrounded by a series of cliffs that are home to several Longtail bird nests. The park and beaches are always open, and admission is free. Public restrooms can be easily found near the beach area.

Just next to Astwood Park is the much more private **Marley Beach**, home to the wonderful clifftop **Marley Beach Cottages**, among the finest seaview accommodations in this parish.

After leaving the beaches of this area, have a great (and affordable) lunch or dinner on the outdoor patio of the laid-back family style **Paw Paws Restaurant**, just across the street on South Road.

Golf & Horseback Riding

If you cross over from Southampton into Warwick parish on **Middle Road**, veer off to the north on **Riddell's Bay Road** and follow it around the bay to reach the **Riddell's Bay Golf and Country Club**. This fine privately owned 18-hole par 69 golf course contains some 5588 yards of beautifully manicured greens and fairways, most of which have memorable views of Great Sound. As Bermuda's oldest golf course (established way back in 1922), Riddell's Bay has become a favorite stop on vacationers' golf holidays. Since the club is private, you must book tee-off times well in advance through either your hotel or with a member (discounts apply if joining a member on the links). Expect to pay about $45 per person each round on weekdays, and about $55 on weekends and holidays, plus cart rentals.

After viewing the golf course and panoramic peninsula around Riddell's Bay, head back to Middle Road and head a bit further east before reaching the signpost for **Spicelands Riding Centre**. This great horseback center offers a selection of rides and private English style riding lessons depending on your skill level and how early you wish to get up in the morning. This equestrian center schedules a nice hour and a half low skill level morning trail ride at 6:45am that will take riders near the beaches of the south shore for $45 each, a few daily one hour rural trail rides for $35 each, 6pm rides may also be available upon request, and private lessons with internationally trained professionals (ask for Sabrina) cost about $30 per half hour.

Back on Middle Road, across from Christ Church (see below), you'll find the reasonably priced **Belmont Hotel, Golf & Country Club** resort, which offers nice rooms. All of the Belmont's guests have the opportunity to enjoy unlimited complimentary golf on its nice 18-hole par 70 golf course of 5777 yards. Non-guests will be charged about $53 per person per round plus cart rentals, and should have their hotel call a few days in advance to make reservations.

The Middle Road Route

When you get back to **Middle Road**, you will be in the parish's most commercial area coming up with the **Warwick Lanes** bowling alley, which charges about $3 per person per game plus shoe rentals. There are also grocery stores, schools, reasonably priced laundromats, and a pizza joint or two. Nearby you can take an exhilarating walk, bicycle ride, or scooter journey up the rural and hilly **Khyber Pass**, just off to the right (south) – but be extremely careful on its narrow turns.

Also in the same general area is an ornithologist's delight at the Allspice tree-laden **Warwick Pond**, which is a sanctuary for several unusual species of birds, and is managed by the Bermuda National Trust. The pond is open from sunrise to sunset, and admssion is free.

As you wander back to Middle Road, the next sight, just before you reach the corner of Orb Road is the quaint **Christ Church** (1719); open between 9am and 4pm daily.

The Harbour Road Route

Harbour Road can be reached by taking Middle Road east into Warwick parish from Southampton, and then turning left (north) onto **Burnt House Hill Road**, which then shifts towards the right (east) and merges into Harbour Road. This lovely stretch of mansions, private estates, and coastline offers little in the way of specific attractions, but it is a wonderful route to enjoy the natural beauty of the north shore and its impressive coastline. An assortment of fine watersports activities and sea excursions can be found at the eastern part of this road.

Over by the **Belmont Wharf** (behind the Belmont Hotel) you can hop on a ferry to Hamilton, or pop into the **Fantasea Diving Ltd.** shop which can take you water-skiing for about $80 per hour, diving for the first time for about $85 with instruction and a wreck dive, and one and two tank dives for those who are PADI certified (call for rates). Many other snorkeling, sailing, and glass bottom boat cruise excursion companies can schedule a special pick-up at this wharf if they are notified at least one day in advance.

A bit further east on Harbour Road at **Darrells Wharf**, which also has ferry service to Hamilton, you can enjoy a great assortment of enjoyable shipwreck snorkeling adventures with the fun staff of **Jessie James Cruises** for as little as $30 per person, or a three and a half swizzle snorkeling and sightseeing trip for $40 per person with **Bermuda Barefoot Cruises**.

NIGHTLIFE & ENTERTAINMENT

This is not the parish to experience any real nightlife. The only choices you have here is to either visit one of the hotel lounges (especially the **Belmont**) or go to Hamilton. Sorry about the inconvenience, but Warwick is not the place to party.

14. PAGET PARISH

The beautiful parish of **Paget**, with its many estates, named after Lord William Paget, is one of the best parishes to stay in while visiting Bermuda. With its central location on the heart of **Great Bermuda Island**, almost any point in Paget is just a few minutes ride away from the capital city of Hamilton, as well as fabulous pink sand beaches, awesome historic mansions, delightful gardens, small seaside paths, adventurous excursions, sporting activities, tranquil harbors, and fine dining.

Paget also contains a seemingly endless array of deluxe seaside resorts, peaceful cottage colonies, nice rental apartments, charming bed and breakfast inns, and quaint guesthouses in all price ranges.

ARRIVALS & DEPARTURES

There are two easy ways to travel between Paget Parish and the **Kindley Field International Airport**. Either you can take a taxi ride for about $21.75 each way, or you contact Bee Line Transportation or Bermuda Hosts Ltd. a day or two in advance and pay around $20.50 per person round trip. Depending on where you're staying, the ride should be about 13 kilometers (8 miles) long and usually takes about 20 minutes.

ORIENTATION

Packed with plenty of sights and natural attractions, sprawling Paget Parish is among my favorite places to spend time just wandering around. Besides offering a great selection of fine seaside hotels and gourmet restaurants, Paget has plenty of charming neighborhoods, cove inlets, and expansive beaches to discover on nice sunny days. While the dramatic coastline alongside South Road is one of the best landmarks to use while exploring this area, the interior is also full of interesting sights such as the Botanical Gardens (which are just as easy to find if you follow Middle Road or Harbour Road instead).

GETTING AROUND

There are several forms of public transportation in this parish, including excellent ferry service from several points on Paget's north shore towards Hamilton and beyond, and several bus routes. The buses that can be found running across Paget will all veer north on **Trimingham Road** to reach the main bus depot into the city of Hamilton, so expect the necessity of a bus transfer if you need to get beyond that intersection. The most commonly used lines are bus route #8 and its continuation with bus route #1 which heads down **South Road**, bus route #8 and its continuation with bus route #3 that follows **Middle Road**, and finally bus route #2 which can be found on **Ord Road**.

If you prefer to walk or ride on bicycles and scooters, you can find many nice little mansion-lined streets and rural lanes (that are easy to get a bit lost on), and taxis are never a problem to find here. Section #4 of the **Railway Trail** cuts through the center of this fine parish.

WHERE TO STAY

ELBOW BEACH-BERMUDA, *South Shore Road, Paget. Tel. 441/236-3535, Fax 441/236-8043. Toll Free Reservations (Hotel Direct) at 800/344-3526 US; 800/447-7462 (Prima Hotels) Canada. Low season rack rates from $205 per double room per night (E.P.). High season rack rates from $415 per double room per night (E.P.). No meal plans available. 244 deluxe rooms, suites, and private cottages with air conditioning and private bathrooms. Four restaurants with two outdoor dining terraces, and two bars. Cash, Traveler's Checks, and all major Credit Cards accepted. Member of "Prima Hotels."*

The Elbow Beach Hotel is located on 52 acres of beautifully landscaped gardens that face onto a mile long stretch of pink sand beach. The hotel is centered around a six story main hotel building which contains an ornate European style marble lobby area, several fine restaurants, and 174 beautifully appointed spacious rooms and suites. On a sea-view hillside just a two minute walk away from the main hotel building are an additional 20 cottages each with several luxurious accommodations, as well as a few super-deluxe independent one and two bedroom villas.

The vast majority of the large rooms and suites here have either dramatic seaview balconies or garden-side terraces, air conditioning, marble bathrooms, imported soaps and shampoos, antique reproduction furnishings, mini-bars, remote control color cable televisions, direct dial telephones with computer modem jacks, executive style desks, mini-safes, hair dryers, pull out sofa beds, large closets with irons and boards, plush cotton bathrobes and slippers, and much more. The private villas also feature huge screened-in living rooms, wet bars, remote control audio and video systems, wood burning fireplaces, exposed wood beam ceilings, and private gardens

There is an Olympic size heated outdoor swimming pool with a hot tub, giant sun decks, a health club with exercise equipment, a health spa and beauty center, five outdoor tennis courts, a high season supervised children's activities programs, opulent meeting rooms and private reception areas, room service, on-sight scooter and bicycle rental, several boutiques and newsstands, wheelchair accessible rooms for the physically challenged, daily afternoon high tea service, a weekly manager's rum swizzle party, optional baby sitters, excursion desks, a putting green, and of course guest access privileges at Bermuda's famed golf courses.

At the beach club, guests can rent water sports gear such as sailboats and snorkeling equipment, rent a private European styled beach cabana, relax on comfortable sun chairs, head over to the Sand Bar for cool drinks and light meals, or learn how to scuba dive or kayak. Dining here is a wonderful experience with a series of gourmet international restaurants to choose from each day. Now that the well respected Monaco-based Rafael Group of Hotels has stepped in to both manage the hotel and to oversee the $30 million investment, the Elbow Beach Hotel has become the finest large resort hotel in Bermuda. Highly Recommended.

Selected as one of my *Best Places to Stay* – see Chapter 10.

HORIZON'S & COTTAGES, *33 South Shore Road, Paget. Tel. 441/236-0048, Fax 441/236-1981. Toll Free Reservations (Relais & Chateaux) at 800/468-4100 US & Canada. Low season rack rates from $230 per double room per night (M.A.P.). High season rack rates from $310 per double room per night (M.A.P.). 48 rooms, suites, and private cottages with air conditioning and private bathrooms. One restaurant with an outdoor terrace, and one bar. Cash, Checks, and Traveler's Checks only, No Credit cards accepted. Member of the "Relais & Chateaux" group of hotels.*

Horizons is a deluxe cottage colony on a hilltop overlooking the sea. The 48 unique rooms, suites, and private cottages are located in either an 18th century manor house, or in one of 13 charming detached pink cottages. Each unit (most are seaview) has a trouser press, ceiling fans, a mini-safe, heated towel racks, bathrobes, hair dryers, telephones, refrigerators, fresh cut flowers, and televisions (upon request). Many of the rooms can adjoin for family use, and several have living rooms with fireplaces and seaview patios.

Facilities include a nine-hole par three golf course, putting green, three tennis courts, an outdoor heated swimming pool, scooter and bicycle rentals and tranquil walking paths. Temporary memberships can also be obtained for guests to use the nearby Coral Beach & Tennis Club's facilities.

Dining at Horizons is amazing experience, with a cooked to order breakfast delivered directly to each unit, and a beautiful country style dining room offering superb gourmet French cuisine and fine international wines served with silver and crystal service. Dine around privileges are available at Waterloo and Newstead as well. Horizons is a perfect place for those who are seeking elegant accommodations, extremely attentive service, and the finest cuisine. Highly Recommended.

Selected as one of my *Best Places to Stay* – see Chapter 10.

FOURWAYS INN & COTTAGE COLONY, *Middle Road, Paget. Tel. 441/236-6517, Fax. 441/236-5528, Toll Free Reservations (Hotel Direct) at 800/962-7654 US. Low season rack rates from $150 per double room per night (C.P.). High season rack rates from $230 per double room per night (C.P.). 11 rooms and suites with air conditioning, balconies, and private bathrooms. Two restaurants, and one bar. Cash, Traveler's Checks, and most major credit cards accepted. M.A.P. meal plan is also available for $42.50 per person per day.*

Fourways Inn and Cottage Colony is a pleasant little cottage colony with a handful of two-floor cottages. Each cottage contains one deluxe double room and a one bedroom suite which may upon request be combined into a wonderful deluxe two bedroom/two bathroom private cottage. All the units have deluxe private bathrooms with dual hair dryers and telephones, either a balcony or patio with Mexican tiles and patio furnishings, remote control cable televisions, direct dial telephones, marble tile floors, antique and reproduction hardwood furnishings, individually controlled air conditioners, original Bermudian artwork, both wet bars and mini-bars, ceiling fans, small fully stocked hideaway kitchenettes, fine English hair and skin care products, mini-safes, well light retractable make up mirrors, plush bathrobes, irons, and lots of space to stretch out in.

Facilities include a heated outdoor freshwater swimming pool and sun deck, complimentary day passes to the beach club at the Stonington Hotel, courtesy introductions and reservations at several golf courses, a complimentary gourmet continental breakfast served daily in each room, laundry and dry cleaning, baby sitting services, and much more. All guests may also take advantage of the expensive gourmet cuisine served in the adjacent Fourways restaurant and less formal Peg Leg Bar during lunch and dinner hours.

Selected as one of my *Best Places to Stay* – see Chapter 10.

STONINGTON BEACH HOTEL, *South Road, Paget. Tel. 441/236-5416, Fax 441/236-0371, Toll Free Reservations (Prima Hotels) at 800/447-7462 US & Canada. Internet Web Site is http://www.bermuda-best.com/StoBeach/. Low season rack rates from $172 per double room per night (B.P.). High season rack rates from $316 per double room per night (B.P.). 64 air conditioned oceanview rooms with air conditioning, private balconies, and private bathrooms. One restaurant and one bar. Cash, Traveler's Checks, and all major Credit Cards accepted. M.A.P. meal plan is also available for $28 per*

person per day upon request. No children under three permitted. Member of the
"Bermuda Collection" of fine hotels.

Stonington is a great beachfront resort hotel with rates that are much lower than I would expect. With a staff that is comprised of a combination of workers who have been here for years, and student interns from the Hospitality and Culinary Institute of Bermuda, this great medium-sized hotel has an amazingly high level of personalized service. Mr. Edmund Tucker, the hotel's extremely friendly Bermudian manager, runs a great operation and plenty of guests keep coming back year after year.

All 64 spacious rooms have sea-views, air conditioning, marble bathrooms, imported hair and skin care products, ceiling fans, remote control cable television, private balconies, direct dial telephones, mini-safes, stunning lithographs by famous local watercolor artists, hardwood furnishings, lavish designer fabrics, ironing sets, mini-refrigerators, and lots of natural sunlight.

The accommodations are housed in a series of modern two story pink buildings near the sea which are a short walk away to the hotel's main reception building. Facilities include a large heated pool with sundeck, a fine pink sand beach, tennis courts, a main lobby with an adjacent bar and fireside library, and the fantastic Norwood Dining Room featuring fine breakfasts and impeccably good dinners. The hotel offers optional meal plans with dine around privileges, afternoon tea, and a Monday night manager's champagne party. Highly Recommended.

HARMONY CLUB, *South Shore Road, Paget. Tel. 441/236-3500, Fax 441/236-2624, Toll Free Reservations (hotel direct) at 800/427-6664 US & Canada. Low season rack rates from $410 per double room per night (A.I.). High season rack rates from $525 per double room per night (A.I.). 68 rooms with air conditioning and private bathrooms. One restaurant with an outdoor terrace, and one bar. Cash, Traveler's Checks, and most major credit cards accepted. No children under 18 allowed.*

This medium-sized, all inclusive resort hotel is located near several fine pink sand beaches. The hotel is comprised of a former manor house that dates back to the 1830's, and a few newer two-story patio laden buildings. As Bermuda's only all inclusive resort, its base price includes all meals, beverages and alcoholic drinks, tennis, gratuities, taxes, service charges, admittance to Elbow Beach with chaise lounge and sun umbrella, and roundtrip airport transfers. This unique system allows guests to avoid taking out their wallets while on property.

The hotel's manager, Mr. Billy Griffith, is part of a local group of investors that have purchased the Harmony Club and has spent several months completely refurbishing the rooms and facilities. Each of the 68 rooms have remote control cable television, private bathrooms, coffee machines, hair dryers, direct dial telephone, and clock radios. Guests also have complimentary use of an outdoor swimming pool, tennis courts, sauna, Jacuzzi, and have dine-around privileges at Hamilton's Little Venice restaurant.

Meals are served either in the tranquil Garden Room or the casual Palm Court Lounge. Afternoon tea with light snacks is available daily at 4pm in the Palm Court Lounge. Smoking is strictly prohibited in the dining areas. Complimentary beer, wine, and cocktails including daily frozen drink specials are available in the relaxing Tavern Bar and can also be delivered the pool area.

NEWSTEAD, *Harbour Road, Paget. Tel. 441/236-6060, Fax 441/236-7454, Toll Free Reservations (Hotel Direct) at 800/468-4111 US, 800/236-2451 Canada. High season rack rates from $315 per double room per night (B.P.). Low season rack rates from $246 per double room per night (B.P.). 42 air conditioned rooms and suites with air conditioning and private bathrooms. One restaurant, one luncheon terrace, and one bar. M.A.P. meal plan available for $40 per person per day upon request. Cash, Traveler's Checks, and all major Credit cards accepted.*

Situated at water's edge just a short ferry ride across the harbor from downtown Hamilton, Newstead is a delightful converted manor house surrounded by adjacent cottage style wings with delightful views. The inn boasts 46 harbor and garden views rooms and suites, each with air conditioning, beautiful hardwood furnishings, direct dial telephones, mini-safes, remote control cable television, heated towel racks, irons with boards, electronic trouser press, and large windows looking out to the water or a series of beautiful gardens. Rates here include a full American breakfast, a wonderful afternoon tea with finger sandwiches and desserts, reduced rate access to the facilities of the nearby Coral Beach & Tennis Club, and much more.

Newstead also offers two tennis courts, a putting green, an outdoor swimming pool, on-site ferry service to downtown Hamilton, peaceful gardens, and several lounges filled with fine antiques and oil paintings. Mediterranean styled menus are offered in both their water-view indoor dining room and their extremely popular outdoor dining terrace. Newstead is a charming place to vacation in Bermuda, and is highly recommended.

Selected as one of my *Best Places to Stay* – see Chapter 10.

SALT KETTLE HOUSE, *Salt Kettle Road, Paget. Tel. 441/236-0407, Fax 441/236-8639. Low season rack rates from $90 per double room per night (B.P.). Low season rack rates from $110 per double room per night (B.P.). Eight rooms and cottage apartments with air conditioning and private bathrooms. No restaurant, but the inn has a breakfast room. Cash, Checks, and Traveler's Checks only, No credit cards accepted.*

The Salt Kettle House is a remarkably friendly inn at the edge of Hamilton Harbour in Salt Kettle. As one of Bermuda's most welcoming family owned and operated bed and breakfast inns, I can easily imagine why guests would never consider staying anywhere else.

The inn is comprised of a main house and a few adjacent cottages which, when combined, have a total of four double guestrooms. There are also four more one and two bedroom apartments with kitchens, all with antiques, nice furnishings, and lots of sunlight. Among my personal favorites is the upstairs Tower Room which has a series of windows that provides almost 360 degrees of panoramic views. Each morning a complimentary home-made breakfast is served to all guests in the inn's main building which also contains a relaxing TV lounge. All guests may also use the main cottage's full common kitchen to prepare meals on their own at any time.

Everything that is so special about this cute waterside guest house is the direct result of all the hard work and persistence of Salt Kettle's charming owner Hazel Lowe, and her manager Margie Smith. The Salt Kettle House is a great value for the money. Make sure to reserve well in advance as the inn tends to sell out during much of the year. Highly Recommended.

Selected as one of my *Best Places to Stay* – see Chapter 10.

PRETTY PENNY GUEST HOUSE, *Cobbs Hill Road, Paget. Tel. 441/ 236-1194; Fax 441/236-1662; Toll Free (Bermuda's Small Prop.) at 800/637-4116 US & Canada. High season rack rate from $125 per double room per night E.P. Low season rack rate from $90 per double room per night E..P. 7 air conditioned studio apartments with private bathroom. No restaurants, but all units have kitchenettes. Cash, Traveler's Checks, and most major credit cards accepted.*

Pretty Penny is a cute converted house with an additional cottage which together contain seven nicely furnished and well maintained garden or pool view studio apartments. Each of the large bright modern units has a kitchen with microwave oven and coffee maker, irons and ironing boards, clock radios, telephones, and a nice patio.

The property is located in the heart of Paget, close to public transportation, beaches, fine restaurants, grocery shops, and sporting activities such as golf and tennis. Facilities on premises include daily maid service, a beautiful swimming pool, nice gardens, rental televisions, and amusing little binders loaded with the owner's restaurant suggestions followed by updated comments from past guests. A great choice for independent travelers looking for nice, quiet, and affordable accommodations at reasonable prices. Highly Recommended.

GRAPE BAY COTTAGES, *Grape Bay Beach, Paget. Tel. 441/236-1194; Fax 441/236-1162; Toll Free (Bermuda's Small Prop.) at 800/637-4116 US & Canada. High season rack rate from $220 per double room per night E.P. Low season rack rate from $160 per double room per night E.P. 2 air conditioned 2* *bedroom cottages with private bathroom. No restaurants, but all units have kitchens. Cash, Travelers Checks, and most major credit cards accepted.*

These two spectacular two-bedroom cottages are situated in an exclusive residential area just off the ocean in Paget parish. Each cottage (one is called Beachcrest and the other is named Beach Home) has two double bedrooms, a private bathroom, fireplace, air conditioning, phone, terrace, full kitchen, wood plank flooring, deluxe furnishings, daily maid service, fantastic seaviews, direct access to the fine reef laden Grape Bay beach, and can sleep up to six people in comfort. Due to Grape Bay's somewhat remote location, scooter rentals should be strongly considered. I suggest booking this place far in advance since it is often sold out. Highly Recommended.

SKY TOP COTTAGES, *South Road, Paget. Tel. 441/236-7984; No Fax. High season rack rate from $90 per double room per night E.P. Low season rack rate from $75 per double room per night E.P. 11 air conditioned studios and apartments with private bathroom. No restaurants, but all units have kitchen facilities. Cash, Travelers Checks, Visa, and MasterCard accepted.*

Sky Top is an extremely peaceful cluster of 4 semiprivate detached pale apricot colored cottages that dot a beautiful hillside garden close to the south shore beaches. Each pretty English style cottage contains a selection of either studio or one bedroom gardenview apartments with their own independent entrances, ceiling fans, telephones with free local calling, rental televisions, and kitchen facilities. All of the units are well decorated and rather comfortable, and are surrounded by a tranquil environment that is so peaceful I could hardly believe it!

The owners (Marion Stubbs and her partner Susan Harvey) have been so careful to preserve the tranquility and natural beauty of their property that they have gone as far as to bury all the utility and electric cables underground. These are all great inexpensive self catering units which offer an outstanding value for the money for couples and families who enjoy cooking.

GREENBANK & COTTAGES, *Salt Kettle, Paget. Tel. 441/236-3615; Fax 441/236-2427; Toll Free (Bermuda's Small Prop.) at 800/637-4116 US & Canada. High season rack rate from $95 per double room per night E.P. Low season rack rate from $70 per double room per night E.P. 11 air conditioned rooms and apartments with private bathroom. No restaurants, but most units have kitchens. Cash, Travelers Checks, and most major credit cards accepted.*

Greenbank boasts 11 comfortable studio apartments and guestrooms, housed in a series of small cottages (some are over 180 years old) on the edge of Hamilton Harbour. All but two of these cozy units come complete with full kitchens, and several have waterviews. Each accommodation contains air conditioning, phones, alarm clock radios, ceiling fans, and plenty of sunlight. The warm and welcoming owners, Cindy & David

Ashton, offer sailboat and Boston Whaler rentals at the dock. Guests are also invited to utilize the main house with its television lounge, pool table, and piano. Additional facilities include a private dock and swimming area, nearby ferry terminal with service to Hamilton, and an excellent location. A nice quiet place to stay.

PARAQUET GUEST APARTMENTS, *South Road, Paget. Tel. 441/ 236-5842, Fax 441/236-1665. Low season rack rates from $122 per double room per night (E.P.). High season rack rates from $132 per double room per night (E.P.). 12 rooms, efficiencies, and apartments with air conditioning and private bathrooms. One restaurant. Cash, Checks, and Traveler's Checks only, No credit cards accepted*

This is a nice and exceedingly well maintained grouping of guestrooms and apartments situated just a few minutes walk from Elbow Beach. This complex contains three large double guestrooms, and six huge studio units, two sun-drenched one bedroom apartments, and a family style two bedroom suite. All of the studios, apartments, and suites have spotless modern kitchens which put most other rental apartments to shame. Each unit has a lot of natural light, television, and a clock radio.

On-site facilities include coin operated laundry machine, terraces, a huge pool (use by permission only), public phones, and access to the surprisingly affordable Paraquet restaurant. Paraquet is a great place for those who want to be able to walk to the beach, and have nice affordable accommodations.

LOUGHLANDS, *South Road, Paget. Tel. 441/236-1253; No Fax. High season rack rate from $114 per double room per night C.P. Low season rack rate from $75 per double room per night C.P. 25 air conditioned guestrooms, most with private bathroom. One breakfast room. Cash, Check, and Traveler's Checks only, no credit cards accepted.*

Loughlands is a huge Bermudian mansion-style inn set among over seven acres of well manicured lawns. Each corner of this unusual inn is filled with fine Victorian era antiques which almost demand you attention while on the premises. The guestrooms are all completely different and range from being large opulent suites with fine period furnishings, to somewhat small guestrooms with little natural sunlight and shared bathrooms. Each of the 25 or so unique single and double accommodations have basic amenities including radios. The inn has some fine public rooms, a dramatic dining room serving daily breakfast, a nice tennis court, sundeck, and swimming pool. A good place to stay if you can avoid getting one of the more basic rooms.

WHERE TO EAT

FOURWAYS INN, *Middle Road, Paget. Tel. 441/236-6517. Open 7:00pm until 10:00pm daily. Dress Code is Jacket and Tie. Reservations are required. Cash, Traveler's Checks, and all major credit cards accepted.*

Fourways Inn originally started life in 1727 as an opulent mansion for famous sherry baron John Harvey of England (founder of Harvey's Bristol Cream sherries). Back in those days Mr. Harvey enjoyed inviting his friends here for lavish dinner parties of legendary proportions. His private estate was later converted into an elegant inn and restaurant, and now this incomparable establishment continues to be the domain of some of the world's most skillful chefs. Besides featuring a magnificent main dining room embellished with exposed antique cedar wood beams and stone arches, there are also several stunning semi-private dining areas, and the picturesque Palm Court dining terrace. Ever since being awarded multiple AAA "4 Diamond" and Wine Spectator "Excellence" awards, it is commonplace to find American politicians, members of European royalty, international movie stars, and reclusive industrialists dining here among the islands' most demanding vacationers.

On my last visit here I enjoyed a fine meal. The team of master chefs create outstanding al la carte menus each night that may include Beluga or Sevruga caviar served on ice, lobster salad with artichoke and snow peas, smoked Scottish salmon with cucumber noodles, seared scallops and giant shrimp on ratatouille with pesto sauce, wild mushroom cannelloni, charcoal grilled rockfish with black olive and lobster paste, fresh broiled Bermuda lobster, strudel of assorted vegetables in basil tomato sauce, grilled shitake mushrooms topped with goat cheese, the best Chateaubriand you will ever have, veal sautéed in lemon butter, roasted rack of lamb, grilled filet mignon, roasted chicken in a light stock, and a many other seasonal favorites. To accompany your delicious dinner the outstanding sommelier will present each guest with one of the largest, most comprehensive, and expensive wine lists in this hemisphere which includes over 7,500 bottles from the world's finest vineyards. After your meal I strongly suggest trying at least one of the superb pastry chef's soufflés or other mouth watering desserts.

Unfortunately, the service at Fourways oftentimes depend entirely on how famous or powerful you are, and the mammoth wine list is more than a bit overpriced in my opinion, but I guess that's what you pay in Bermuda for the privilege of dining at the island's most famous restaurant. Those on somewhat more restrictive budgets may avail themselves of Fourway's special low season dine-around program and traditional roast beef dinner menus, while those looking for the ultimate in gastronomic delights can request details about the restaurant's special gourmet menu. Expect an incredible dinner for two from the al la carte menu to cost somewhere around $180, not including wine.

HORIZON'S & COTTAGES, *33 South Shore Road, Paget. Tel. 441/ 236-0048. Open 7:30pm until 10:00pm daily. Dress code is Jacket & Tie. Reservations Required. Cash, Checks, and Traveler's Checks only, No Credit Cards accepted.*

Horizon's stunning candle-lit dining room is an extraordinary place to enjoy some of Bermuda's finest culinary artistry. Beautifully decorated in the English colonial style that Horizons has become famous for, this intimate gourmet restaurant has consistently impressed me with its world class cuisine. Service is highly professional yet warm and personal. The restaurant's Sheffield silver settings, fine crystal stemware, and regal bone china add even more to the elegant ambiance here.

Unlike most other restaurants, the menu here is never posted until after 11am that same day. This is because head chef Jonathan Roberts and his excellent kitchen staff don't even begin to plan the daily offerings until after they have carefully inspected and selected the finest ingredients from local suppliers, and have looked at what just arrived on the special airplane that jets in to deliver the freshest possible imported produce and meats. I have dined here many times before, and have almost never seen the same dishes repeated.

During my most recent visit, the kitchen staff conjured up remarkably delicious cream of broccoli soup topped with thin slices of roasted almond, smoked local fish pate served atop a horseradish tart, an amazing fillet of pan seared sole with basil pesto couscous, perfectly roasted breast of chicken, grilled rib of beef in a rich Port wine reduction served with wild mushrooms and sauteed garlic, and several wonderful desserts including their incredible mousse of Bermuda bananas which cover a dark chocolate brownie. They also offer a great vegetarian menu, as well as cater to those with special dietary concerns if advised in advance.

As in the past, the wine list here is equally impressive with such fine vintage offerings such as '81 Mouton Rothschild, '86 Chateau D'Yquem, '94 Cakebread Estate Reserve Cabernet, '90 Cos D'Estornel, '92 Marchese di Barolo, '95 Far Niente Chardonnay, '88 Veuve Cliquot La Gran Dame Champagne, dozens more European and New World labels, and the largest selection of half bottles (in all price ranges) I've seen just about anywhere. Horizons is an essential part of any gourmand's visit to Bermuda and is highly recommended.

CAFÉ LIDO at *Elbow Beach-Bermuda, South Road, Paget. Tel. 441/236-9884. Open 12noon until 3:00pm daily (April through October), and year round from 6:45pm until 10:00pm daily. Dress code is Smart Casual. Reservations Strongly Suggested. Cash, Checks, Traveler's Checks, and most major credit cards accepted.*

Café Lido is a fantastic beach-front dining establishment that serves up some of the best Italian-inspired cuisine in Bermuda. Stunningly located on the edge of Elbow Beach, this beautiful and charming restaurant is a true delight. During the warmer months the Café puts up a terrace awning so that clients can dine al fresco style accompanied by the sounds of cresting waves. The main dining room itself is surrounded by giant picture windows with views out over both the sea and the remarkably landscaped hibiscus gardens of the resort at Elbow Beach. The 40 or so candle-lit tables with white linen are exceedingly comfortable, and every plate coming out of the kitchen is beautifully plated. Certainly one of the island's most romantic settings for a fine gourmet sunset dinner, Café Lido (and its adjacent Mickey's beach-front bistro) deserves each and every award that it has won over the past few years.

The exceptional lunch menu here features chilled fresh fruit salads, Parma ham served atop sweet melon, sliced broiled chicken with mango and avocado in a light creamy curry sauce, giant bacon-cheese burgers with country style fries, pan seared catch of the day, and superb pastas and pizzas. The more lavish dinner offerings include an outstanding lobster salad in orange sauce, grilled sausage of wild boar, whole wheat penne pasta tossed with sautéed shrimp and zucchini, skewers of grilled jumbo prawns with balsamic vinegar seasoned vegetables, mint marinated grilled lamb chops, veal scaloppini in a Port wine glaze, and an amazing seafood casserole slow simmered in white wine and herbed tomatoes. The massive wine list has many, many bottles from Italy, France, and the New World and is an example of great value for the money. Desserts change daily, but are always incredible, and the service here is superior. An evening here will be remembered for years to come.

SEAHORSE GRILL at *Elbow Beach-Bermuda, South Shore Road, Paget. Tel. 441/236-3535. Open 6:30pm until 10:00pm daily. Dress code is Smart Casual. Reservations Suggested. Cash, Traveler's Checks, and all major credit cards accepted.*

Bermuda finally has a refreshing new dining experience that offers a unique take on the next evolution of Bermudian cuisine. Comprised of several adjoining dining rooms, each with its own style of post-modern architecture and furnishings, this remarkable new dining venue has become quite popular with both locals and visitors looking for an alternative to the high-fat content Continental cuisine offered almost everywhere else. Michael Mooris, one of the island's few Bermudian

Maitre D's, will make sure to seat you in a great spot and even help to suggest a nice half or full bottle of wine from the extensive list available here. Make sure to inquire about the daily specials, and feel free to request alterations in the menu if you are vegetarian or on a special diet.

This ultra-modern grillroom does a wonderful job in fusing classic Bermudian recipes with strong influences from Europe, Asia, and the West Indies. Using more local ingredients than any other hotel-based dining venue, Executive Chef Neville King has created a truly spectacular menu featuring such delicious and innovative dishes as tartar of fresh yellowfin tuna with loquat baked tomatoes, outstanding shark hash spring rolls topped with loquat black rum barbeque sauce and Bermudian slaw, salad with foie gras and Surinam cherry vinaigrette, char-grilled local Wahoo on plantain and coconut rice cakes with rum salsa, allspice and honey glazed breast of duck with root vegetables ragout, a wonderful rich and creamy Bermuda fish and seafood bouillabaisse, lobster burritos served atop pureed black beans and imported sausages, and sweet casava pie stuffed with apples and pears with a tropical coulis. This is a good place to head for if you want to try something quite out of the ordinary.

PEG LEG BAR, *Fourways Inn, Middle Road, Paget. Tel. 441/236-6517. Open 11:30pm until 3:00pm daily. Dress Code is Smart Casual. Reservations are suggested but not always required. Cash, Traveler's Checks, and all major credit cards accepted.*

This cozy traditional English-style wood paneled tavern and restaurant in a side wing of the famous Fourways Inn restaurant is a wonderful place to enjoy an afternoon meal. Their delicious lunch menu includes a good assortment of international favorites at affordable prices, including smoked Norwegian salmon, wild mushroom cannelloni, fresh asparagus with Parma ham, chef's salad, Caesar salad, spinach salad with bacon and chopped egg, Bermuda fish chowder, fresh soup of the day, triple decker club sandwiches, free range chicken burgers, filet mignon, codfish cakes with fried rice, vegetable pasta in cream sauce, pan fried catch of the day, roasted baby chicken, grilled shitake mushrooms with goat cheese, dark and stormy cake, home-made ice creams & sorbets, and fresh fruit salad. A typical hearty gourmet lunch here will set each couple back around $40 plus drinks. Highly Recommended.

THE PARAQUET RESTAURANT, *South Road, Paget. Tel. 441/236-9884. Open 9:30am until 1:30am daily. Dress code is Informal. Reservations are not necessary. Cash and Traveler's Checks only, no credit cards accepted.*

Paraquet is a nice big city diner style restaurant with a lunch counter and two adjacent rooms with table service for about 75 people. This is the perfect place to pop in for a totally down to earth home-made meal and prompt friendly service. The clientele here ranges from local office and hotel workers in suits, to uniformed off duty cops and tourists in shorts and T-shirts searching for an inexpensive tasty meal.

The menu features typical items such as omelets, jumbo burgers, club sandwiches, grilled cheese sandwiches, BLT's, roast beef with gravy, T-bone steaks, deep fried scallops, grilled pork chops, codfish cakes, BBQ chicken fillets, ice cream sundaes, and what may very well be the world's biggest lemon marangue pies. The restaurant also has a large magazine rack, and can make items to take out. Expect lunch to only set you back about $15 or less per couple. A great local eating establishment.

AFTER HOURS, *South Road, Paget. Tel. 441/236-8563. Open 9pm until 3:45am. Monday through Saturday. Dress code is Informal. Reservations are not necessary. Cash and Traveler's Checks only, no credit cards accepted.*

While not gourmet dining, this fun late night spot offers the only possibility for late sit-down meals. I have eaten here on several occasions, and have never been disappointed. The bizarre menu features eggs and omelets, red bean soup, assorted 10" and 14" pizzas made to order, fettucine Alfredo, burgers, fries with or without curry sauce, shrimp platters, goat roti, lamb roti, curried chicken, curried goat, and apple pie a la mode. This is the place for those of you who are not all dressed up, but still have no place to go.

ICE QUEEN, *Rural Hill Plaza, Middle Road, Paget. Tel. 441/236-3136. Open 10am until 5am daily. Dress code is Informal. Reservations are not necessary. Cash and Traveler's Checks Only, no Credit cards accepted.*

Ice Queen is nothing more than an amusing little fast food takeout shop that happens to be open extremely late. While the menu may not impress you, where else can you get a burger at 4:30am? The fun really gets started after 3am when the big clubs in Hamilton close. All kinds of blasted club patrons will line up here and feed their bad cases of the munchies. This is a great place to people-watch late at night. The menu offers decent pizza, cheap burgers, fish sandwiches, huge orders of fries, cold soda, and ice cream.

SEEING THE SIGHTS
The South Road Route, Part 1

After crossing into Paget from Warwick parish on **South Road**, you will first pass by on the right (south) side of the road the private entrance way leading to the exclusive **Coral Beach & Tennis Club**. Unfortunately, this great seaside resort and sports club is only open to members and invited guests, so don't even think about trying to gain access to its fine beach, pool, tennis courts, or restaurant.

Fortunately, almost directly across the street you will find the stone pillar marked entrance to the romantic **Horizons and Cottages** resort, much more accessible to the general public. This excellent hilltop cottage colony, with its spectacular 18th century main clubhouse, offers beautiful rooms, suites, and private cottages that have great views out over the stunning flower-filled grounds and across the way to the ocean.

One of the most impressive aspects of this deluxe resort property is its world class restaurant. Since Horizons is rather fortunate to employ what may be Bermuda's finest French chef, its extraordinary dining room and candlelit outdoor terrace offer some of the finest gourmet meals, wine lists, and service found anywhere in the world. All guests here have access, for a small surcharge as an invited guest, to the Coral Beach & Tennis Club. Horizons' on-site **Mashie Golf Course** is a nice 9 hole par 3 links which is open to the public with advance notice for only $20 per person during the week and $25 per person during weekends and holidays. Just keep in mind that golf carts are not available.

As you head back down onto South Road and continue to the left (east), the next must-see stop is the luxurious and newly refurbished **Elbow Beach Hotel**. Besides being my favorite large seaside hotel in Bermuda, this fine deluxe resort offers several dozen breathtaking acres of enchanting seaview grounds that are full of activities that can be enjoyed by both guests and visitors alike.

The best rooms, suites, and lanais here face out onto the fantastic **Elbow Beach Surf Club** (free for guests, and about $3 per person for visitors), which is one of the best spots in Bermuda to swim, suntan, and meet other people. The beach club staff will gladly direct you towards the restrooms, changing rooms, showers, snack bar, and for a small fee visitors can rent beach chairs, umbrellas, flotation rafts, and snorkeling equipment.

One of the most charming facilities at Elbow Beach is its delightful **Cafe Lido** beachfront restaurant. This is Bermuda's only truly casual romantic seaside Italian restaurant with affordable prices, and the food is as good as anything in New York, Boston, Philadelphia, or Toronto.

The hotel also contains a few other fine eating establishments that are also quite enjoyable. As you can see by my description, it is relatively easy to spend at least a whole week at the Elbow Beach Hotel without even venturing off property more than once or twice.

Eastward on South Road

When you return to South Road and keep going to the right (east), you will soon see the inexpensive **Paraquet Restaurant**, one of the best diner-style eating establishments to stop in for a totally casual home-made lunch or dinner. Just behind the restaurant is the equally affordable **Paraquet Guest Apartments** complex. Of all the reasonably priced apartment complexes that have seaview units with nice kitchens and daily rates, this is perhaps the best choice.

Just a bit further down the road, also on the right (south) side, is the **Art House Gallery** which displays pretty watercolor landscape paintings and prints by local artist Joan Forbes. The gallery is open from 10am until 4pm on weekdays and 10am until 1pm on high season weekends, and admission is free.

Next on the right (south) side of the road you'll see **Bermuda College** and its world class **Hospitality and Culinary Institute**, which is linked with **The Stonington Beach Hotel**. This moderately priced modern beachfront hotel is a great alternative for those who enjoy nice seaview rooms and fine meals at bargain prices. The rooms all face onto the end of Elbow Beach, and the cuisine at the hotel's famed **Norwood Room** is also superb. Since over 20 perrcentof the staff here are on temporary internships from the college, they work extremely hard to please both the hotel's management and each client in order to have a chance at a more permanent position. The result is that every guest feels like they are being treated like a king.

BECOME A GOURMET CHEF...
THEN EAT THE GOODIES!

*On several Wednesday nights, the **Hospitality and Culinary Institute** opens its doors to visitors who have called in advance and wish to learn how to prepare multiple course gourmet meals, which are then promptly eaten by the participants and master chefs. The cost is about $35 per person, and the experience is worth every penny.*

A few hundred meters (yards) further east on South Road, you can pop into the **Trimingham's** and **Bermuda Railway Co.** shops for great deals on T-shirts and gifts. On the opposite side of South Road you'll find the entrance driveways that lead to a series of charming guesthouses, bed and breakfast inns, and small resorts including **Sky Top Cottages**, **Loughlands Guest House**, and the all inclusive **Harmony Club**.

Just after this point, you'll see a stoplight signaling the merging of South Road and Middle Road. I should mention that at this intersection, just a few meters (yards) before the signal light, there is an unusual little late night restaurant called **After Hours**. With a basic down home ambiance and a menu loaded with items such as burgers, pizzas, omelets, goat roti, fisherman's platters, and curried meats, this is the only place in Bermuda to enjoy a fairly good sit down meal as late as 3:45am (closed on Sunday). After a long night of partying, its nice to know there is still somewhere to get a hearty meal.

Since South Road is now merged with (and is known as) Middle Road for a while after this stop light, please read the following Middle Road and the South Road Route Part 2 sections for what to see and do next.

The Middle Road Route

After heading east onto Middle Road in Paget from Warwick parish, you will soon pass **Fourways Inn** with its ornate restaurant, bar, and bakery, just after the intersection of Cobbs Hill Road. This is the country's most famous and expensive gourmet restaurant, and its opulent evening dining room attracts a wealthy and powerful clientele who don't mind paying thousands of dollars for a special vintage of Bordeaux.

Its adjacent **Peg Leg** bar is a much more casual and affordable alternative for the average visitor and serves a fine lunch. Fourways' bakery also sells mouth watering cakes and pastries. The inn itself offer a series of delightfully decorated but somewhat pricey deluxe poolside suites that can be rented by the day or week.

Continue eastward on Middle Road and soon you will pass by an assortment of huge private residences not open to the public, and lots of cute side streets. There is little of specific interest to tourists, until you reach the intersection of Valley Road; to the left (north) on Valley Road are the main offices of **Oleander Cycles Ltd.** (a great place to rent scooters and mopeds). Across the street from Oleander, you can pop into the **Bermuda Cottage Crafts** shop which offers a selection of inexpensive Bermudian hand-crafted gift items for sale. Another good scooter, moped, and mountain bicycle rental agency can be found a few yards further east on Middle Road at **Eve's Cycle Livery.** Also in this same general area you can visit the pretty but not overly historical **St. Paul's Anglican Church**, open and free of charge to the public daily.

As you move east to the stop light where Middle Road and South Road merge together (see above *South Road Route Part 1* section), you will soon pass the **Rural Hill Plaza** on the right (south) side. This quaint little shopping center is home to a **24 hour ATM** machine, the **Paget Pharmacy** which also sells sundries and newspapers, and most interesting of all, the **Ice Queen** takeout restaurant. This famous late night snack shop is open until about 5am and offers ice cream, cheap burgers and fish sandwiches, pizzas, and great french fries. This is the place that most hungry club and bar patrons mingle just after most of Hamilton's nightspots close. A great place to meet all kinds of unusual (and often drunk) people late at night!

A bit further east on Middle Road you will find a side street called Stowe Hill Road, which branches off to the left (north), where you'll find fine locally produced art. The **Birdsey Studio** is the best place on these islands to find original works by Bermuda's most famous scenic watercolor artist Alfred Birdsey and other members of his family. The gallery is open from 9am until 4pm on most weekdays, and admission is free.

As you go back on Middle Road and keep on going east, you will have no choice but to try to navigate around the traffic circle which will shortly confront you (be extremely careful to give way to those entering before you, and take the second exit to the left). Now you have merged back onto South Road, and Middle Road sort of temporarily disappears as it heads north towards the city of Hamilton.

The South Road Route, Part 2

Now that you have no choice but to again travel east on South Road for the time being, a few more attractions await you. A few minutes' ride down the road will be the entrance to the wonderful **Bermuda Botanical Gardens**. First opened in 1898, this dramatic collection of some 36 acres is filled with incredibly well maintained gardens and indoor horticultural exhibits that must be seen by all visitors to Bermuda.

Among the many worthwhile attractions inside the property are the cacti and succulent collection, the palm garden, the Montrose orchard, the exotic plant house, the impressive rose garden, an aviary filled with exotic birds, the beautiful formal gardens, and several buildings which contain all sorts of different exhibits. Since this is a rather large area to cover, I suggest that you pick up a copy of the free *A Guide to the Bermuda Botanical Gardens* pamphlet that is handed out upon request at the main visitor's center. Many of the trees and exhibits are marked by well located and easy to read explanatory plaques. The gardens also feature several public restrooms, and a snack shop and gift shop staffed by additional volunteers in the visitor's center.

GUIDED TOURS THROUGH THE BOTANICAL GARDENS

While admission to the Botanical Gardens is free from sunrise to sunset on a daily basis, the best way to see most of these gardens might very well be to join one of the free guided tours. Given by several gifted and knowledgeable volunteers from the Bermuda Botanical Society like Nell Johnson and Dianne Herr, these one hour walking tours depart at 10:30am each Tuesday and Friday with occasional additional tours on Wednesdays during the high season. The guides will be glad to answer even the most specific questions as they walk your group from sight to sight. Be careful not to get hit in the head by a falling scarlet cordia fruit!

Located within the grounds of the gardens is the fantastically beautiful official residence of the Premier of Bermuda known as **Camden**. Although used only for state functions, this early 18th century seaview mansion is surrounded by pretty gardens and a cute fountain. A free self guided walking tour can take visitors up inside the mansion to view the fine cedar staircase and panelling, handmade cabinetry, beautiful brass and crystal chandeliers, fine period furnishings, and several portraits of former Premiers. The house is open on Tuesdays and Fridays from 12noon until 2pm, and admission is free.

After the gardens, you have pretty much seen all the major sights available on South Road in Paget parish.

The Harbour Road Route

As you travel eastward on Harbour Road in Paget from Warwick, the first sight you will see on the north shore is the budget **Palm Reef Hotel**, with 94 nice, basic rooms, many of which look out onto Hamilton Harbour. The hotel is a great choice for people who desire clean and fairly basic waterview accommodations at affordable rates.

The hotel is also the home of several lounges, including **The Gombey Room** which hosts the *Bermuda Follies* show in the high season (10pm from Monday through Saturday). The show is an amusing blend of magic, animal tricks, comedy, dancing, videos, audience participation, and songs which are based (loosely) on the history and culture of Bermuda. The cast consists of four sexy female dancers (former Seattle Mariners' cheerleaders), a lead singer (the lovely Ms. Kristen Kite) with a powerful voice and a revealing costume, and a magician named Max. Although not exactly Broadway quality, this show has been running for the past 15 or so years. Admission is $25 per person with one free drink included, or $49 per person with dinner and one free drink included.

As Harbour Road winds its way a few hundred meters (yards) east from the hotel, take the first left turn onto Salt Kettle Road. Besides the **Salt Kettle ferry landing** that goes towards Hamilton, the **Salt Kettle peninsula** is also home to a coupe of nice bed and breakfast inns and a boat rental marina.

The most impressive of these inns is the delightful **Salt Kettle House**, with a nice selection of guestrooms, and apartments with cooking facilities, in an English/Bermudian family owned and managed setting. The inn has perhaps the finest and friendliest possible waterview accommodations in this price range in Bermuda.

Also in the same general area is the rustic cottage and apartment units of **Greenbank & Cottages**, also rather comfortable. At Greenbank's dock, visitors will find **Salt Kettle Boat Rentals Ltd.**, offering two hour rentals of Boston Whalers for $60 and Sunfish for $40, as well as a three hour sailing motor yacht snorkeling excursions that start at aboout $35 per person and depart most days during the high season. In general, Salt Kettle is a pretty little area that is well worth a visit.

When you get back to Harbour Road, continue eastbound and you'll pass the gardens and antique-filled manor house that has been lovingly converted into the opulent main building of the beautiful **Newstead Hotel**. The units here are quite nice, and most have enjoyable harbour views. During the high season, Newstead offers spectacular and moderately priced lunches and dinners at its famed **'Brellas** terrace restaurant.

A bit further down the road you will first pass the **Hodson's Ferry** and the **Lower Ferry** landings, with service to Hamilton. Just after Lower Ferry you will pass by the **Red Hole cove**; stay to the left (north) at the next fork in the road. Although you are now on **Pomander Road**, you will be able to get to the last remaining sight that I'll suggest in this parish.

The **Waterville House** is an early 18th century manor house that once belonged to the Trimingham family of local department store fame, and was where their first retail shop was born. These days it has become the **Bermuda National Trust Headquarters**, and can be visited to tour its lovely restored rooms, filled with period furnishings, shop in its cute **Trustworthy** gift shop with local handicrafts and items that feature the Trust's palmetto logo, or ask questions and get brochures about the other properties managed by the Trust.

This historic home is open to the public from 9am until 5pm on weekdays, while the shop is open from 10am until 4pm from Tuesday through Saturday. Admission to both the shop and home is free.

Now you can head to the end of this road and meet up with the traffic circle which can take you to wherever you want.

15. PEMBROKE PARISH

Located on a wide peninsula that juts out from **Great Bermuda Island** into the sea, **Pembroke** is this nation's busiest and most often gridlocked parish. Originally named after the third Earl of Pembroke, this cosmopolitan parish contains about 24 percent of the population.

The most obvious reason for the congestion and vast popularity of Pembroke is its most famous attraction, the city of **Hamilton**, which became the capital of Bermuda in 1815. For many years, a group of prominent local merchants and businessmen, known locally as the *Forty Thiefs*, controlled much of the political and economic decisions that shaped the future of Bermuda. With a huge assortment of fine shops, restaurants, nightclubs, pubs, hotels, charming inns, international business headquarters, historical sights, museums, and government offices, Hamilton is the most logical starting point of your journey through this parish.

What many visitors to Pembroke parish don't seem to realize is that just outside of town there are many wonderful back roads and mansion-lined country lanes that are perfect for half day walks and rides. In the *Seeing the Sights* section of this chapter, I'll guide you on a brisk walking tour of Hamilton's best sights, shops, restaurants, and attractions that should take about six hours including lunch. Then I will direct you on a circular route through some of the more secluded corners and lesser known points of interest on the outskirts of this parish.

ARRIVALS & DEPARTURES

For those traveling between the inns and hotels of Pembroke Parish and the **Kindley Field International Airport**, there are a couple of possibilities for quick and easy transportation. Either you can take a taxi ride for around $22 each way, or you contact Bee Line Transportation or Bermuda Hosts Ltd. a day or two in advance and pay about $20 per person round trip. Depending on where you're staying, the ride should be about 11 kilometers (7 miles) long and usually takes about 20 minutes depending on traffic conditions in downtown Hamilton.

ORIENTATION

Almost all visitors to this large peninsula will find themselves spending much of their time walking around the capital city of **Hamilton**. The various towers of churches and government buildings in the heart of the city can be seen from far away; when cruise ships dock alongside Front Street they too are good landmarks to use while navigating around town.

GETTING AROUND

There is certainly no lack of transportation to, from, and within Pembroke. All public buses in Bermuda either begin or end their routes at the **Central Bus Terminal** on **Washington Street** in the heart of Hamilton. From here you can transfer to any other bus, including bus route #4 which goes northwest of town to the **Spanish Point** area, and bus routes #10 and #11 which head northeast of town towards the north shore and on to Devonshire.

Ferry service is also abundant to and from the city of Hamilton, with frequent service linking several points in western Bermuda to the main **Ferry Terminal Building** just off Front Street. For those of you who like to travel around town the old fashioned way, horse-drawn carriages can be found waiting in front of this terminal to pick up passengers during the warmer months.

If taking a taxi, bicycle, bus, or scooter into Pembroke, keep in mind that there is plenty of rush hour traffic to be dealt with if passing anywhere near Hamilton. In fact, one of the most interesting people in town is the cheerful Johnny Barnes who can be seen each morning waving at frustrated drivers stuck at the last traffic circle before entering the city. For those of you who prefer to walk, unfortunately the **Railway Trail** does not cross through this parish at all.

WHERE TO STAY

WATERLOO HOUSE, *Pitts Bay Road, (City of Hamilton), Pembroke. Tel. 441/295-4480, Fax 441/295-2585, Toll Free Reservations (Relais & Chateaux) at 800/468-4100 US & Canada. Internet: www.bermudasbest.com. Low season rack rates from $190 per double room per night (B.P.). High season rack rates from $260 per double room per night (B.P.). 30 rooms and suites with air conditioning and private bathrooms. One restaurant, one luncheon terrace, and one bar. M.A.P. meal plan is available from $40 per person per day. Cash, Traveler's Checks, and all major credit cards accepted. Member of "Relais & Chateaux" hotels.*

This exquisite inn is based around an old 19th century estate on the harbor just steps away from downtown Hamilton. With a clientele base that would never consider staying anywhere else, this small luxury hotel caters to an upscale European and North American clientele.

The inn is housed within a few adjacent historical buildings that were once used as ships' warehouses for rum and other goods. Every one of the 30 unique deluxe rooms and suites are decorated with antiques and beautiful artwork. Two additional deluxe one bedroom suites are also available in a beautiful waterfront cottage for daily or monthly rental. Each of these accommodations contain heated towel rails, huge private bathrooms (some with jacuzzi), remote control air conditioners, mini safes, electric trouser presses, patio areas, and come with a complimentary full breakfast. The inn's fantastically ornate public rooms contain museum quality art, including some pieces on loan from the Masterworks Foundation.

Dining here is a serious experience, with a wonderful afternoon tea and European inspired gourmet meals served with superior service and a definite touch of class in their stunning main dining room and its outdoor terrace. The inn's own motor launch can take guests across the harbor for a relaxed dinner at their sister hotel's (Newstead) affiliated restaurant, or on romantic picnic lunch excursions to small secluded islands. Guests can arrange access to the private Coral Beach & Tennis Club. The ambiance is upscale, a bit formal, and somewhat exclusive. If you are the type of client that demands the finest, you will not be disappointed.

Selected as one of my *Best Places to Stay* – see Chapter 10.

CANADIAN PACIFIC HAMILTON PRINCESS HOTEL, *Pitts Bay Road, Hamilton, Pembroke. Tel. 441/295-3000, Fax 441/295-1914. Toll Free Reservations (Canadian Pacific Hotels) at 800/441-1414 US & Canada. Internet: www.cphotels.com. Low season rack rates from $119 per double room per night (E.P.). High season rack rates from $289 per double room per night (E.P.). 413 air conditioned rooms and suites with private bathrooms. Three restaurants, one bar, and one showroom. Dine Around (M.A.P.) meal plan is also available from $45 per person per day upon request. Cash, Traveler's Checks, and all major Credit Cards accepted.*

As the only deluxe full service resort hotel located within walking distance from downtown Hamilton, I have enjoyed staying here on several occasions. The hotel was originally opened in 1884 and named after Princess Louise of England who became one of the first notable tourists to this then tranquil island paradise.

Over the years the Princess hotel has had an adventurous existence, including its infamous 5 year stint as the unofficial Bermuda headquarters of Allied intelligence operations during the second world war. To this day, several local and international celebrities can be found lounging on the patios of their top floor super deluxe presidential suites. For regular people like you and me, the Princess offers a seemingly endless array of facilities and activities for both leisure and business clientele alike.

The hotel has more thant 400 full and partial harborview rooms and suites, many with waterview terraces, in its main and side wings which all contain cable television, radio, large private bathrooms, mini safes, deluxe furnishings, designer fabrics, and direct dial phones. The facilities include a health club, two swimming pools, a putting green, and private ferry service and total access to the Southampton Princess hotel and its fabulous golf course, tennis courts, and beach club. Dining choices include the gourmet Continental Tiara Room, the relaxed English style Colony Pub and piano bar, and the suprisingly good and affordable Harley's Bistro. Live entertainment is presented on most nights at the Gazebo Lounge.

Selected as one of my *Best Places to Stay* – see Chapter 10.

OXFORD HOUSE, *Woodbourne Ave., Hamilton, Pembroke. Tel. 441/ 295-0503, Fax 441/295-0250, Toll Free Reservations (Hotel Direct) at 800/ 548-7758 US & Canada. Low season rack rates from $131 per double room per night (B.P.). High season rack rates from $145 per double room per night (B.P.). 12 rooms and suites with air conditioning and private bathrooms. No restaurant, but the inn has a breakfast room. One Breakfast Room. Cash, Traveler's Checks, and most major credit cards accepted.*

Of all the affordable English style bed and breakfast inns in all of Bermuda, this is the one I would put on the top of my list. Located on a residential street just a few minutes walk away from downtown Hamilton, this charming little inn is lovingly owned and managed by Smith family. If I could design the perfect little romantic country inn, I am sure it would be rather similar to the Oxford House. Each of its spacious and bright rooms are traditionally furnished, exceedingly well maintained, and feature quaint floral interiors, televisions, phones, coffee machines, and a daily continental breakfast.

With the ability to add a couple of cots inside most rooms, families will be pleased to know that children are warmly welcome here. The inn has memorable public rooms, a central spiral staircase, and terraced front lawns. The personable staff always seem to be smiling, and are quite happy to assist each guest. This is one of Bermuda's undiscovered little treasures.

ROYAL PALMS HOTEL, *Rosemont Ave., Hamilton, Pembroke. Tel. 441/292-1854, Fax 441/292-1946. Toll Free Reservations (Hotel Direct) at 800/ 678-0783 US: 800/ 799-0824 Canada. Low season rack rates from $143 per double room per night (C.P.). High season rack rates from $180 per double room per night (C.P.). M.A.P. meal plan available for $43 per person per night. 9 rooms, 11 mini-suites, 4 deluxe one bedroom suites, and one deluxe self-standing cottage, all with garden views, air conditioning and private bathrooms. One restaurant with an outdoor dining terrace, and one bar. Cash, Traveler's Checks, and all major credit cards accepted.*

The Royal Palms is a nice full service inn, which is perfect for those seeking high end accommodations in a casual yet sophisticated environment. This lovely mansion, converted and managed by Richard Smith, has 11 impressive rooms and a one bedroom suite that look out over extensive gardens and a nice pool area. Each room has huge windows, traditional furnishings, telephones, television, and refrigerators that can be requested.

Situated on a hilly residential suburb just an 8 minute walk from Hamilton, the inn is surrounded by peace and tranquility. Mornings are a delightful time at the inn, with a fine continental breakfast featuring fresh pastries from Fourways being served to all guests. During the evenings, the fortunate guests may choose to enjoy the Ascots restaurant whose fine cuisine is only upstaged by its fabulous interior and outdoor terrace. Service at both the inn and the restaurant is top notch, and you can tell that no corners have been cut to provide clients with the best of everything.

ROSEMONT, *Rosemont Ave., Hamilton, Pembroke. Tel. 441/292-1055, Fax 441/295-3913, Toll Free Reservations (Hotel Direct) at 800/367-0040 US; 800/267-0040 Canada. Low season rack rates from $100 per double studio apartment per night (E.P.). High season rack rates from $130 per double studio apartment per night (E.P.). 37 studio and suite apartments with air conditioning, kitchens, and private bathrooms. One restaurant. Cash, Traveler's Checks, and most major credit cards accepted.*

Rosemont is a great medium-sized apartment complex with nice studio and luxurious 1-bedroom apartments which can comfortably accommodate up to four people each. Situated on a hill above Hamilton Harbour, this great complex is about a 10 minute walk away from the heart of town.

Each of the 37 tastefully decorated units have full modern kitchens, color television, telephones with free local calling, new comfortable furnishings, and some of the suites even come with jacuzzis. Based around a modern 3 story wing, some of the rooms have poolviews, while others have dramatic patios with panoramic views over the harbor. Just next door are a handful of traditional Bermudian cabana style buildings that house nice but more basic garden view rooms.

Under the caring direction of Karen Cooper-Olsen, this fine establishment provides wonderful self catering accommodations for a lot less than what I would expect to pay. Many guests come here for extended stays because the ambiance is so laid-back. Coin operated laundry and vending machines are located on site. I certainly suggest this property to families and couples alike.

ROSEDON, *Pitts Bay Road, Hamilton, Pembroke. Tel. 441/295-1640, Fax 441/295-5904, Toll Free Reservations (hotel direct) at 800/742-5008 US & Canada. Low season rack rates from $118 per double room per night (B.P.). High season rack rates from $152 per double room per night (B.P.). 43 rooms with air conditioning and private bathrooms. One restaurant. Cash, Traveler's Checks, and most major credit cards accepted.*

Rosedon is nice casual hotel with an attractive antique manor house and a new wing which is located behind the manor itself facing the outdoor pool. This popular small hotel is located just a few minutes walk from downtown Hamilton and is surrounded by gardens. The manor contains the four most attractive guestrooms, while the newer 60's style wing has another 39 basic and modern double rooms with patios, television, wall safe, coffee machine, and refrigerators. Guests also receive complimentary taxi service to Elbow Beach.

The hotel features a restaurant serving 3 meals daily, nightly movie screenings, a well stocked honor bar, afternoon tea and refreshments, a weekly swizzle party, and some of the most relaxing public rooms and lounges in Bermuda. This friendly home away from home is lovingly staffed by employees (who have in many cases worked here for decades) who work under the guidance of Mrs. Muriel Richardson, Rosedon's delightful General Manager.

PLEASANT VIEW, *Princess Estate, Pembroke. Tel. 441/292-4520; Fax: None. High season rack rate from $110 per double room per night C.P. Low season rack rate from $90 per double room per night C.P. 6 air conditioned rooms and apartments with private bathroom. No restaurant; apartments have kitchenettes. Cash, Checks, and Traveler's Checks only, no credit cards accepted.*

Pleasant View is located in the north suburbs of Pembroke parish near North Shore Road which is about a 10 minute ride into Hamilton. This moderately priced guesthouse offers 4 large and comfortable guestrooms with ceiling fans, cable television, am-fm clock radios, and telephones, as well as one studio and another bedsitter apartment which both have kitchenettes. The inn itself faces past a nice freshwater pool and onto the ocean. Inside its pink building, Pleasant View offers a home style lounge area which is a perfect spot to relax and read the morning paper.

EDGEHILL MANOR, *Rosemont Ave., Hamilton, Pembroke. Tel. 441/295-7124, Fax 441/295-3850. Low season rack rates from $86 per double room per night (C.P.). High season rack rates from $110 per double room per night (C.P.). nine rooms with air conditioning and private bathrooms. One Breakfast Room. Cash, Checks, and Traveler's Checks only, no credit cards accepted.*

This cozy bed and breakfast style guesthouse is set in an old mansion on a lush hillside a few minutes walk outside of Hamilton. Edgehill's 9 large and airy guestrooms offer lots of sun, television, and either private balconies or patios. The top floor of the guesthouse contains three fine rooms which have partial harbor views and cute outdoor sitting areas. This is a truly affordable property with a loyal clientele base of Americans and Canadians who return year after year.

Some of the rooms can accommodate up to four guests, and children are welcome here. A continental (home-made) breakfast is included daily, and afternoon tea is available upon request. The atmosphere at Edgehill is casual, welcoming, and low key, especially at the outdoor pool and sundeck. A good budget selection.

WHERE TO EAT

LA COQUILLE, *at the Bermuda Underwater Exploration Institute, East Broadway (Front Street's extension), Hamilton, Pembroke. Tel. 441/292-6122. Open from 11:30am until 2:30pm and again from 6:300pm until 10:00pm daily. Dress code is Smart Casual. Reservations are Strongly Suggested. Cash, Travelers Checks, and most major credit cards accepted.*

Beautifully situated alongside Hamilton's famous harbor, this new French-inspired restaurant has become one of the very best gourmet restaurants in all of Bermuda. Housed in the ground level of the B.U.E.I. pavilion just a few minutes walk or ride from downtown, La Coquille has become the favored location for serious power lunches as well as romantic candle-lit dinners. Meals are served either inside their modern white glass enclosed main dining room, or if weather permits there is also a fantastic harbor-front al fresco luncheon terrace where you can even dock your yacht. The ambiance here is casual yet somehow elegant and the service is first-rate for all that walk through their doors.

Swiss master chef Serge Bottelli has done a wonderful job in creating a superb menu of innovative European courses that are works of culinary artistry. My latest lunch-time meal here featured a simply outstanding cold gazpacho soup with lobster chunks, the best salad Nicoise I have ever tasted with fresh pan-seared tuna and French beans with hard boiled egg slices, and a grilled minute steak sandwich served on a fresh baguette with sautéed onions and rosemary sauce. Although I was already convinced that this was someplace quite special, nothing could possibly prepare me for the sumptuous dinner feast a few days later. Serge and his staff must have been hard at work for hours to prepare such delicious items as the terrine of ripe tomatoes with basil and goat cheese, amazing miniature crepes filled with morels and a mixture of seafood sprinkled with truffle dressing, a roasted free range chicken stuffed with herb and sun dried tomato rice served atop a saffron risotto pancake, and my personal favorite, the grilled jumbo prawns and sea scallops accented with a Pernod-lime-black bean sauce.

Besides truly memorable steak, fish, seafood, and game dishes, the menu here is also filled to the brim with lavish dessert offerings such as pistachio flavored profiteroles with almond creme Anglais, a frozen chocolate five spice soufflé, and their unique pear dessert soup with a red wine and fresh ginger base.

After my two meals here it was easy to see why the people of Bermuda have recently voted La Coquille the best restaurant in Bermuda, and why I can fully agree. The extensive wine list is both intelligently selected (none of this 75 page nonsense) and reasonably priced, thus including many fantastic bottles for less than $50 each as well as fine reds, whites, champagnes, and Ports by the glass. This is a great place to go for either lunch or dinner and deserves my highest praise. A great al la carte lunch for two here will set you back at least $48 plus drinks, while a splendid evening event should cost somewhere in the range of $120 per couple plus wine. I had a wonderful time dining here, and I am sure you will too.

ASCOTS RESTAURANT, *Royal Palms Hotel, Rosemont Ave., Hamilton, Pembroke. Tel. 441/295-9644. Open 12 noon until 2:30pm (every day except Saturday) and again from 6:30pm until 10:30pm daily. Dress code is Smart Casual. Reservations are strongly suggested. Cash, Travelers Checks, and most major credit cards accepted.*

Located in a magnificent old Bermudian mansion just a few minutes' walk or ride from downtown Hamilton, Ascots has matured into one of the finest unpretentious gourmet restaurants in Bermuda. What continues to make this opulent yet relaxed restaurant so remarkably delightful is that it offers a unique combination of superb gourmet European/Bermudian cuisine, flawless personalized service with a smile, and quite possibly the most romantic ambiance imaginable.

Set amidst beautiful gardens of scented flowers and hand-carved stone fountains, this amazing little bastion of gastronomy offers seating in their two intimate Victorian styled fireside dining rooms which are accented with chandeliers, as well as on adjacent al fresco dining verandahs and a cozy new gazebo. Tables here are set with purposely-mismatched antique china, imported crystal and silver, candles, and fresh flowers. The charming antique brass and Bermudian cedar-wood bar area is also beautifully designed and offers an outstanding selection of vintage Ports, single malt Whiskies, Cognacs, Grappa, and exotic liqueurs.

Owned and operated by a master chef (Dublin born Edmund Smith) and his charming Maitre D' (Angelo Armano from southern Italy), all of the staff at Ascots truly understand the art of providing gracious hospitality. Extremely popular for lunch, dinner and Sunday carvery, the menu is a fine example of modern provincial Mediterranean cuisine utilizing as much fresh Bermudian produce as possible. Chef Smith's specialty is incorporating local produce, imported meats, and fresh regional seafood into his own interpretation of both classic and nouveau European recipes.

His sauces and garnishes are delicate yet just strong enough to perfectly enhance the flavor of the dishes they are dressing.

The menu changes several times each year, but during my latest two evenings I was seriously impressed with their chilled Bermuda banana soup with almonds and black rum, their own home-cured local Wahoo gravlax in a lemongrass infused balsamic vinaigrette, warmed creamy Bermuda goat cheese wrapped inside marinated grapevine leaves, salad of roasted duck with cashews finished in a creamy raspberry sauce, soy marinated black tiger shrimp presented on a bed of citrus drizzled Jicama accompanied with mango-tomato salsa, an unbelievably tasty pasta St. Tropez with grilled Mediterranean vegetables and sun-dried tomatoes, Thai marinated sesame encrusted fresh tuna steaks served on glass noodles, and a superb classic sirloin steak with roasted shallots.

Desserts here are made fresh daily and include mouth-watering banana and dark chocolate crepes Garabaldi, rich mascarpone ice cream, tropical fruit sorbet, and several other unusual creations of the day. Angelo, the friendliest Maitre D' on the island these days, is continuously selecting dozens of new labels for their award-winning (and quite reasonably priced) wine list.

Winner of multiple Best of Bermuda awards as well as other highly respected international honors, there has recently been talk of the chef also offering a surprise six course menu, with the option of six specially selected accompanying wines, which I am convinced will set a new standard for gourmet dining in Bermuda. The average price for a great lunch for two will be about $42, while a four course al la carte dinner will cost around $105 per couple plus wine. Dining at Ascots is a wonderful experience that should not be missed by any visitor to these shores.

WATERLOO HOUSE, *Pitts Bay Road, Hamilton, Pembroke. Tel. 441/ 295-4480. Open 7:00pm until 9:30pm daily. Dress code Jacket and Tie. Reservations required. Cash, Travelers Checks, and most major credit cards accepted.*

The stunning gourmet dining room at the intimate Waterloo House inn rests a few steps away from the shores of Hamilton's harbor, just a short two block walk away from Front Street. Housed in a elegantly appointed 19th century Bermudian estate mansion, this unusually welcoming gourmet restaurant is among the very finest dining venues in all of Bermuda and offers innovative European cuisine served with great style and grace. Meals here are delicious offerings presented in a magnificent dining room and its adjacent waterside terrace, both with a charming English country ambiance.

The kitchen is presided over by executive chef Brent Price who was trained by, and continues to consult with, the acclaimed London-based master chef Anton Mosimann. Chef Price and his team create outstanding sumptuous al la carte lunch and dinner menus that change every day. Their special blend of classic and nouveau cuisine is light and refreshing. The gracious wait staff is a delight to be served by, and never show the slightest hint of pretentiousness that I have seen all too often at other perhaps more famous and expensive Bermudian dining establishments. The two dozen or so spacious tables here covered by linen and are set with a stunning collection of imported bone china, sterling silver, and crystal.

After being warmly greeted at the door by Maitre D' (and head sommelier) Angelo Buglione, each guest is gently guided to their seats and offered their choice of aperitifs before being presented with an extensive menu and informed of the chef's suggestions for the day. During my latest casual lunch here I was fortunate enough to indulge my palate with such delicious European and Asian influenced fusion dishes such as dishes as a fresh fruit salad with homemade tropical fruit sorbet, Caesar salad with sautéed shrimp and scallops, a quiche of roasted cauliflower and zucchini, duck breast marinated with Chinese hoisin sauce perched atop oriental noodles, and marinated penne pasta with vegetable laced basil pesto. The dinners here are much more elegant and formal, with an amazing seasonal menu that recently featured the best rum and sherry pepper infused Bermuda fish chowder I have ever tasted, Bermuda goat cheese and spinach ravioli in a classic French white lemon-butter sauce, sautéed black tiger prawns atop a creamy saffron spiced risotto, grilled black grouper, lamb cutlets with Stilton mousse, and a stuffed breast of chicken filled with Feta cheese and sun-dried tomatoes along with seasonal vegetables, and upwards of eight different tempting desserts.

Their excellent wine list has well over 200 different vintages from all corners of the globe and includes an extensive selection of rare finds such as '89 Chateau Latour, '95 Jadot Chevalier Montrachet, '96 Far Niente Chardonnay, '94 Rocchetta Sassicaia, '94 Antinori Tigananello, and '63 Croft vintage port. The staff here will also be pleased to suggest a superb half bottle or a selection of wines by the glass. A wonderful relaxed lunch here will usually cost upwards of $46 per couple, while an extravagant full four course gourmet dinner for two averages about $118 plus wine.

FRESCO'S RESTAURANT & WINE BAR, *Chancery Lane, Hamilton, Pembroke. Tel. 441/295-5058. Open 11:30am until 2:30pm on Weekdays and from 6pm until at least 11:45pm daily. Dress code is Smart Casual. Reservations Suggested. Cash, Traveler's Checks, and all major credit cards accepted.*

This brand new split-level gourmet restaurant and wine bar is another real gem in the dining scene of downtown Hamilton. Fresco's is the creation of well known Italian restaurateur Claudio Vigilante who has been associated with several other successful Bermuda based dining establishments for well over a decade now. As his new venture, Fresco's presents a unique concept by combining fine dining with a wonderful European-based lunch and dinner menu, the only real wine bar with over twenty wines available by the glass every day, and a late night café that serves delicious specialty coffees, tapas and gourmet desserts for the after theater set.

Executive chef Olivier Ramos is an expert in conjuring up delicious cuisine, which is beautifully presented and feature such tempting selections as his goat cheese terrine with roasted red pimentos and eggplant, carpaccio of seared duck breast sautéed in walnut oil and spice, superb fresh spinach and arugula salads with lamb jus and balsamic vinegar, Cajun spiced blackend halibut surrounded by a red wine reduction alongside a creamy vanilla sauce, Mediterranean style seafood cassolette in a light lobster sauce, whole wheat fettuccine tossed with a variety of sun dried southern European vegetables and anchovies, and last but not least their orange and lavender caramelized crust rack of lamb.

A special dessert menu may list such delicious offerings as a soufflé du jour and their famous warm chocolate mousse cake with jasmine tea infused custard. The service here is professional, polite, and friendly, and the overall ambiance on both floors is welcoming and intimate. Fresco's wine list is a true delight with more than enough choice for even the most discriminating wine lover. The average lunch bill per couple here is some $51 plus wine while a seriously good al la carte dinner should cost around $93 plus wine per couple.

PORT O'CALL RESTAURANT, *87 Front Street, Hamilton, Pembroke. Tel. 441/295-5373. Open 12 noon until 2:30pm on Weekdays and from 6pm until at least 10:00pm daily. Dress code is Smart Casual. Reservations Suggested. Cash, Traveler's Checks, and all major credit cards accepted.*

Port O'Call is a remarkable little steak and fresh seafood restaurant located on Front Street in downtown Hamilton. Well respected by locals and visitors alike for providing superb cuisine in a casual yet elegant nautical setting, complete with ribbed cedar paneling and brass portals, this cozy restaurant is popular during both lunch and dinner hours. One of the many aspects that makes Port O'Call so unique is that often local fisherman literally burst through the front door with an unexpected supply of freshly caught seafood, which Chef Martin Fickinger immediately proceeds to incorporate into his amazing daily specials.

Lunchtime here is a real treat with a large menu that includes such delicious dishes as Caesar salads topped with either blackened chicken or teriyaki sirloin steak, piping hot focaccia bread stuffed with thin slices of grilled wahoo or roasted vegetables and goat cheese, and main courses such as oven roasted snapper on a bed of mushrooms with a lemon butter sauce, and vegetarian pasta with seasonal vegetables. Dinner here is a bit more elegant without being formal and features an outstanding array of

Asian and European accented Bermudian courses which may include sesame encrusted shrimp served on Thai noodles with cilantro, fresh mussels simmered in white wine and garlic, lobster bisque, slow roasted Barbarie duck topped off by an orange rosemary glaze, herb crusted rack of New Zealand lamb, tandoori red snapper with cucumber relish, and sea scallops seared in red chili and basil puree.

Owners George Heracleous and Marco Zanuccoli have transformed this cozy 72 seat venue and adjoining bistro style al fresco terrace, into on of the island's premier restaurants, and their efforts have really paid off. Besides their massive menu, Port O'Call also offers great desserts and cappuccinos, over 30 different wines by the glass at reasonable prices, and a more extensive wine list of bottles from around the globe. This is a truly special place, and I highly recommend it for those that love to experience what a great chef and friendly wait staff can do to make a meal really special. Expect a lunch here top cost somewhere around $39 per couple plus drinks, and a lovely al la carte dinner to set you back around $85 for two people plus wine.

THE HARBOURFRONT, *21 Front Street West, Hamilton, Pembroke. Tel. 441/295-4207. Open 11:40am until 10:00pm daily. Closed on Sundays. Reservations Suggested for dinner. Dress Code is Smart Casual. Cash, Travelers Checks, and all major credit cards accepted.*

The Harbourfront is an excellent dining establishment with a great harbor-view location atop a charming old building along the western edge of downtown Hamilton's front Street. Packed with locals during sunny afternoons and weekend evenings, this welcoming medium sized eating establishment is Bermuda's originator of fusion cuisine and has been successful in offering two very different types of international cuisine, both of high quality and great value for the money. The Mediterranean white and blue accented interior of its two adjacent dining rooms is quite attractive, they have a delightful cedar lined bar area, and their truly panoramic outdoor harbor-view terrace is a delight in the summer.

The specialty here has always been the freshest possible seafood and meat dishes with a decidedly European twist. I was totally blown away by such offerings as their Harrington Sound Bouillabaisse with a great sampling of local seafood and daily fish chucks, the Chardonnay sautéed lobster served in phillo pastry, a superb New Zealand rack of lamb Provencial, the sliced roasted duck breast glazed with Curacao, a great vegetarian penne pasta Mediterranean with feta cheese and roasted veggies, the panfried Bermuda Wahoo with Bermuda bananas, and their famed lobster Marco Polo simmered in garlic-white wine sauce with sun-dried tomatoes over pasta.

Besides a vast array of delightful desserts, to further accompany your meal the waiter will be glad to suggest a great bottle from their *Wine*

Spectator award-winning list of over 200 different vintages from around the globe, all at reasonable prices.

Besides these wonderful French and Italian inspired dishes, what has made The Harbourfront such a great success is the fact that they also offer a full variety of Japanese dishes and freshly rolled sushi. While many customers mix and match both European and Asian dishes, I sat down one evening and really enjoyed a sampling of Miso soup with shrimp, crispy and light vegetable tempura, fresh yellowfin sashimi, red snapper nigiri, spicy tuna temaki, and a huge bottle of Saporo beer.

The service here is exceptional, with sushi orders taking a bit of extra time since they are rolled to order, and the staff under the direction of seemingly ever-present manager Pierangelo Lanfranchi really took care of every table as if it were filled with members of royalty. This has become one of my favorite places to dine in Hamilton and is really worth the experience. The average al la carte lunch for two should cost about $37 plus drinks, while a more exotic international gourmet dinner will set you back around $86 plus wine. They also offer an early bird dinner menu with a choice of several starters, main courses, desserts, and coffee from just $19.95 a head plus beverages.

LE FIGARO BISTRO, *63 Reid Street, Hamilton, Pembroke. Tel. 441/ 296-4991. Open 12noon until 2:30pm on Weekdays and again from 6pm until 10:30pm daily. Dress code is Casual. Reservations Required. Cash, Traveler's Checks, and all major credit cards accepted.*

For the past several months I been hearing great things about this fantastic new Parisian-styled French bistro in downtown Hamilton. When I finally arrived at Le Figaro I was impressed with its casual yet romantic ambiance and the warm welcome that guests receive from the staff. Owned and managed by an extremely friendly German restaurateur named Frank Schmitz, Le Figaro represents the best value for the money in the mid-priced fine cuisine restaurant category. Packed at lunchtime with government officials and insurance executives, and equally full at night with couples and friends looking for a relaxing venue for a delicious meal at affordable prices, the bistro and its adjoining wine shop have become an overnight success.

Le Figaro's superb Chef de Cuisine, Mr. Paul Duclos, manages to create an outstanding array of sumptuous French bistro dishes including a Marseilles style fish soup, imported escargot simmered in Chablis laced garlic butter, vegetarian ratatouille sprinkled with melted Gruyere cheese, a giant grilled ribeye steak with crispy homemade real French fries, braised free range chicken marinated in Beaujolais wine, fresh mussels steamed in white wine and pastis cream, and an amazing pan-seared salmon filet served on a wonderfully prepared rice pilaf. Desserts here are equally impressive and include the best chocolate creme brulee I have ever had in my life. Your waiter may suggest one of the dozens of fine wines from around the globe including a special list of fifteen outstanding French wines that cost $25 per bottle. The service here is polite and friendly. Expect a casual lunch to cost somewhere around $42 per couple plus drinks, or a more complex three course dinner to set you back around $77 for two plus wine. This cozy bistro place is a real gem, and is highly recommended for those that appreciate fine French cuisine served in a relaxing and welcoming setting.

LITTLE VENICE, *32 Bermudiana Road, Hamilton, Pembroke. Tel. 441/ 295-3503. Open 1135 to 3:00pm on weekdays and 6:30pm until 10:00pm daily. Dress code is Smart Casual. Reservations accepted but not usually required. Cash, Traveler's Checks, and all major credit cards accepted.*

Located on a quiet side street full of good restaurants, this great little Italian restaurant has long been a favorite of both locals and visitors alike. The exposed brick and molded ceiling panel interior offers and intimate setting in which to enjoy delicious made-to-order traditional Italian cuisine in style.

The extensive menu here includes a wonderful roasted antipasto with artichokes and eggplant beside Parma ham, their famous calamari which is so light and crispy it is hard to believe, a superb St. Giusto salad with grilled chicken breast and portobello mushrooms atop fresh spinach leaves, an authentic minestrone soup, vegetarian cannelloni filled with ricotta and seasonal vegetables, pan-fried tender veal scaloppini, grilled fresh swordfish, and all sorts of daily made pastas and pizzas. The deserts here are also delicious (especially the tiramisu), and the wine list is extensive. Service here is polite and prompt, and the overall experience is rather enjoyable. Expect a dinner for two to cost somewhere in the range of $93 plus drinks.

THE SURF CLUB, *Front Street, Hamilton, Pembroke. Tel. 441/2892- 6566. Open from 5pm until at least 11:45pm daily. Dress code is Smart Casual. Reservations Suggested. Cash, Traveler's Checks, and all major credit cards accepted.*

The Surf Club is a brand new restaurant, microbrewery and entertainment center located along the harbor-front in the heart of downtown's bustling Front Street commercial district. Each afternoon the Surf Club begins its offerings at a popular after work happy hour with a selection of snack items served alongside several fine ales and stouts brewed right here in brass fermentation tanks operated by staff from Bermuda's Triangle Brewing Co.

As the evening sets in, a team of Asian sushi chefs begin to hand roll an assortment of delicious sushi and sashimi which can be filled with a selection of local and imported fresh fish such as yellowfin tuna and lobster or shrimp and crab with cucumber slices. By 7pm or so the live music kicks in on most nights, and the main steak house kitchen grill-room works its magic on USDA prime cuts of beef as well as ribs and tender free range chicken dishes and seafood brochettes.

Sometime around 9pm on several nights a week, legendary piano-man and comedian Jimmy Keys starts his first set of live music which is one of the island's funniest events. No one is spared from his side comments, especially honeymooners or those who leave before his set is over. The overall experience here is quite nice, the music is superb, and both the food and brew is tasty. Expect an evening of laughs and good simple steak and seafood or delicious sushi ton set you back around $76 or so per couple.

THE COLONY PUB STEAK HOUSE, *Canadian Pacific Hamilton Princess Hotel, Pitts Bay Road, Hamilton, Pembroke. Tel. 441/295-3000. Open 11:30am until at least 10:00pm daily. Dress code is Smart Casual. Reservations accepted but not usually required. Cash, Traveler's Checks, and all major credit cards accepted.*

If you're in the mood for a relaxing pub styled meal, then head straight for this delightful little steak, seafood, and deli sandwich venue in the lobby of Hamilton's Princess Hotel. This casual traditional English styled wood paneled steak house presents a carefully selected lunchtime menu of well prepared Bermudian/American dishes such as zesty shrimp cocktails, spicy chicken wings with blue cheese sauce, triple decker club sandwiches, fish and chips, and thick burgers.

As the day turns into night, the Colony Pub switches to an extensive dinner menu with much more choice. Along with a full selection of English and local beer on tap (as well a good international wine list), the evening menu features such delicious offerings as their wonderful Bermuda fish chowder with dark rum and sherry pepper sauces, garlic infused escargot, fresh blue point oysters on the half shell, mixed green salads, juicy USDA Grade A prime rib, tender roasted chicken, giant sea scallops served with garlic on wild rice, and grilled 22 once lamb chops; you have your choice of sauces for your meats of Bernaise, Pergourdine, Bercy, or green peppercorn. The portions are large, and the service is good. On most evenings there is also live jazz music, and the bar area serves a selection of Cuban cigars and Port wines. Expect a wonderful three-course dinner here to set you back around $73 per couple plus drinks.

PORTOFINO, *Bermudiana Road, Hamilton, Pembroke. Tel. 441/295-6090. Open 6pm until 11:45pm daily. Dress Code is Casual. Reservations are suggested. Cash, and Traveler's Checks, and most major credit cards accepted.*

Portofino is without doubt one of downtown Hamilton's busiest restaurants. This small and often overcrowded Italian restaurant has a lively ambiance, and a staff which seem to always be in a rush to go nowhere fast. As with all good things, a little patience is the key to enjoying this bustling eating establishment. When the high season kicks in, it is not uncommon to find long lines of tourists and local residents waiting up to an hour to get inside.

Most who people come here seem to take advantage of the moderately priced items on the menu, which include hearty minestrone soup, a good Caesar salad, fettucini Alfredo, pasta primavera, veal parmigana, steak pizzaiola, lasagne, plump chicken cacciatore, excellent risotto, and over a dozen kinds of delicious thin crusted pizzas. A great place to enjoy simple classic Italian dishes, especially later at night. Dinner for two can be as low as $50 without wine.

RESTAURANTE PRIMAVERA, *Pitts Bay Road, Hamilton, Pembroke. Tel. 441/295-2167. Open 11:30am until 2:30pm (on weekdays only) and from 6:30pm until 10:30pm daily. Dress code is Smart Casual. Reservations accepted but not usually required. Cash, Traveler's Checks, and all major credit cards accepted.*

Located just steps away from the Princess Hotel on the edge of downtown Hamilton, this friendly Italian restaurant features classic pasta, meat, and seafood dishes for both lunch and dinner. Portions are generous. On my last visit to Primavera, the menu featured imported ham with melon, seafood soup, antipasto salad, minestrone soup, shrimp cocktails, mushrooms sauteèd in garlic butter, penne with pesto, mushroom ravioli in tomato sauce, gnocchi in walnut and Gorgonzola cheese sauce, spaghetti Bolognese, fettuccine with shrimp and calamari, mussels marinara, shrimp scampi, chicken breast in brandy sauce, veal scaloppini, tiramisu, and many more items. Special lunch menus bring the average price for two down to under $35 plus wine, while a typical dinner for two will cost around $75 plus drinks.

HARLEY'S BISTRO, *Canadian Pacific Hamilton Princess Hotel, Pitts Bay Road, Hamilton, Pembroke. Tel. 441/295-3000. Open 1135 to 3:00pm daily and 6:30pm until 10:30pm Wednesday through Monday in high season only. Dress code is Smart Casual. Reservations accepted but not usually required. Cash, Traveler's Checks, and all major credit cards accepted.*

Situated on a harbor-front section of the famous Hamilton Princess Hotel just a few blocks away from downtown Hamilton, this good Mediterranean styled bistro is a real hit with both locals and hotel guests alike. From the moment you arrive at the restaurant's front door you are warmly greeted and then seated at a large oval table with plenty of space and even more charm.

The spacious pastel waterfront dining area is nicely decorated with hanging plants and European designed trim. Popular with couples and families looking for casual dining in a friendly environment, Harley's offers an extensive menu that is sure to suit just about any taste. On my most recent visit here the menu included such tasty items as scallops served on saffron-ginger sauce, crispy fried calamari, traditional Caesar salad with plenty of Parmesan, pan-seared fresh red snapper with roasted sweet peppers, penne pasta with sun dried tomato pesto, fine USDA Grade A veal and beef steaks, and of course tasty pizzas and huge desserts. A hearty 3 course dinner here will set you back about $70 per couple plus beverages.

BOMBAY BICYCLE CLUB, *75 Reid Street, Hamilton, Pembroke. Tel. 441/292-0048. Open 12noon until 2:30pm weekdays, and 6:30pm until 11pm daily. Dress Code is Smart Casual. Reservations are suggested. Cash, and Traveler's Checks, and most major credit cards accepted.*

This slightly out of the way Indian restaurant can be found on the 3rd floor of a large building at the east end of Reid Street in Hamilton. As Bermuda's only Indian restaurant, it provides a spicy dining alternative well worth pursuing. The restaurant has a delightfully refreshing rattan-laden interior, and soft spoken staff who will gladly prepare meals to your requested level of spice.

The menu here is loaded with perfectly prepared Indian specialties including mullagatawny soup, aj ki yakni soup, crispy onion fritters, pleasant saffron flavored rice, zesty shrimp vindaloo, vegetable curry, roganjosh lamb curry, chicken tandoori, paratha bread, beef biryani, and lots of unusual condiments. An excellent value for the money! Dinner for two will end up costing about $60 without wine.

THE PICKLED ONION, *53 Front Street, 2nd floor, Hamilton, Pembroke. Tel. 441/295-2263. Open 11:30am until at least 10:00pm daily. Dress code is Casual. Reservations accepted but not usually required. Cash, Traveler's Checks, and all major credit cards accepted.*

This new international restaurant has become one of downtown Hamilton's most popular dinner and drinking establishments. Located on the site of a former pub, the Pickled Onion is an architectural curiosity complete with an exposed beam and Bermuda stone chapel ceiling, art nouveau chandeliers, bright pastel wall surfacing, imported Italian fabrics, world beat music, and plenty of modern art on the walls. The dining rooms have round tables, several comfy booths, and a wonderful al fresco dining terrace overlooking Front Street and the cruise ship terminal.

The fusion-style fare here is pretty good and features dozens of favorites from around the globe, including a delicious chilled gazpacho, yellowfin tuna served on Japanese soba noodles, BBQ chicken pizzas, local mussel stew with Spanish sausage, Caesar salads, and lots of pastas and roasts. The wine list is extensive and includes many varieties served by the glass as well as the bottle, and the full service bar gets packed at night with the polo wearing single yuppie crowd that mingle as they gulp down colorful cocktails. This is a good place for those who like to try something a bit out of the ordinary, but still want the choice of playing it safe. A good hearty dinner for two here will be around $64 plus drinks. **ROMANCING THE SCONE**, *Front Street, Hamilton, Pembroke. Tel. 441/295-3961. Open 10am until 4pm. Closed Sunday. Dress Code is Casual. Reservations are suggested, but not always necessary. Cash, Traveler's Checks, and most major credit cards accepted.*

This small lunch terrace restaurant on the 2nd floor of A.S. Cooper & Sons department store is casual, refined, and friendly. The dozen or small tables that overlook Hamilton Harbour help create one of the best spots in town to enjoy a charming breakfast, traditional afternoon tea, or a superb light lunch. The delicate menu offers Caesar salads, cobb salads, baked avocado with shrimp, vegetarian lasagne, albacore tuna sandwiches, croissants with egg and bacon, scones, bagels with cream cheese, and fresh fruit. The last time I ate here, I must have stayed two hours just relaxing and people watching. Lunch for two will cost about $25.

THE HOG PENNY, *Burnaby Street, Hamilton, Pembroke. Tel. 441/292-2534. Open 11:30am until 4pm and 5:30pm until 10:30pm. Closed Sundays. Dress Code is Casual. Reservations are suggested. Cash, Traveler's Checks, and most major credit cards accepted.*

This English-style wood paneled pub and restaurant is situated just off the corner of Front Street and Burnaby Street in the heart of downtown Hamilton. This a great place to have some fun while enjoying a casual and reasonably priced meal. The service is a bit slow at times, but if you order a few beers before dinner, you won't even notice it.

The menu here is a combination of typical pub fare and more sophisticated Indian, Bermudian, American, and English inspired offerings such as fish chowder, spinach salads, wings, calamari, shrimp cocktails, fish and chips, steak and kidney pie, burgers, roganjosh lamb curry, chicken satay, fish cakes with curry and banana chutney, shepards pie, angus sirloin steaks, Bavarian apple strudel, apple fritters, and English sherry trifle. On most evenings, the pub offers live entertainment. A good choice for those who miss down to earth food at prices they can afford. Dinner will cost about $60 per couple plus drinks.

CHIT CHAT BOULEVARD CAFE, *27 Queen Street, Hamilton, Pembroke. Tel. 441/ 292-3400. Open 11:00am until 11:00pm daily. Dress code is Casual. Reservations are not necessary. Cash, Traveler's Checks, and all major credit cards accepted.*

This family-style pizzeria and international restaurant in the heart of downtown Hamilton continues to be popular with budget conscious casual diners of all ages. The concept here is that each evening they offer a menu featuring the cuisine of a foreign country such as Mexico, India, Italy, etc., as well as lunchtime offerings of soups, salads, pizzas, rotis, and burritos. The food is prepared in small open kitchens located near the tables, and is of good quality. The interior of the restaurant is designed to resemble a small city center complete with rambling lanes, inner courtyards, alcoves, and terrace areas. While far from fancy, this is a good place for a light meal, and the kids will love it. Expect a filling lunch or dinner for two to cost around $39 plus drinks.

M.R. ONIONS, *Par-la-Ville Road, Hamilton, Pembroke. Tel. 441/292-5012. Open 12noon until 3pm weekdays, and 5pm until 9:45pm daily. Dress Code is Casual. Reservations are suggested, but not always necessary. Cash, Traveler's Checks, and most major credit cards accepted.*

Every city seems to have their own immensely popular bar/restaurant where the local office workers instinctivly head to after the office closes. Full of loud music, walls strewn with memorabilia, hanging plants, and a huge long bar with brass trim, M.R. Onions has successfully created what they refer to as "a fun place to eat and drink."

The menu includes an assortment of both typical bar snacks, and much more sophisticated house specialties including lots of their signature onion soup, huge salads, potato skins, big burgers, fish and chips, barbecued ribs, Cajun-style blackened fish, and chicken dishes. The restaurant also offers a great children's menu and daily specials. While far from gourmet cuisine, Onions is the place to enjoy a rollicking two hour happy hour starting weekdays at 5pm, have a small snack between sightseeing adventures, or save some serious dollars during their daily early bird specials served until 6:30pm. Expect a filling dinner for 2 to cost somewhere about $40 before adding in a pitcher or two of beer.

CHOPSTIX, *Reid Street, Hamilton, Pembroke. Tel. 441/292-0791. Open 12noon until 2:30pm weekdays, and 6pm until 11pm daily. Dress Code is Casual. Reservations are suggested, but not always necessary. Cash, Traveler's Checks, and most major credit cards accepted.*

Chopstix is certainly the best Chinese restaurant in Bermuda. The large eat-in and take-out menus offer an assortment of Hunan, Szechuan, Cantonese, Singapore, and Thai-style items which are well prepared and presented. Among the many fine selections, I suggest trying the Thai rolls, hot and sour soup, baby back ribs, vegetable fried noodles, Panang beef, kung pao chicken, Singapore fried rice, lemon chicken, evil jungle prince vegetables, or Phoenix prawns. While the food here is rather good, even the Szechuan dishes are normally prepared fairly mild. Ask for hot chili sauce if you want to breath some fire. Dinner for two should cost about $50 without drinks.

PARADISO CAFE, *Washington Mall, Reid Street, Hamilton, Pembroke. Tel. 441/295-3263. Open 7:00am until 5:00pm Monday through Saturday. Dress code is Casual. Reservations not accepted. Cash, Traveler's Checks, and Mastercard accepted.*

When you've just about finished your morning shopping excursions through downtown Hamilton and you want to rest your feet for a while, head to the Paradiso and treat yourself to a great freshly prepared lunch. This cozy modern high-end deli, bakery, coffee house, and rendezvous point has huge picture windows facing directly onto Reid Street and makes some of the best cold sandwiches and pasta salads in town.

The 18 tables here are almost always full (average wait time of five minutes for a table to become available) with locals sipping strong cappuccino and snacking on delicate dishes. Their menu features dozens of favorites such as tuna sandwiches on French bread, cold pasta salad with pesto and black olives, shrimp and spinach quiche, fresh blueberry tarts, and both hot and iced imported coffees made by European machines. The portions are reasonably large and rather tasty, and the prices are moderate. Expect a nice tranquil lunch for two with dessert to cost about $34 or so.

ROSA'S CANTINA, *Front Street, Hamilton, Pembroke. Tel. 441/295-1912. Open 12noon until 2:30pm weekdays, and 5pm until 11:45pm daily. Dress Code is Casual. Reservations are suggested, but not always necessary. Cash, Traveler's Checks, and most major credit cards accepted.*

With its new location on the east end of Front Street in Hamilton, this second floor restaurant and dining terrace offers good Mexican food. The typically young and fun-loving clientele can be seen gulping down the huge frozen Margaritas well after their meals are finished.

The menu has changed little since its relocation from Reid Street, and still features such typical Mexican specialties as black bean soup, 8 layer nachos, taco salads, guacamole, chili, shrimp or chicken quesadillas, tacos, bean and beef burritos, enchiladas, steak or chicken fajitas, barbecued ribs, chimichangas, mesquite grilled steak, and several other items which can be prepared as spicy as you prefer. Dinner for two will cost about $45 without drinks.

MANNIE'S SNACK BAR, *Washington Lane, Hamilton, Pembroke. Tel. 441/295-3890. Open 6am until 3pm. Closed Sundays. Dress Code is Informal. Reservations are not necessary. Cash and Traveler's Checks only, no credit cards accepted.*

Mannie's is a fun little unpretentious luncheonette, perfect for those of you who want to avoid costly hotel breakfasts while touring Hamilton. This narrow little spot is loaded with local gossip and flavor, and makes delicious and inexpensive home-style breakfast and lunch items. Although the menu is fairly small, you should consider trying their onion omelet, codfish cakes on a roll, fish and chips, and cheeseburgers. A great breakfast here will only set couples back about $12, and lunch will cost only slightly more.

SEEING THE SIGHTS
The City of Hamilton

Depending on how you decided to get to town, you may end up starting your visit to Bermuda's only real city from one of several different points. Scooter parking can be found on every major street in town, but 250 or so dedicated moped spaces fill up fast. Be persistent because after a few attempts you will find an open spot with free parking. I have included a fair amount of listings for cultural, excursion, and shopping activities because these are equally popular destinations for tourists visiting this city. For the most part, you should count on at least one full day to fully explore this pretty little city.

Start at the **Visitors Service Bureau** office, adjacent to the ferry terminal at 8 Front Street on Hamilton's waterfront. The bureau itself is a great place to pick up free maps of town, shopping brochures and guides, calendars of local events, helpful sightseeing hints, and even additional ferry and bus tokens. The bureau staff are extremely helpful and friendly, and the offices are open from 9am until about 4:30pm on weekdays.

WALKING TOURS OF HAMILTON

*During the low season, park rangers lead free guided walking tours of Hamilton on most Mondays departing from the front of the Visitors Service Bureau at 10am. This great introduction to the sights and history of this city ends at the traditional bagpipe **Skirling Ceremony** at Fort Hamilton.*

Let Me Take You On a Sea Cruise!

The small docks next to the Visitors Service Bureau are the departure slips for several sea excursions. Among the vast assortment of exciting adventures (usually from April through November only) that leave from these docks are the following, in order of my recommendations:

- **Jessie James Cruises** – an excellent three and a half hour reef and sea gardens snorkeling cruise twice a day, Sunday through Friday, aboard their 57' motor yacht for $35 per person including masks, fins, and snorkels.
- **Hayward's Snorkeling & Glass Bottom Boat Cruises** – fantastic 3-hour morning and afternoon trips daily on a 54' motor yacht for $38 per person including all the necessary gear.
- **Sail Bermuda** – take a peaceful half-day or sunset outings aboard their beautiful sailing yachts each day for $25 per person and up.

HAMILTON'S TROLLEY TOURS - COMING SOON!

There are plans underway to begin offering a special **city tour** *to be operated by* **Bermuda Train Co.** *Similar to their Royal Naval Dockyard train-like trolley, this proposed ride will offer passengers the ability to get on and off as many times as they like at stops beginning at the Bermuda Underwater Exploration Institute and continuing along to Hamilton area sights and attractions including downtown's Front Strèet, Albouy's Point, Reid Street, the National Gallery, Fort Hamilton, the Cathedral, and the Botanical Gardens. Perfect for both landlubbers and cruise ship passengers, this tourist train is scheduled to operated daily (high season for sure, low season depending is not definite) and will begin at 9:30am and run continuously until about 4:00pm. The full day price for the ride will include paid admission fees to all the above sights and is expected to cost $25 per adult, $12.50 per child from 6 to 12, and free for kids under 6.*

- **Bermuda Water Tours** – several unique excursions each week including a full day lunch cruise for $30 per person which lets its clients not only snorkel and swim along the way, but also includes a full lunch at the Waterside Inn and admission fees to the Maritime Museum at the Dockyard.
- **Reef Roamers** – twice daily on a 2-hour glass bottom boat trips (high season only) to the sea gardens and a shipwreck for $30 per person.
- **Bermuda Island Cruises** – tacky theme dinner-cruise excursions like their Pirate Party Night with entertainment and a dinner buffet for $65 per person each Tuesday, Wednesday, Friday, and Saturday at 7pm.

Just behind the Visitors Service Bureau are a few little shops such as the **Hodge Podge Souvenir Shop**, offering inexpensive gifts, and the **King Midas Jewelry Store** for silver chains, pendants, and trinkets. Also in the same general area you can utilize the public restrooms, a telephone booth, or just sit down and watch the yachts sailing through **Hamilton Harbour** from the lawns and benches of the tranquil harborfront **Point Pleasant Park**.

After visiting the park, follow the park's adjacent **Point Pleasant Road** and turn right (north) towards Front Street. Peek to your left for a glimpse of the prestigious private **Royal Bermuda Yacht Club**, which occasionally hosts sailing regattas and match cup races through the harbor.

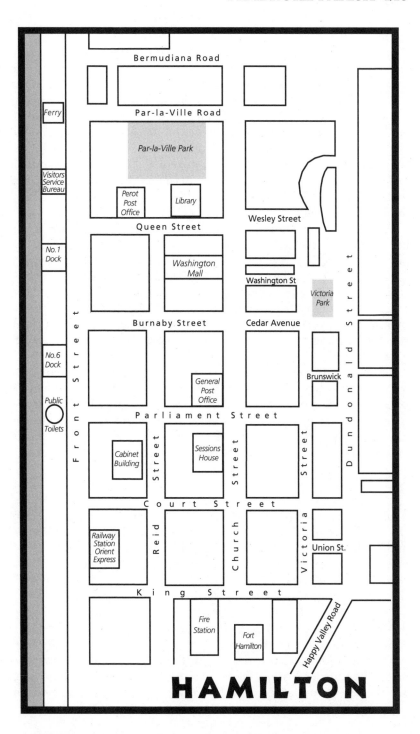

Front Street

Now that you have found yourself on **Front Street**, you have hours and hours of excellent shopping, eating, historical, and cultural diversions awaiting. As you head up (east) on Front Street, you can't help but notice the large modern facade of the **Bank of Bermuda Building** just steps away. Besides being the headquarters of this large international bank, the building's mezzanine houses a wonderful collection of antique Spanish, British, and Bermudian coins which must be seen. The highlight of the exhibit are the so called Hog Money coins, which date back to 1615 and are the oldest currency minted in Bermuda. The collection is open to the public from 9:30am until 3pm on Mondays through Thursdays and until 4:30pm on Fridays, and admission is free.

As you continue up Front Street you will see several other boutiques just across the street including the **Otto Wurz Co.** silver shop, **Bananas** gift and T-shirt shop, **Walker Christopher Ltd.** goldsmiths, the **Vera P. Card** figurine and collectible shop, **Cecile** European designer women's clothing, the **E.R. Aubrey Jeweller** shop (be advised of their phony 75% off sale; most items seem to be tagged at 300% above what I have priced them at in New York), **Wadson's** T-shirt store, the tempting **Harbourfront** restaurant, **Smuggler's Reef** T-shirt and gift shop, and the fabulous **Irish Linen Shop**.

Although dozens more fine boutiques, restaurants, pubs, and nightclubs can be found in the pretty pastel-colored buildings that line the upcoming section of Front Street, we will save them for a bit later on this tour. During the high season, two huge cruise ships moor themselves at the wharfs along this street and release thousands of additional tourists onto this normally manageable street.

Queen Street

At this point you should have reached the first major intersection, where you'll turn left (north) onto Queen Street. Just before turning, you can't help but notice the round **Birdcage** traffic box platform in the middle of the intersection. During rush hour you will find a uniformed policeman (complete with Bermuda shorts) directing traffic and gladly posing for photos.

As you turn up on the left (west) side of Queen Street, you will first pass by the **Bermuda Book Store**, owned by the Zuill family and who are noted historians and authors in their own right. If you are looking for either current bestsellers or special interest books to help identify local geography, wildlife, history, and culture, then this is the place. Next is the huge **Riihiluoma's Flying Colors** T-shirt shop, and the adorable little **Scottish Wool Shop** where I picked up a couple of fantastic Shetland sweaters for less than $28 each.

Now you'll wander past the entrance to Hamilton's most serene attraction, the **Par-La-Ville Park**. This wonderful palm and shrub-filled public park was once the private garden of fabled Bermudian postmaster William Bennet Perot. His lovingly manicured gardens of exotic plants and trees have become a peaceful location for both businessmen and tourists alike to relax and enjoy box lunches upon its many benches. As you wander through the lovely stone-topped trails and peaceful gardens it is hard to believe that you are actually in the middle of a bustling city. The park also has public restrooms and nearby pay telephones for your added convenience. Admission to the park is free, and it is open daily from sunrise to sunset.

The next building you'll pass is the **Perot Post Office**. This cute two story 19th century building with its trademark shutters and cedar beams is Bermuda's first official post office. Bermuda's original postmaster, William Bennet Perot, would greet arriving sea vessels at the wharfs to get the incoming mail, and then walk around town to personally deliver these letters. In 1848 he decided to print and sign Bermuda's first stamps to further minimize his workload, and assure that the correct postage was paid for outgoing letters. Less than a dozen of these highly valued original hand-signed stamps still exist today. This fine example of Bermudian architecture still operates as a branch post office complete with an original antique wooden counter, extremely friendly and patient postal employees, oil paintings of Mr. Perot and Queen Victoria, and sometimes lines of tourists who pay 60 cents to mail their cards and letters back to America. The post office is open from 9am until 5pm weekdays, and admission is free.

A few meters (yards) up from the post office, you will see a large rubber tree that Mr. Perot planted here, in his house's front yard, from a seed in 1847. His former home has become the **Bermuda Library & Historical Society Museum** building. The library itself offers a vast reference section full of rare historical books about Bermuda, and a full range of more modern reference and reading materials. Non-Bermudians may be permitted to withdraw books here if they inquire upstairs.

The 3-room museum exhibit area displays a series of antiques and artifacts including paintings of the founders and former governors of Bermuda, 18th century European furniture, scale models of the *Sea Venture*, beautiful old clocks, antique coins, 17th century maps of Bermuda, old Bermudian family heirlooms, and if you inquire with the staff, perhaps they will let you take a peek at the 1775 letter from George Washington written to the inhabitants of Bermuda asking for help in obtaining gunpowder for the Revolutionary War. Unfortunately, most of the exhibits have no descriptive plaques.

The library is open from 9:30am until 6pm Monday through Friday, and until 5pm on Saturday and admission is free. The museum is open from 9:30am until 12:30pm and 2pm until 4:30pm Monday through Saturday and a $2 donation is requested.

After the museum, I suggest a bit of browsing and window shopping on the way to the next cultural attraction. Directly across Queen Street from the Bermuda Library you should first take a peek in the **Windsor Place Mall**. Inside the mall there are several great boutiques including the **Queen Street Glass** shop where you can purchase hand-blown glass miniatures from the **Bermuda Glass Blowing Studios**.

In the heart of this small shopping center is the fantastic little **Fourways Gourmet Shop** which is a moderately priced casual cafeteria style restaurant for huge sandwiches, salads, iced cappuccinos, and delightful pastries. Also inside the mall is a back entrance to the huge **Phoenix Pharmacy Centre** which sells everything from cold remedies and film to books and toys, a 24-hour ATM bank machine, the second floor **Air Canada** reservations and ticketing offices, and a pay phone.

A bit further up this side of Queen Street you will find a few more places worth a good look at, including the fantastic **Crissons** jewelers where I have found some serious bargains on Swiss watches, one-of-a-kind European gold bracelets, and cute sterling pendants.

A couple of doors further up you will first pass by the **Little Theater** with its twice daily screenings of first run American movies, and a rather odd pari-mutuel betting parlor appropriately named **Sea Horses Turf Accountants**.

City Hall & Arts Centre

Now that you are at the intersection, cross the street and make a right turn onto the far (north) side of **Church Street**. On the next block you are confronted by the impressive circular driveway, charming fountains, white Bermudian style facade, and towering bronze *Sea Venture*-topped weather vane of **City Hall & Arts Centre**, designed in the late 1950's by Wilfred Onions. From the minute you step inside this fine building's massive cedar doors, you are surrounded by elaborate chandeliers, impressive paneling, and portraits of Queen Elizabeth and former mayors which are all protected by remarkably cold air conditioning. During the summer I have spent hours at a time here to escape the blistering heat.

Several side rooms contain small local exhibits like the **Benbow Stamp Collection**, an intimate theater that hosts live music events, and private municipal government offices including those of the mayor. Upstairs you will find some of the most incredible works of art to be found in all of Bermuda. City Hall is open from 9am until 5pm Monday through

Friday, and 9am until 12noon on Saturdays, and admission is always free. Public restrooms are available at this location.

The **East Wing** on the second floor of City Hall is home to the **Bermuda National Gallery**. This dramatic gallery houses several outstanding collections of fine art. The first installation of art works is the Herewald T. Watlinton Collection, named after a local millionaire who willed his private collection to Bermuda. This permanent exhibit contains 18 wonderful European paintings from artists such as Gainsborough, Murillo, Romney, Palma Vecchio, de Vos, and others.

The world famous **Masterworks Bermudiana Collection** is comprised of paintings by internationally renowned artists like Georgia O'Keefe, Ross Turner, Albert Gleizes, Winslow Homer, who have all visited Bermuda and painted their impressions in these very canvasses. The non-profit Masterworks Foundation has tracked down these masterpieces and brought them back home to Bermuda. Several other wings and galleries also display exhibits which change each season and feature other international touring exhibits. The National Gallery also has a small gift shop which sells posters, art cards, and gifts. *Excellent free guided tours are usually held on Tuesdays and Fridays at 10:30am, and on some weekends at 2:30pm. The National Gallery is open from 10am until 4pm Monday through Saturday, and 12:30pm until 4pm on Sundays. Admission is $3 per adult and children under 16 are invited for free.*

ENJOY MUSIC & ART AT THE
ANNUAL BERMUDA FESTIVAL

*Each winter between the first week of January and the last week of February, Hamilton hosts the famous **Bermuda Festival**. This is one of those special events that brings out all of Bermuda's leading citizens in a show of support for the arts. Events range from casual jazz concerts and art exhibitions, to more dressy events like chamber music recitals and theatrical performances by world renowned artists. If you happen to be planning a stay in town during these weeks, make sure you call well in advance for these tickets. Prices generally range from $20 to $30 for regular events, $50 for gala evenings, and students can receive up to 40% off. Events take place at both the City Hall Theater, and several other locations around Hamilton.*

For exact schedules, event prices, reserved advance seating, and further information call the festival organizers at Tel. 441/295-1291 for a copy of the complete program. These shows are an excellent way to spend a few evenings, and perhaps meet some interesting new friends from the local community.

Last, but certainly not least, is the upstairs **West Wing** of City Hall, which has become the home of the **Bermuda Society of Arts Gallery**. This is a more informal collection of the society's local member artists' best work. Since the exhibits are constantly changing, you may be able to view local watercolors, oil paintings, photography, sculptures, modern stained glass, and batik works. Admission to this gallery is free and is open from 10am until 4pm from Monday to Saturday.

Further Along Church Street

After departing City Hall, continue walking down the same side of Church Street until you have reached the next corner. Here you can't help but notice the **Central Bus Terminal**, home base of all public bus routes through Bermuda. If you need any tokens, tickets, passes, directions, or transit maps, then you really should stop here.

Further down (east) on Church Street is the unmistakable Neo-Gothic tower and facade of the **Cathedral of the Most Holy Trinity**. This outrageously ornate Anglican church is also known to locals as the **Bermuda Cathedral**. This huge church, designed by William Hays of Scotland, was inspired by several 8th-12th century English cathedrals and was finally completed in 1911 using limestone, granite, and marble from all over the world. Inside this house of prayer you will find many treasures including hand-carved oak pews with locally embroidered cushions, dramatic stained glass windows, beautifully carved choir stalls, and a memorable marble altar. The Cathedral is open daily from 8am until 6pm and admission is free.

Heading further down (east) on Church Street, the next place you may wish to see is the **Bermuda Department of Tourism** office at 43 Church Street in the building known as Global House. After you have passed by the security guard in the lobby, he will direct you to the office where you can pick up dozens of different free maps, calendars of events, tourist brochures, hotel guides, golf guides, and other useful literature.

At the next corner is the oldest church in town, **St. Andrew's Presbyterian Church**, open from 8am until 7pm daily; no fee. Built in 1846, this Neo-Gothic structure was constructed on land donated by then-Governor Lieutenant Colonel William Reid. Over the years several new additions have been added including its bold organ and choir chancel, bell tower, and administration offices.

Court Street

Now you are at the intersection of Court Street, where you will be taking a right (south) turn and walking down its righthand (west) side. The massive 19th century **Sessions House** was originally completed in 1817, with the Italian-inspired terra cotta **Jubilee Clocktower** and colonnade added in the later part of the 19th century. During much of the year, the **House of Assembly** sessions take place on the top floor.

With its Old World English-style proceedings and customs, you may want to take a few hours out of your day to watch one of these meetings from the upstairs visitors gallery. When no session is taking place, the Sergeant at Arms might just open the chambers for you to look at if asked politely. The lower floor is home to Bermuda's **Supreme Court**, which also invites the general public to watch the robed and wigged participants argue their cases from a visitors gallery.

Call 292-7408 to find out if a House of Assembly or Supreme Court session is scheduled while you're in town; watching this is a great once in a lifetime experience. The building itself is open to the public from 9am until 5pm on weekdays, and admission is free.

TOUR THE HOUSE OF ASSEMBLY

During the low season, a free 30 minute guided walking tour through the Sessions House is hosted by a clerk of the House of Assembly at 11:15am on most Mondays. An in-depth discussion of Parliament's role in making Bermudian laws and policy is held during and immediately following the tour.

Fort Hamilton

Retrace your steps (north) back up Court Street until again reaching the intersection of Church Street, where you will turn right (east). After following Church Street for another two blocks or so, you will come to a dead end where you should turn left (north) onto King Street towards the back end of town. After a block and a half you will find a turnoff on the right (east) side of the road onto **Happy Valley Road**, which you will follow for quite a brisk walk until finally reaching the entrance of **Fort Hamilton**.

This restored 19th century fort was ordered to be built by the Duke of Wellington to protect Hamilton from attack. Although never used in any battle to defend the city, its massive angular fortifications, slathouse, shrub filled moats, stone tunnels, and 1-ton gun placements are a perfect spot to get a great panoramic view over the downtown waterfront area. During the restoration process, much of the fort's landscaping was altered slightly to accommodate gardens and a large green.

A small and moderately priced tearoom offers refreshments during the afternoon hours. *The fort is open from 9:30am until 5pm Monday through Friday, and admission is free.*

BAGPIPE MUSIC AT THE FORT

During low season, the traditionally-dressed **Bermuda Isles Pipe Band** *hosts a bagpipe and skirling ceremony on the fort's lush green each Monday at noontime. This is without doubt the best time to visit the fort.*

After a good walk around the fort, wander back over to King Street, turn left (south), and follow it down all the way to its end at the intersection of Front Street. As you turn right (west) onto Front Street, walk for another block or so; you'll pass several eating and drinking establishments including the **Docksider Pub** and the adjacent **Rosa's Cantina** Mexican restaurant.

Next you will find the gates surrounding the understated **Cabinet Building**. This fine mansion-style building dates back to 1838, and now houses the offices of the extremely personable Premier of Bermuda, Sir John Swan, and his cabinet. This is the scene of several serious closed-door Cabinet meetings each month. The **Senate** also meets here, with the general public invited to view its weekly Wednesday sessions. The building contains several beautiful antiques and portraits. On the front lawn is a huge limestone **Cenotaph**, dedicated to those Bermudians who perished during World Wars I and II. The Cabinet Building is open to the public from 9am until 5pm on weekdays, and admission is free.

DON'T MISS HARBOUR NIGHT!

On Wednesday evenings during the summer from 7pm until about 10pm, all of Front Street is closed off to vehicles for the enchanting **Harbour Night** *street festivals. These harbour nights attract locals and tourists of all ages who wish to socialize and wander over towards streetside vendors selling local handicrafts, stalls serving spicy Caribbean food, amusing sidewalk fashion shows, excellent live bands, and extended store opening hours (some close after 10pm). This is a highly enjoyable experience for adults and kids alike. Try to attend at least one Harbour Night if you are here during high season.*

Back to Front Street

After departing the Cabinet Building, keep heading west on Front Street, Hamilton's most important shopping road. Soon you will pass several great places to eat, drink, and shop 'till you drop. In order of what you will be seeing while heading west on this block of Front Street (between **Parliament Street** and **Burnaby Street**), these are a few of my favorite spots to pop into: the **Vera P. Card** collectibles shop, **Goslings** wine and spirit shop, tiny **Bermudiana House Lane** where you can stroll up to see fantastic pieces at the **Masterworks** art gallery or the **Windjammer** art gallery, a quaint pedestrian only side street known as **Chancery Lane** with several small boutiques (including the inexpensive little **Swiss Timing** watch shop and the intimate **Chancery Wine Bar and Restaurant**).

You'll also pass the airline ticketing offices for **British Air**, **US Air**, and **Delta Airlines**, the **Port O' Call** steak and seafood restaurant, a high end **Astwood Dickinson** jewelry shop, **Traders Gate** gift and - shirt shop, the opulent but affordable **Crissons** jewelry boutique, and finally the **Emporium Mall** that contains several additional boutiques and a couple of great nightspots including **Flanagan's** Irish pub (with live music most nights), and the infamous **Oasis** nightclub, open until 3am, featuring the town's most serious high intensity dance music.

The brand new **Tienda de Tabaco** cigar shop has just opened in the Emporium mall This is a popular destination for American visitors looking for superb Cuban cigar brands, such as Cohiba (long rumored to be Fidel Castro's favorite brand) and Montecristo. Unfortunately, US customs does not permit anyone to bring these back into America due to long-standing trade sanctions against Cuba.

The next block of Front Street, between Burnaby Street and Queen Street, is the most congested shopping area in all of Hamilton. As you walk west you'll see a number of excellent shopping and dining possibilities. The first major attraction is the famed **A.S. Cooper & Sons** department store with four floors of fine imported crystal, china, clothing, and unique gifts. The store is also home to a lunch-only restaurant called **Romancing the Scone**, which offers afternoon tea and delicious lunches on their open air harborview patio.

A bit further down the street you will come to the **55 Front Street Mall** where you will find another fine **Crissons** jewelry store as well as a small **Triminghams** gift & perfume boutique, the **Body Shop**, a 24 hour **ATM** bank machine, and the upstairs patio and restaurant area of **Pink's** delicatessen.

Next on the list is the always busy **Ye Old Cock & Feather** pub and restaurant, followed by the **Burrows Lightbourne** liquor store and **Penniston Brown** perfumes. Then you will find the **Archie Brown & Son** and **English Sports Shop** clothing stores where you should stop in to compare prices before heading next door to the world famous main branch of **Triminghams**. This massive upscale department store contains over three floors of the finest quality imported fragrances, men's and women's clothing, and unique gift items. On the top floor is the relaxing

Botanic Garden Tea Room which serves breakfast. lunch, and a casual afternoon tea. The last, but not least, shops on this major block are **H.A. & E Smiths** department store, and on the corner is **Goslings**, my favorite liquor and wine shop in Bermuda.

Up to Reid Street

If you have some extra time to shop, I suggest a walk up to **Reid Street**, which is just behind and runs parallel to Front Street. On the first couple of blocks on the far (north) side of this large commercial street you will find such retail business as the **Harbourmaster** luggage and leather goods shop and the main entrance to the **Phoenix Centre** pharmacy, just before the **Washington Mall**. This mall has several good shops including the **Tie Deck**, the **Mall Magazines** kiosk, the **Mall Photo Studio**, the **London Beauty Clinic**, and the sinfully delicious **Fourways Pastry Shop**.

FREE ACTIVITIES & SPECIAL EVENTS

The #1 Passenger Terminal (where the cruise ships dock) near the Visitors Service Bureau on Front Street hosts a vast assortment of special events during the low season. Among the free activities are a fashion show and afternoon tea each Monday at 3pm, a folk art and Gombey dancing revue on Tuesdays at 3pm, and a Bermudian cuisine cookery demonstration at 2:30pm on Wednesdays. Stop by either the Department of Tourism offices on Reid Street, or any branch of the Visitors Service Bureau for further details.

A bit further down the street you will also run into the **Yankee Store** gift shop, the **Bermuda Railway Co.** clothing store, the tiny **Red Carpet** restaurant, **Blue Ribbon Cleaners**, and finally a bit further down will be an the undiscovered gem of Hamilton's casual dining scene, **Archimedes** Greek restaurant, and the **Bombay Bicycle Club** Indian restaurant. On the near (south) side of Reid Street there's the **Aston & Gunn** and **Stephanel** clothing shops, **Bermuda Photo Craftsmen**, the **Coconut Rock** restaurant and club, **Crissons** jewelry shop, and, if you're hungry, you can grab a quick egg roll at **Chopstix** Chinese restaurant.

The Bermuda Underwater Exploration Institute (B.U.E.I.)

Located on the edge of Hamilton Harbour just alongside East Broadway (not far from downtown Hamilton's bustling Front Street) is the **Bermuda Underwater Exploration Institute**. This state of the art multimedia museum has become one of the islands' most popular and interesting venues for adults and children of all ages.

The B.U.E.I. is housed in a brand new two-floor waterside complex that has been specially designed to enclose dozens of special self-guided interactive exhibits that explore the past, present, and future of sea exploration along the reefs that surround Bermuda, as well as along the famous nearby sea mount that drops an incredible depth of 12,000 feet just off the island's south coast. It is this unusually steep decent to the ocean bottom that has made Bermuda the center of groundbreaking international oceanographic research for several decades now.

As soon as you enter the Institute's ultra-modern public lobby you may browse around the gift-shop or perhaps pop into one of the daily free screenings of sea related educational films in their magnificent 148-seat auditorium and lecture hall (it is not necessary to pay the B.U.E.I. admission fee to view these movies) and then purchase your ticket for the rest of the exhibits. The first exhibit, known as "**The Ocean Revealed**," focuses attention on the effects of the ocean on the rest of the planet. Among the more interesting elements on display here are exhibits showing the effects of undersea pressure on humans and machines, examples of early helmet diving and scuba gear, deep sea submersibles, and a full scale replica of the Bathysphere that was used by Drs. Beebe and Barton to descend a record breaking 3,028 feet below the surface back in 1934.

The next exhibit space you will encounter will be "**Underwater Bermuda**" which among other topics will also explain once and for all just why the sand along much of Bermuda is pink, and then compares it with sand samples from other famous beaches in America, Europe, Hawaii and Australia. Further along is the "**Lightbourn Shell Room**" which is lined by beautifully lit glass cases filled with an awesome collection of sea shells belonging to Jack Lightbourn, a Bermudian conchologist who is the only person on the island with a permit to collect shells. His vast assortment of multi-colored oysters, scallops, conch, and other rare specimens, is one of the finest in the world.

After leaving the shell collection you are then guided towards "**The Dive**," a twenty-seat multimedia deep sea capsule descent simulator. Before entering the simulator you will be shown a video narrated by author/diver Peter Benchley that will explain some of what to expect to see along your "voyage" stops at various points until reaching the bottom of the sea some 12,000 feet below. Upon entering the ride you will be seated and then briefed before the three-minute ride begins. Several video monitors display views outside the capsule as well as simulated readings from various navigational systems.

As the narrated "descent" begins you will feel movement and a change in depth as, at various depths, you can run across whales, jellyfish, sharks, and even giant squid, which are displayed across a large video screen. For adults and kids alike the ride is perhaps the most exciting part of you adventure at B.U.E.I.

Upon departing the ride you will enter the lower level of the building and proceed into "**The Sea Floor**" exhibit. Here you can listen to the sounds of marine animals at several state of the art listening posts, learn more about plate tectonics, see the effects of garbage dumping on the marine environment, study an echo sonar chart of the sea floor, and play an amusing interactive laser guided game called laser diver. Next on the agenda are a series of rooms called "**The Reef Area and Shipwreck Gallery**" that display locations and historical data about famous shipwrecks, artifacts and antiquities found nearby by famed Bermudian treasure hunter Teddy Tucker, and a new exhibit of gold and silver coins and jewelry found inside of wrecks.

The Bermuda Underwater Exploration Institute is a privately funded non-profit organization dedicated to the education of Bermudians and visitors alike. It is operated under the direction of a special foundation whose international advisory board includes famous marine biologists, treasure hunters such as Teddy Tucker, and renowned divers such as Peter Benchley (of "Jaws" fame). There is also a wonderful gourmet restaurant known as La Coquille serving fantastic lunches and dinners daily, several private meeting rooms, boutiques and logo shops, plenty of free parking, wheelchair accessible ramps and elevators, and volunteer guides to explain various elements of the submerged world.

B.U.E.I. is open from 10:00am until 6:00pm daily and has an admission fee of $9.75 per adult, $7.80 for senior citizens, $5 for children between 7 and 12 years of age, and is free for kids 6 and under when accompanied by an adult. Guided tours conducted by B.U.E.I. volunteers are scheduled on Tuesdays at 10:30am. For more details please contact their offices at Tel. 441/292-7219 or via Internet at www.buei.org.

The Circular Tour of Pembroke Parish

There are an assortment of several fine country lanes and roads leading out of Hamilton and into more residential areas. While most of these roads are far from being packed with major attractions, they offer a superb chance to see off the beaten path curiosities and the exclusive private residences of Pembroke parish.

The easiest of these routes would take you down the western edge of Front Street as it turns into **Pitts Bay Road**. As you walk or ride down this beautiful road it will first lead past a couple of fine shops at the edge of town including **William Bluck & Co.** with its English antiques, china, and crystal. Next door is the **Heritage House** that sells imported porcelain and pewter gifts, and contains an art and antique gallery. Across the street is the **Pegasus** old map and antique print shop.

A bit further down you will then pass the harborfront **Barr's Bay Park**, the exclusive **Waterloo House** inn, the large pink structure of the deluxe **Princess Hotel**, and then the suburbs. This area has several private estates that can be easily admired from the roadside. If you are walking, turn back into Hamilton when you start to run out of steam. Those of you on cycles and scooters should continue up the Pitts Bay Road as it winds its way towards the northwest sectors of Pembroke Parish.

For those interested in seeing native plants and trees in their natural environment, turn left (west) onto **Point Shares Road** for a short side trip to **Point Shares**. This beautiful untamed oceanfront area is home to several varieties of local flora and fauna such as the Bermuda Palmetto and Sedge that are protected in the **Butterfield Nature Reserve**. The reserve is always open, and admission is free. After a quick walk around the reserve, head back to Pitts Bay Road to continue your journey towards the tip of Pembroke. The street you are traveling on will soon merge into Spanish Point Road that will lead you into **Spanish Point**.

This suburban area faces onto the oceanfront **Spanish Point Park** with its small and rather basic swimming section, seaview picnic tables, a few fishing boat moorings, and an adjacent private boat club. The park is open from sunrise to sunset, and admission is free. This whole community is studded with somewhat hidden neighborhoods filled with plush multimillion dollar homes. Just take any of the side roads that veer to the left (south) near the park and head towards **Buck Point**, and you will be amazed at the opulence of this area. Spanish Point itself is less than impressive, but it may have been briefly inhabited by Spanish sailors as far back as in 1603. The park is open from sunrise to sunset, and there is no admission fee.

After a quick rest at the park, turn back onto Spanish Point Road, and head back (southeast) for a couple of minutes until reaching a better swimming area at **Admiralty House Park**. The park itself is based around the massive grounds of a private estate, once used to house the regional commander of the Royal Navy. These days it is just a tranquil spot for cliff walking, cave crawling, sunbathing, and fantastic swimming on its seldom visited **Clarence Cove** beach. The last time I was here there were even public bathrooms available. The park and the beach are open from sunrise to sunset, and admission is free.

The road forks at this point; stay to the left (north) and merge gently onto **North Shore Road**. Just a few minutes ride down this road lies the righthand (south) turnoff for **Langton Hill** where the dramatic **Government House** can be seen from a distance. Although not open to the public, this massive property is the official residence of the Governor of Bermuda, who is appointed by the Queen of England. The house and its luscious gardens have hosted many visiting dignitaries and foreign heads of state, and is worth a quick look from behind the fence. It was on these grounds in 1973 that then-Governor Sir Richard Sharples and his top aide were shot and killed by a militant Bermudian revolutionary who was later executed for his crimes.

When you return to North Shore Road, the next turnoff to the right (south) is for **Black Watch Pass**. This road leads to the fabled **Black Watch Well**. During a period of drought in the mid-19th century, British Black Watch Battalion troops began drilling deep down into this mostly limestone cliff to look for a new source of drinking water. While their efforts certainly paid off, an additional excavation of over 2.4 million cubic feet of rock was completed in the 1930's, in order to create the present-day pass. The pass is not very exciting.

From here, follow this road until it ends at the next intersection, where you will bear right (west) onto **Marsh Folly Road**. A couple of dozen meters (yards) down, turn left onto **Cedar Avenue**, which will lead past the **Government Tennis Stadium** with its 13 clay and plexi cushion courts (three are night-lit) that rent for as little as $5 per hour. Also nearby is **Bernard Park** where several weekly soccer, cricket, and softball games that can be watched for free. I have checked out some rather competitive and amusing amateur softball games here during the high season, and it's a way to meet the more spirited locals.

Cedar Avenue leads back into the rear of Hamilton, and passes the Spanish-style facade of **St. Teresa's Cathedral** (Roman Catholic), opened in 1927. Inside the open interior of this vast church you can view a gold and silver chalice given by Pope John Paul VI on his official visit to Bermuda in 1968. The church is open from 8am to 7pm daily with no admission fee.

TAXIS & SAFETY

Finding taxis in downtown Hamilton, or calling a taxi from any point in Bermuda, is never difficult. Since visitors and residents alike have been known to drink more than their fair share of alcohol, and the back of town (especially near Court Street) is not particularly the safest place to be walking around alone at night, I suggest spending the money to take a taxi back to your hotel after dark. Make sure to exercise the same cautions you would in an American city.

A couple of blocks further down the same street, you will pass along the side of **Victoria Park**. This beautiful five acre park contains impressive sunken gardens, nice shrub-laden walking paths, and a central Victorian bandstand where summertime concerts are held. The park is open from 8am until sunset daily, and admission is free.

Now that you are back in town (just behind City Hall), I suggest navigating the somewhat frustrating maze of one-way streets to return to your favorite spot for a meal or drink.

NIGHTLIFE & ENTERTAINMENT

Unlike most of the other parishes, the nightlife scene in Pembroke is centered within Hamilton, which full of all sorts of different places that stay open to either 1am, 3am, or in a few cases even until sunrise. The activities gets started pretty early.

Just after the offices close at around 5:00pm there are several bars that offer good happy hour specials. Among my favorites are **M.R. Onions** on Par-la-Ville Road, the **Hog Penny** pub on Burnaby Street, the crowded **Pickled Onion** upstairs restaurant and cocktail bar with live top 40 rock music on Front Street, and the extremely fun **Fresco's Wine Bar** on Chancery Lane. For folks that love jazz, a small local hang out called **Hubie's** on Angle Street (just off Court Street in a somewhat tough part of town) has great free live jazz music (and occasional jam sessions) on Friday and Saturday nights from 7:00pm until 10:00pm.

A bit later on, perhaps by 9:30pm, several places like the split level **Robin Hood** pub just a few minutes walk from downtown on Richmond Road and **Flanagan's Irish Bar** on Front Street, offer more lively live music to pull in the early party animals. Recently a new sushi bar/steakhouse/microbrewery called the **Surf Club** opened up on downtown Hamilton's harbor-front and has contracted popular entertainer Jimmy Keys to perform his pianoman/comedy show here on 5 night per week.

Shortly after midnight, the discos begin to fill up. While most discos' cover charges range from $5 to $20 per person depending on the hour of entrance, some hotel front desks can give you special reduced rate or complimentary admission passes. The 19 to 30 year old set hangs out at either the **Oasis** disco, **The Club** hip hop disco on Bermudiana Road, or the Aussie styled **The Beach** bar and electronic casino on Front Street.

Other hot spots, with more local patrons, include the **Spinning Wheel** on Court Street (be extremely careful around this part of town!), **Oscar's** on Victoria Street, and last but not least, the **Ambassadors Club** after-hours joint on Reid Street.

16. DEVONSHIRE PARISH

· The sleepy residential parish of **Devonshire**, named after the first Earl of Devonshire, is a collection of lush hilly interior lands and dramatic seaside estates. Situated in the geographic center of Bermuda on **Great Bermuda Island**, the parish has been able to maintain much of its peaceful non-commercial existence over the years – almost no hotels, restaurants, or large businesses can be found here.

Although there are fewer tourist attractions here than in any other parish in Bermuda, there are still some excellent places to visit and wander around. As you travel through Devonshire, you can see several private estates owned by wealthy individuals and multinational corporations, set back behind secure gates and fences, which contain wonderful gardens and even a few stables that are open to the public. The small windswept parks and hamlets that dot the northern coastline also provide a fantastic side trip when the weather is nice.

ARRIVALS & DEPARTURES

Those needing to be transported between any hotel or cottage colony in Devonshire Parish and the **Kindley Field International Airport** can take a taxi ride for about $20. The ride is about nine kilometers (6 miles) and usually takes about 15 minutes.

ORIENTATION

Devonshire Parish is a nice quiet place to get away from it all. While there are relatively few places to stay and dine in this area, it does offer several beaches and areas of splendid natural beauty such as the **Arboretum** and **Devonshire Bay Park**. While the seaside along **South Road** makes for a great point of reference, the small winding county lanes that pass along giant private estates are also well worth the effort to explore. As I have stated in various other parish orientations, to avoid getting completely lost you really should carry a copy of the free *Bermuda Handy Reference Map*, available at any Visitor's Service Bureau office.

GETTING AROUND

The north coast of Devonshire can be accessed by the appropriately named **North Shore Road**, which is served by the #11 public bus route. The peaceful countryside interior of the parish is dissected by **Middle Road** where you can hop on the #3 bus route.

Over on the southern coast, you will find the famed **South Road** where the #1 bus route can be found. No ferries serve this parish, and taxis can be rather hard to find unless you call for one of them to pick you up. The parish does offer nice walking alternatives, with its section #5 of the **Railway Trail**.

WHERE TO STAY

ARIEL SANDS BEACH CLUB, *South Shore Road, Devonshire. Tel. 441/236-1010, Fax 441/236-0087, Toll Free Reservations (Hotel Direct) at 800/468-6610 US & Canada. Internet:www.arielsands.com. Low season rack rates from $220 per double room per night (B.P.). High season rack rates from $340 per double room per night (B.P.). 47 ocean-view rooms, suites, and private cottages with air conditioning, private terraces or balconies, and private bathrooms. One restaurant, one outdoor dining terrace, and two bars. Cash, Traveler's Checks, and all major Credit Cards accepted. M.A.P. meal plan available for $40 per person per day. Member of "The Bermuda Collection" of fine hotels.*

The newly upgraded Ariel Sands Beach Club is a picture-perfect colony club resting along a sandy beach in quiet Devonshire Parish. Owned and operated by the friendly Dill family for several decades, it has recently gone through an impressive multi-million dollar renovation project. Besides a centrally located main clubhouse and dining area, the property is based around a series of traditional Bermudian style cottages dotting 14 acres of gently rolling hills with pretty views out onto the ocean.

Each of the 46 rooms, suites, and deluxe cottages feature seaview terraces or patios, bleached pine furnishings, remote control color cable television, direct dial telephone, walk-in closets with mini-safes, mini-refrigerators, coffee machines, hair dryers, and Bermudian artwork. Among the many new or improved facilities are a wonderful restaurant and outdoor seaside dining terrace, a European-style hydratherapy spa center, a conference center, an outdoor hot tub with Jacuzzi, a sauna, a fitness center, a unisex beauty salon, two of the island's only saltwater ocean reef swimming pools, an outdoor heated freshwater swimming pool, three outdoor tennis courts, a putting green, massage, room service, and a lovely beach area. Ariel Sands has become among the most relaxing and enjoyable places to stay in Bermuda.

Selected as one of my *Best Places to Stay* – see Chapter 10.

BURCH'S GUEST APARTMENTS, *North Shore Road, Devonshire. Tel. 441/ 292-5746; No Fax. High season rack rate from $80 per double room per night E.P. Low season rack rate from $80 per double room per night E.P. 10 air conditioned units with shared or private bathroom. No restaurant, but all of the apartments have kitchenettes. Cash, Check, and Traveler's Checks only, no credit cards accepted.*

This is a small converted home with five double bedrooms (three of them share bathroom facilities), and an additional wing with five small but comfortable one bedroom apartments with private bathrooms. Located just off the sea on the north coast of Devonshire, these are the most affordable accommodations in the whole parish.

This casual guest house offers a great location near the #10 and #11 public bus routes, and contains a nice little garden and pool area. Each of the guestrooms have television, radios, and telephones, while the apartments contain a reasonably sized kitchenette.

WHERE TO EAT

CALIBAN'S, *Ariel Sands Beach Club, South Shore Road, Devonshire. Tel. 441/236-1010. Open 12:00noon until 3:00pm and again from 7:00pm until 10:15pm daily. Dress code is Smart Casual. Reservations are suggested. Cash, Traveler's Checks, and all major credit cards accepted.*

Situated just off a remarkably beautiful stretch of sandy beach, Caliban's is a great place to enjoy a delicious and affordable meal. The restaurant's cozy indoor dining area is used during inclement weather and throughout much of the low season, while its fantastic palm lined split level outdoor dining terraces are full to capacity when the nice weather arrives.

Under the constant supervision of chef Carsten Stelzer from Germany, Caliban's presents a fresh approach to fine dining in a comfortable and relaxed waterfront setting. During lunchtime, you can feast on overstuffed tuna, chicken, and crab sandwiches, bacon beef burgers, deep fried shrimp and scallop platters, New York strip steaks cooked to order, towering club sandwiches, grilled chicken breast on a bun, croissants filled with smoked salmon, and some of the best grilled BLT's and club sandwiches in Bermuda.

The extensive dinner menu includes lobster and crab ravioli with brandy sauce, filo dough pastry stuffed with sautèed wild mushrooms in Port wine sauce, a great Bermuda fish chowder, chilled lobster salad, potato leek soup, Caesar salad, Mediterranean salad, roast rack of lamb with mint mousse, grouper filet stuffed with spinach and tiger prawns, grilled veal chops with mushroom sauce, coconut coated chicken in mango salsa, char-broiled beef tenderloin, and a host of seasonal specials and awesome desserts. During Bermuda's long lobster season there is also a special menu with either broiled or thermador locally caught spiny lobster served with all the trimmings. The restaurant also has a good selection of international wines at bargain prices.

The service here is first-rate, and the ambiance is most welcoming. A delicious lunch will cost about $40 per couple, while a four course dinner will set you back around $90 for two, plus drinks. Highly Recommended.

SEEING THE SIGHTS

The North Shore Route

As you take **North Shore Road** towards the east, across into Devonshire from its border with Pembroke parish, you will soon pass by the rather active **Devonshire Dock**. This is where several local fishing boats unload their daily catch amidst a swirl of hungry sea gulls. The best fish are often purchased by local residents waiting patiently at dockside each afternoon. Some people can even be found trying their own fishing skills from the edge of the dock once the boats have left.

Golf Diversion

About a kilometer (1,000 yards) further up the same road, you can't help but notice the pretty seaview links of the **Ocean View Golf Course** stretching across the right (south) side of the street. This 9-hole government-owned par 35 course with 2,956 yards of well manicured fairways and elevated tees offers a great rate of $25 per person during the day for either 9 or 18 holes, and an even better sunset special after 3:45pm of $12 per person, plus cart rentals.

Back to the North Shore Route

On the left (north) side of **North Shore Road**, facing the Atlantic Ocean, there is a large abandoned (and presumably haunted) mansion close to the equally unmaintained seafront **Robinson's Bay Park**. The last time I went to this park, the only thing I saw was a bunch of empty beer cans and a couple of laughing lovers sitting on the rocks.

A few hundred meters (yards) up the road, the next attraction that you will pass is a tranquil oceanview open space called the **Palmetto Park**, filled with trees and benches. Stop here on a sunny day to rest or picnic while enjoying a great view of the picturesque northern coastline. The park is open daily from sunrise to sunset and admission is free. This is also the area where section # 5 of the **Railway Trail** begins, and continues to run just about parallel to the seafront.

A couple of minutes further you will pass the entrance to the 18th century crucifix shaped **Palmetto House**. This odd manor house has changed little since it was first constructed, and now belongs to the

Bermuda National Trust. It contains a few rooms that are open to the public and display many unusual original period furnishings. Admission is free, but it is open on Thursdays only from 10am until 5pm.

As North Shore Road continues easterly up the coastline, there are no additional sights of specific interest to see, besides perhaps the huge seafront **Clay House Inn** bar and nightclub complex, offering live jazz and calypso music nights which may even include a performing hypnotist act, and the moderately priced **Burch's Guest Apartments**.

The Middle Road Route

When departing the outskirts of Hamilton and entering Devonshire via **Middle Road**, you will soon come to **Montpelier Arboretum**. This 20 acre park was developed by the government's Department of Agriculture, Fisheries, and Parks to help assure the future of several varieties of flora and fauna. It is a delightful place to visit, and has a few paths that can be hiked upon to view both the trees and several different types of birds. The arboretum is open from sunrise to sunset daily, and admission is free.

About another kilometer or so up Middle Road on the left side, you can wander up Tribe Road #1 to get to the **Lee Bow Riding Centre** which specializes in private instruction and $25 one hour group trail rides for kids 18 and under.

As Middle Road continues slicing eastward through the interior of this calm parish, the next stop that you should consider is over at the beautiful English-inspired **Old Devonshire Church**. Although originally built in the early 17th century, this simple little limestone and cedar beam church was completely rebuilt twice during its lifetime. The first rebuilding was in 1716, while an explosion in 1970 forced the structure to undergo a major restoration.

What can now be seen inside this small cottage-like building are several original surviving 16th century pieces of silver, cedar furnishings, and an old cross. Don't get confused by walking into the adjacent 19th century New Devonshire Church instead, a common mistake for first time visitors.

Almost directly across from the church, on the left (north) side of the road, you can be one of the few tourists to brave the wilds of the **Devonshire Marsh**. This untamed natural water basin consists of both the Freer Cox Memorial and Firefly nature reserves, which provide 10 acres of undeveloped marshlands set aside as a sanctuary for nature and bird lovers to observe unusual native plants, orchids, and endangered wild birds. The marsh, managed by the Bermuda Audubon Society, is always open, and admission is free.

Spectator Sports, Squash, & Pony Rides

A few hundred meters (yards) further east on Middle Road you can pop into the **National Sports Club**, which hosts an array of exciting spectator sports including weekend hockey, rugby, and cricket matches. Just next door, you can pop inside to reserve a stress relieving game of squash for about $6 per hour plus a $5 guest fee at one of 4 courts at the fully equipped **Bermuda Squash Racquets Association** clubhouse.

If you take the next right (south) turnoff onto **Chaingate Road**, which then bears left (west) and merges into **Watlington Road**, you will soon find the **Shiloh Ranch** – a great place to enjoy pony and hay rides. The rest of **Middle Road** has little of interest besides some fine private estates.

The South Shore Route

When you follow South Road to the east from Paget parish into Devonshire, you will first pass by the entrance of the oceanfront **Ariel Sands** resort. Continue onward to the marked right (south) side access road for **Palm Grove**. This beautiful private estate allows tourists to view its unusual pond, which contains a grass covered relief map of Bermuda. The pond itself is located near some citrus trees and Desmond Fountain statues. Please do not disturb the inhabitants of the mansion atop this pristine private estate. The pond is open to the public from 9am until 5pm each weekday, and admission is free.

Just a few dozen meters (yards) down South Road from the entrance to the pond, you should turn right (south) onto Devonshire Bay Road. At the end of this road you will come to **Devonshire Bay** with its fishing harbor, sheltered cove swimming area, old 19th century fortress, and walking trails with seabirds circling above. You have now reached the border of this fine parish.

NIGHTLIFE & ENTERTAINMENT

About the only nightlife that takes place in this sleepy community is over at the **Clay House Inn** on North Shore Road. Here you can catch one of their high season calypso/dance/local musical revues for about $25 per person including 2 drinks, or with a bit of luck you can watch a special live concert featuring internationally know jazz or reggae stars from about $35 per ticket.

17. SMITH'S PARISH

The parish of **Smith's**, originally named after Sir Thomas Smith, is situated on the eastern portion of **Great Bermuda Island**. With its abundant supply of both historical and natural attractions, this part of the country is perfect for a pleasant half day of relaxed sightseeing. The main points of commerce and vehicular traffic in Smith's can be found in the old pirate haven of **Flatts Village**, home to several restaurants and exceptional inns. Surrounded by the Atlantic Ocean to its north and south, and **Harrington Sound** on its eastern border, there is no lack of dramatic craggy coastlines and waterside parks to explore.

ARRIVALS & DEPARTURES

For transportation between Smith's Parish and the **Kindley Field International Airport**, you can either take a taxi ride for about $12 each way or contact Bee Line Transportation or Bermuda Hosts Ltd. a day or two in advance and pay around $14.50 per person round trip. The ride is about 7.5 kilometers (5 miles) long and usually takes about 10 minutes.

ORIENTATION

Smith's Parish is a tranquil area to spend a stress-free vacation and is located near plenty of interesting sights. Bordered by the Atlantic Ocean to the north and south, it also has a nice stretch of waterfront on **Harrington Sound**. The former pirate haven of **Flatts Village** and the **Spittal Pond Nature Reserve** make the best landmarks, but there are also several nice beaches around **John Smith's Bay** that are worth a visit.

GETTING AROUND

The parish's main byways include the windswept **North Shore Road** with service via the #10 and #11 public bus lines, and the ever popular South Road where you can catch the #1 bus. These two roads both run the full length of the parish and are connected by the estate-filled **Harrington Sound Road**.

Additional bus transportation on the # 3 line can be found along the central **Middle Road** and its extension of **Flatts Hill Road**.

Taxis can usually be found along the major roads, and a portion of section 5 of the **Railway Trail** can be followed along the parish's northernmost reaches.

WHERE TO STAY

PINK BEACH CLUB & COTTAGES, *South Road, Smith's. Tel. 441/ 293-1666, Fax 441/293-8935. Low season rack rates from $230 per double room per night (M.A.P.). High season rack rates from $340 per double room per night (M.A.P.). 81 rooms and suites with air conditioning, terraces or balconies, and private bathrooms. Two restaurants, one outdoor dining terrace, and one bar. Cash, Traveler's Checks, and all major Credit Cards accepted. Member of "Small Luxury Hotels of the World."*

This older cottage colony and its adjacent condo complex are situated on 16.5 acres of landscaped gardens that slope down to a wide sandy pink beach off the famous Tucker's Town district. Pink Beach offers 81 refurbished rooms and suites (many adjoin) in a series of colonial styled low-rise cottages. Most of the units have sea views and contain individually controlled air conditioners, private bathrooms, hair dryers, hardwood furnishings, balconies, color cable television, direct dial telephone, walk-in closets with mini-safes, am-fm clock radios, irons, available mini-refrigerators, toasters, hair dryers, and pull out sofas.

Among the many facilities here are a restaurant and outdoor seaside dining terrace, a freshwater swimming pool with sun deck, two outdoor tennis courts, a fireside lounge, business meeting and reception rooms, express laundry and dry cleaning, available babysitting, a daily high season schedule of activities and live entertainment, temporary membership privileges at many golf clubs, complimentary room service, and of course a superb beach with a fine nearby snorkeling reef that is full of friendly fish. Major ongoing condominium construction on the property may be of some concern to you.

ANGEL'S GROTTO, *Harrington Sound Road, Smith's. Tel. 441/295-6437; Fax 441/292-1243; Toll Free (Bermuda's Small Prop.) at Tel. 800/637-4116 US & Canada. High season rack rate from $110 per double room per night E.P. Low season rack rate from $90 per double room per night E.P. 7 air conditioned apartments with private bathroom. No restaurant, but all apartments have kitchens. Cash, Traveler's Checks, and most major cards accepted.*

Angel's Grotto consists of three white Bermudian style houses that face a private dock on the edge of the water on beautiful Harrington Sound. The property contains 7 modern and well furnished one and two bedroom apartments (most are soundview and have patios) all with telephone, television, huge kitchens, wall to wall carpeting, ceiling fans, additional pull-out sofas, and coffee machines. Located just a few minutes outside of Flatts Village, Angel's Grotto is quite close to several excursions, restaurants, and attractions. One of the best values in all of Bermuda might be this inn's massive 2 bedroom/2 bath soundview top floor apartment that can sleep up to 6 adults in total comfort.

BRIGHTSIDE APARTMENTS, *Flatts Village, Smith's. Tel. 441/292-8410; Fax 441/295-6968. High season rack rate from $75 per double room per night E.P. Low season rack rate from $75 per double room per night E.P. 13 air conditioned rooms and apartments with private bathroom. No restaurant, but all the apartment units have kitchens. Cash, Traveler's Checks, and all major cards accepted.*

Brightside is a nice modern family-owned and managed apartment complex just steps away from Flatts Village. It contains a couple of white Bermudian-style soundview buildings and an adjacent private cottage that are surrounded by fruit growing trees and large gardens.

The complex contains 2 double guestrooms, nine huge apartments (most are waterview), and a gigantic family sized two bedroom soundview cottage. The apartments and the cottage have great full-sized kitchens, televisions, telephones, radios, ceiling fans, simple wooden furnishings, sofas, and patios.

Facilities include excursions aboard their private 46' motor yacht, outdoor pool and sundeck, barbecue pit, soda and laundry machines, and an extremely friendly manager (Mr. Lightbourne) who will be glad to answer sightseeing questions, and even pick fresh fruit for you from the gardens.

WHERE TO EAT

NORTH ROCK BREWING CO., *10 South Shore Road, Smith's. Tel. 441/ 235-6633. Open 11:30am until 1:00am daily. Dress code is Casual. Reservations are not necessary. Cash, Traveler's Checks, and all major credit cards accepted.*

Located about two kilometer from the Bermuda Botanical Gardens, this wonderful English pub-style microbrewery, bar, and international restaurant is a true delight. Owners David & Heather Littlejohn have succeeded in creating a friendly and unusually affordable little restaurant that serves up some of the biggest and best casual lunches in all Bermuda. To top it all off, David also just happens to brew as many as eight different delicious varieties of tasty European-style beers in the exposed copper fermentation tanks located alongside the tables. The restaurant has an outdoor dining terrace as well as a brass and dark wood panel lined main dining room and bar area.

The menu here is a real mixture of influences from around the globe, but house specialties include their dark beer and Bermuda onion soup, the giant Mediterranean pasta salad with feta and tuna, tempura of Cajun spice marinated shrimp, chicken teriyaki kebabs with Thai ginger sauce, huge burger plates with fresh and crispy French fries, pan-fried snapper topped with bananas and almonds, lots of daily specials, and pasta primavera in a chunky tomato sauce. Perfect for either lunch or dinner, work up a big appetite before coming this way for one of the island's top values in relaxed dining. Expect a large tasty dinner for two to set you back somewhere around $49 plus brew, and a hearty home made lunch to cost even less.

THE HALFWAY HOUSE, *Flatts Village, Smith's. Tel. 441/295-5212. Open 7am until 11pm daily. Dress Code is Informal. Reservations are not necessary. Cash and Traveler's Checks only, no credit cards accepted.*

This small and unassuming little bar and restaurant on the outskirts of Flatts Village has a simple interior that will not impress you nearly as much as the great meals they create. Besides preparing the best home style breakfast this side of Hamilton, the friendly Bermudian chefs and waiters serve up a delicious assortment of down home cuisine including Portuguese red bean soup, Bermuda fish chowder, chef's salad, chicken salad, fish cakes on a bun (excellent!), steak sandwiches, croque monsieur, fried fish sandwiches, BLTs, burgers with toppings like avocado and Swiss cheese, the island's best french fries, chili, cheese ravioli, lamb curry, chicken parmigiana, deep fried fishermen's platters, 12 oz. sirloin steaks, and panfried wahoo.

The bar will gladly serve you anything from cappuccinos to a large selection of mixed drinks and imported beers. Dinner for two will only cost about $40, and lunch for 2 will be as little as $18, before adding beer.

SPECIALTY INN, *South Road, Smith's. Tel. 441/236-3133. Open 7:30am until 9pm daily. Dress Code is Informal. Reservations are not necessary. Cash and Traveler's Checks only, no credit cards accepted.*

This is your basic local restaurant where you can easily overhear all of the day's local gossip. Specialty Inn is located just below Collector's Hill on the western edge of Smith's parish. The menu here contains an assortment of American, Bermudian, and Italian selections including full breakfasts with eggs and omelets, dozens of sandwiches, Bermuda fish chowder, fried shrimp in the basket, chicken salad sandwiches, garden salads, cheeseburgers, fries, roast beef, steaks, cheese ravioli, fettucine Alfredo, lasagne, assorted 10" pizzas, and ice cream and home-made pies for dessert. This may be the least expensive place to enjoy a simple lunch or dinner, with a full dinner for two costing about $35 without wine.

SEEING THE SIGHTS

The North Shore Route

After taking **North Shore Road** to cross over the parish's western border with Devonshire, you will fist come upon **Penhurst Park**. This well-maintained 15 acre coastal park contains a few short walking trails, good places to fish, some wooden picnic tables, and a small swimming area. As you continue east for another 700 meters (yards) along the same street, you will soon see a small offshore island called **Gibbet Island** where local residents suspected of black magic and witchcraft were once burned at the stake.

North Shore Road dips south to trace its way around **Flatts Inlet**. This inlet is the primary source of the saltwater and aquatic life that fill **Harrington Sound**, and also is the main point of access for local boats to reach the open sea. In the old days of privateers and pirates, the most successful smugglers would unload their cargo here under a vail of darkness to avoid being searched by customs officials. These days, this side of the inlet is surrounded by a series of multimillion dollar waterview condominiums with their own yacht moorings and docks.

Across the street from the modern high-rise condos you will find the affordable **Halfway House** restaurant which serves fantastic breakfasts and lunches. At this point you have found yourself at one of the busiest intersections in this end of the country. Be patient here to avoid accidents, especially during rush hours when these roads get quite busy.

Just about here you will find a small pink cottage, which is the office of **Bronson Hartley's Underwater Wonderland**. Without the slightest doubt, this is Bermuda's most unusual and compelling sea excursion. They run a three and a half hour excursion aboard a 50' motor yacht with a special twist. This amazing trip climaxes with a 30 minute guided walk on the sea bottom during which clients wear large brass helmets (big enough to wear glasses under) and can actually reach out and touch the fish and sea anemones near several coral reef areas. They have both morning and afternoon departures (high season only), and this worth-while adventure only costs about $40 per person.

If you bear left (north) at the next intersection and head up the other side of the inlet and its border with Harrington Sound, you will first pass by the entrance to the **Palmetto Hotel** and its charming **Inlet Restaurant**. The next structure you will come to will be the **Flatts Bridge** that marks the border of this parish and leads to the various attractions on the east side of **Flatts Village**, which is actually in Hamilton parish.

The Harrington Sound Route

If you instead had turned right (south) at the last intersection before the **Flatts Bridge**, you will have merged onto **Harrington Sound Road**. This spectacular tree-shaded road curves towards the south and follows alongside the edge of peaceful **Harrington Sound**. This part of the sound is surrounded by dozens of Bermuda's most expensive mansions which are hidden from the roadside by centuries old stone walls. Every now and then you can try to catch a glimpse of one of these opulent waterfront estates.

At the southernmost point of the sound, you will see signs leading to the famous **Devil's Hole Aquarium**. The aquarium is actually a privately owned salt water cave that is connected to the sea by a series of underground tunnels. First opened as a tourist attraction in the 1840's, the owners have been charging the public to stand on covered wooden terraces overlooking a vast array of reef fish, turtles, eels, and sharks that inhabit the cave. The management supplies complimentary fishing lines with unhooked bait for visitors to feed the sea creatures with, and a small gift shop and the **Angels Wings Cafe** are also on premises. The aquarium is open from 9am until 5pm daily, and admission is $5 per adult and $2 per child under 13.

After feeding the captive fish, return to Harrington Sound Road as it now starts its curve around the east side of the sound. Soon you will find yourself passing right by the enchanting **Angel's Grotto Inn** with its breathtaking soundview apartments, before crossing into the southern part of Hamilton parish.

The South Shore Route

If you've taken **South Road** heading east from Devonshire you will cross into Smith's parish. Keep your eyes open for a side street on the left (north) side called **Collector's Hill Road**. After turning left onto this street (named after the local tax collector that once lived here), follow it to the very top until seeing the signs marking the entrance to **Verdmont**. This beautiful Georgian-style hilltop mansion dates back to 1710, and contains a large collection of antique period furnishings that have been assembled by the Bermuda National Trust.

When you visit this fine example of early 18th century architecture, make sure to spend some time seeing each of the 8 fireplace-filled rooms on its two charming floors and upstairs attic that are all connected by a fine cedar staircase. The first floor contains a Parlour Room with 18th century Bermudian cedar cabinetry and an English piano from the same period, the Drawing Room has 18th and 19th century portraits of former residents (the Smith Family) originally lit by the various hurricane candle shades like the ones on display, and a vast Dining Room featuring an early 18th century Bermudian gateleg table and cedar Wainscot chairs.

The second floor can be visited to see the two bedrooms containing four poster cedar beds and cedar highboy chairs, as well a secondary Parlour which exhibits a fine Chippendale cabinet and side chairs along with fine 18th century Chinese porcelain, and a French blue and gold tea set said to have been captured by local pirates while en route to America in 1815.

The third floor attic nursery contains an unusual assortment of curiosities including children's toys and an old rocking horse. Since many of the items are not marked with descriptive tags, be sure to ask for a free copy of the Verdmont Historic House pamphlet which details the stories of the unusual antiques, residents, and history of this fine estate. The mansion is open from 10am until 4pm from Monday through Saturday, and admission costs $4 per adult, no charge for kids under 12.

When you return to South Road and continue heading east for about 1.5 kilometers (1500 yards), the next attraction is **Spittal Pond Nature Reserve**. The park's Spittal Pond (now partially fenced in to protect the birds) is the heart of a 59 acre wildlife sanctuary that is managed by the Bermuda National Trust. This nature preserve, the largest in all of Bermuda, is home to hundreds of different lizards, crab, and bird species. There are a number of different trails that start at the reserve's east and west parking lots and head past the pond. If you visit here during the off season, you stand an excellent chance of seeing hundreds of migratory birds without even using binoculars.

The impressive nature trails then take you past cactus-filled coastal lookouts and towards the strange **Checker Board** of giant rectangular geological formations at land's end. Although at first it may seem a bit bizarre, this is the most magical spot in the whole country, and has captivated me for hours at a time.

Continue wandering down the poorly marked trails and you'll pass desolate seacliffs with Longtail nesting sites, scary open caves, and onward to the so-called **Spanish Rock**. This large boulder stands on a bluff overlooking the sea and carries an inscription containing a cross with the initials R.P. and the date of 1543. Although the rock was initially thought to have been carved on by Spanish sailors (hence the name Spanish Rock), most historians now believe that this was the work of shipwrecked Portuguese sailors. After decades of locals and tourists carving their own initials next to the original inscription, and the heavy erosion caused by the constant spray of sea water, the ancient cipher was replaced by a bronze replica. Unfortunately, some of the less intelligent visitors to this area have since started carving their own messages into the bronze plaque.

GUIDED TOUR OF SPITTAL POND

During the low season, a series of one hour free guided tours are given around Spittal Pond and its environs, starting at the eastern parking lot at 10:30am on Tuesdays, and 1pm on Fridays.

While walking through the reserve, please keep on the trails as not to disturb the somewhat nervous wildlife in the area. The reserve and its trails are open daily from sunrise to sunset and admission is free.

When you return to South Road and keep heading east, you will pass a series of smaller seaside nature reserves and parks that can all be visited, including **Watch Hill**, **Winterhaven**, and **Summerhaven**. The next interesting spot to pop into along the way, a few hundred meters (yards) up from the pond, is the **Harrington Hundreds** gourmet grocery store on the left (north) side of South Road. This is certainly the best place in Bermuda to buy fine imported foods at reasonable prices. Even if you are staying all the way on the other side of the country, I still suggest doing some of your grocery shopping here.

The last sight to stop in, before crossing the border into Hamilton parish, is **John Smith's Bay**. The roadside bay is home to a wide sandy beach that attracts fewer tourists than locals to its calm waters. The beach also has a few shallow areas that are great for snorkeling. There's a lifeguard and an inexpensive snack wagon during the summer and public restrooms. If you are looking for a nice uncrowded beach to be left alone on while touring Smith's, then this is the place!

NIGHTLIFE & ENTERTAINMENT

There is little in the form of nightlife in this parish beside the hotel-based pubs and lounges. Try the great **Ha'Penny Pub** in the Palmetto Hotel, or call to find out what's going on over at **Pink Beach**.

18. HAMILTON PARISH

The small yet heavily traveled parish of **Hamilton**, named after the Marquis of Hamilton, is located on the eastern end of **Great Bermuda Island**. So much of this wonderful parish is surrounded by salt water that no matter where you are, you are always just a few minutes away from either the sea, sound, or harbor.

On any given day, hundreds of tourists converge to Hamilton's dozens of interesting sights that provide much of the economy for this part of the country. No matter what your interest is, you will find enough things to do in this parish to keep you busy for at least one day, and perhaps keep you here well into the night. This is one of the easiest parts of Bermuda to walk around, since most of the commonly visited sights are well within walking distance of each other.

ARRIVALS & DEPARTURES

Transportation between the hotels of Hamilton Parish and the **Kindley Field International Airport** is both easy and affordable. Visitors can either take a taxi ride for about $13.75 each way, or you can contact Bee Line Transportation or Bermuda Hosts Ltd. a day or two in advance and pay around $12 per person round trip. The ride is about five kilometers (four miles) long and takes about five or six minutes.

ORIENTATION

Glamorous Hamilton Parish is home to some of Bermuda's wealthiest residents, best golf courses, and a good selection of accommodations in all price ranges. The area is bordered by the Atlantic Ocean as well as **Castle Harbour**, and is divided by a series of picturesque main roads. While getting lost here is hard to imagine, I suggest that you utilize the seashore as a major landmark and point of reference while wandering around.

GETTING AROUND

The parish's main roads include its coastal North Shore Road upon which you will have no trouble finding the #10 and #11 public buses, and the action-packed Harrington Sound Road which is served by the #1 and #3 buses.

Taxis are never a problem to find, and section 6 of the **Railway Trail** can also be hiked upon on the north shore.

WHERE TO STAY

CASTLE HARBOUR RESORT, *Harrington Sound Road, Hamilton. Tel. 441/293-2040; Fax 441/293-8288; Toll Free (HDQ) at Tel. 800/223-6388 US & Canada. High season rack rate from $251 per double room per night B.P. Low season rack rate from $130 per double room per night E.P. 420 air conditioned rooms and suites with private bathroom. Five restaurants with 2 additional outdoor terraces and several bars. Cash, Traveler's Checks, and all major credit cards accepted.*

Castle Harbour is a deluxe harborfront resort hotel located on a huge 245 acre property at the edge of exclusive Tucker's Town. The dramatic main wing was constructed in England in the 1920's and was shipped to Bermuda piece by piece, although modern terraced wings have since been added. All of the 420 beautiful rooms and suites have cable television, telephones, clock radios, hair dryers, ironing boards and irons, mini refrigerators, and fine furnishings. Most rooms have a balcony facing either the harbor, pool, or gardens.

Facilities include a private 18 hole championship golf course, three outdoor pools with sundecks, 2 hot tubs, 2 private beaches, saunas, a health club, 6 tennis courts, cruise excursions, and a scuba and watersports center. Other services include supervised high season children's programs, in room movies, room service, soda machines, a beauty salon, several boutiques, and dedicated non-smoking floors. There is an abundance of fine eating establishments ranging from the formal Windsor to Terrace Pool snackbar, and the Mikado Japanese restaurant and sushi bar. Castle Harbour has the rooms, views, service, facilities, and amenities to please just about everybody. Highly Recommended.

GROTTO BAY BEACH RESORT, *Blue Hole Hill, Hamilton. Tel. 441/293-8333; Fax 441/293-2306; Toll Free (Direct) at Tel. 800/582-3190 US; Tel. 800/463-0851 Canada. High season rack rate from $180 per double room per night C.P. Low season rack rate from $110 per double room per night C.P. 201 air conditioned rooms and suites with private bathroom. Two restaurants with an additional outdoor terrace and 2 bars. Cash, Traveler's Checks, and all major credit cards accepted.*

Grotto Bay is a large affordable bayfront resort hotel situated on 21 acres of peaceful grounds in the Bailey's Bay area. The resort is comprised of a series of 11 modern 2- and 3-story terraced waterview lodges which surround the main reception and facilities building, each containing between 15 and 30 nice waterview rooms and suites which are well maintained. All of the property's 198 bright and airy pastel colored rooms are identically designed and contain television, radio, telephone, mini safes, small refrigerators, hair dryer, coffee maker, comfortable bleached pine furnishings, and private terraces. Many rooms can be made to adjoin for family use, and there are 3 huge two bedroom suites.

Meals can be taken at either the centrally located Hibiscus Room, or in the afternoons at the Pool Terrace. A complimentary afternoon tea is presented in the Greenhouse Room, while cocktails are served in the Rum House Lounge. Facilities here include a calm private beach, heated outdoor pool with swim up bar and sundeck, hot tub, natural caves to both explore and swim in, 4 tennis courts, glass bottom boat, sailboats, windsurfing, waterskiing, snorkeling, and scuba. A full day supervised children's program with off-site excursions and kids-only dinners are available for free during the high season. Grotto is a great place to stay for people of all ages. Highly Recommended.

CLEAR VIEW SUITES, *North Shore Road, Hamilton. Tel. 441/293-0484; Fax 441/293-0267; Toll Free (Direct) at Tel. 800/468-9600 US. High season rack rate from $170 per double room per night E.P. Low season rack rate from $110 per double room per night E.P. 12 air conditioned suites and apartments with private bathroom. No restaurant, but several units have kitchenettes. Cash, Traveler's Checks, and most major Credit cards accepted.*

Clear View is a collection of modern pink seaside cottage buildings not far from Flatts Village with several one, two, and three bedroom suites and apartments. With its tranquil location atop a rocky bluff on the north shore, this small and intimate suite complex offers moderately priced seaview accommodations withTVs, phones, radios, living rooms, and a private terrace. Some units also offer kitchenettes and fireplaces.

The facilities at this property include two swimming pools, a tennis court, a small cove swimming area which is also great for fishing, an outdoor barbecue grill, and a nearby bus stop with service to several restaurants, shops, and attractions. A favorite haunt of visiting artists, this casual and friendly property is in a great location for vacationers of all ages. Children are warmly welcome here, and both cribs and hourly babysitting services are available upon request.

WHERE TO EAT

TOM MOORE'S TAVERN, *Walsingham Lane, Hamilton. Tel. 441/293-8020. Open 7pm until 9:30pm daily. Dress code is Jacket Required and Tie requested. Reservations required. Cash, Traveler's Checks, and all major credit cards accepted.*

A fantastic gourmet restaurant located inside of an opulent 17th century mansion loaded with historical links to the legendary Irish poet Tom Moore who spent several days writing in this house and its gardens back in 1804. The building was converted into a tavern for several years until being taken over by Bruno Fiocca and lovingly transformed into one of the world's finest dining establishments.

The restaurant features several intimate dining rooms on two floors, and a beautiful wooden upstairs bar. The restaurant is embellished with casement windows, cedar walls, a fine central fireplace, beautiful imported fabrics, and the finest European silver, china, and crystal settings. Service here is exceptional, with a rather experienced and professional staff. Executive chef Benon Leszkowski has created a superb a la carte menu featuring incredible French and Italian inspired offerings like their delicious oysters wrapped in spinach and poached in champagne, quenelles with crayfish sauce, an unbelievably light scallop mouse, escargots with garlic, Bermuda fish chowder, cream of corn soup with sorrell and smoked scallops, zesty scampis broiled in wine and garlic, a superb parchment baked filet of sole, fresh Bermuda lobster, veal tenderloin flamed with sherry and shallots, an amazing sirloin steak flamed with cognac and peppercorns, lamb chops sauteed with truffles and herbs, roast duckling with raspberry vinegar, and quail baked in a pastry puff after being stuffed with truffels, morels, and goose liver.

The equally serious dessert menu contains a daily souffle, crepes Suzzete prepared at your tableside, and a selection of fruits, pastries, sherbets, and cheeses which are brought by on a silver Parisian dessert trolley. An extensive 26 page wine list includes hundreds of vintages from all over the world including '88 Cristal Champagne, half bottles of '81 Chateau D'Yquem, '61 Chateau Lafite Rothschild, '87 Batard Montrachet, '85 Chateau Ducru-Beaucaillou, '89 Antinori Tiganello, '88 Brunello di Montalchino, '86 Opus One, '91 Napa Valley Cakebread, and glasses of '63 Croft Vintage Port, Martell L'Or Cognac, '45 Laubade Armagnac, and assorted Calvados, Eau de Vie, and Grappa. To sum this all up properly, if I could only have one fine dinner in Bermuda, I would choose to have it here! A fine dinner for two without wine will end up costing about $165. Highly Recommended.

MIKADO, *Castle Harbour Resort, Harrington Sound Rd., Hamilton. Tel. 441/293-8020. Open 6:30pm until 10pm. Closed on some Mondays. Dress code is Smart Casual. Reservations required. Cash, Traveler's Checks, and all major credit cards accepted.*

I didn't expect to enjoy Bermuda's only Japanese Steak House, but in fact I was pleasantly surprised. The restaurant is located on the ground floor of the Castle Harbour hotel and is decked out with a lacquered modern oriental decor. You can choose to be seated at either the modern sushi bar, traditional low rise Japanese style tables, or better yet at one of several 8 person hibachi grill tables where the theatrical Teppanyaki chefs prepare your meals with acrobatic throws of their knives.

The large menu features such classic selections as Tori soup, Miso soup, shrimp tempura, vegetable tempura, vegetable fried rice, a huge assortment of sushi and sashimi, Norimaki, and a choice of complete five-course Teppanyaki dinners featuring either chicken, sirloin, filet mignon, lobster tail, shrimp, scallops, or salmon, all of which are cooked while you watch. The desserts include fried ice cream, grasshopper mint pie, green tea ice cream, and fresh fruit. They also offer a good choice of Japanese sake, plum wine, beer, and mixed drinks. Expect a complete dinner for two without drinks to cost about $85.

SWIZZLE INN, *Blue Hole Inn, Hamilton. Tel. 441/293-9300. Open 11am until 10:30pm daily. Closed Mondays from December to March. The Bar serves drinks until 1am. Dress code is Informal. Reservations are not necessary. Cash, Traveler's Checks, and all major credit cards accepted.*

With its perfect roadside location amidst the many attractions of Bailey's Bay, this extremely popular antique bar and restaurant is packed almost all the time. The simple wood interior is studded with patrons' business cards plastered all over the walls. The lively crowd of tourists and locals that tend to frequent this rather amusing establishment usually end up getting fairly inebriated within the first 10 minutes of their visit.

Besides turning out hundreds of pitchers each day of Bermuda's most potent Rum Swizzles (thus the phrase "Swizzle Inn - Swagger Out"), they serve up some great pub fare including crab bisque, red bean soup, Caesar salads, conch fritters, shepard's pie, gigantic Swizzle burgers, fish sand-wiches, English-style fish and chips, onion rings, Herman's lemon chicken, coconut shrimp, and the famous Johnnie's bread pudding with brandy sauce. You can sit either in one of the simple dining rooms indoors, but if the weather is good I suggest opting for a table on the upstairs patio. You can even play darts while you wait for your table.

Expect a lunch here to set 2 people back about $26, and dinner to start at around $50 per couple, without Swizzles or drinks included.

SEEING THE SIGHTS
The North Shore Route

After crossing over the **Flatts Bridge** into the eastern side of **Flatts Village**, you have just crossed into Hamilton parish. This side of the village contains a few great spots to view, including the fantastic **Bermuda Aquarium, Natural History Museum, and Zoo**, which besides the beach has become Bermuda's number one tourist attraction. Founded in 1942, this large soundview complex has recently been able to acquire an additional $1.5 million to renovate and expand the facilities, which attract over 120,000 visitors yearly. Presently, the complex offers a wide range of exciting exhibits which should be seen by all visitors to the nation. Upon entry, you will first find yourself inside the two-room indoor **Bermuda Aquarium** wing with its 26 tanks filled with unfiltered seawater from Harrington Sound. Make sure to pick up one of the complimentary audio wands which will help guide you past the various tanks containing spiny lobsters, tilefish, groupers, moray eels, sergeant major fish, sea anemone, blue angle fish, parrotfish, squirrelfish, bream, flounder, pudding wife, jewelfish, and squid, and sardines who are kept under conditions that, although somewhat cramped, tend to mimic their natural environment. The most memorable sights in this wing are without doubt the queen triggerfish, loggerhead turtles, molly miller, clawed spiney lobster, Nassau grouper, cowfish, rainbow parrotfish, and the adopted green turtle named Stitch who was rescued after being washed ashore on Elbow Beach.

After passing by the outdoor harbor seal pools, you will be led inside the **Bermuda Natural History Museum**. This part of the complex was designed as an entertaining and educationally motivated collection of local geology, ecology, and scientific exhibits that are all rather well explained. This fine museum is currently under the expert direction of famed curator and marine biologist Dr. Wolfgang Sterrer, author of the wonderful book *Bermuda's Marine Life*. You will find well presented photos, maps, and diagrammatic explanations about the islands' volcanic origins, indigenous plant and tree life, migratory birds, ocean currents, climate, caves, seacoast, and interior lands. One of the more unusual items on display is the documentation and 2 ton circular Bathysphere used by New York Zoological Society's Dr. William Beebe in 1930 to dive a record 3028 feet off the coast of Bermuda. Also at the exit of this building you can take a quick look at all of the world's record game fish catches achieved in this country.

After leaving the museum, you will then pass by a series of outdoor cages, aviaries, ponds, and pens that comprise the **Bermuda Zoo**. Here you can watch many unusual as well as common creatures from all over the world including otters, two toed sloths, golden lion tamarins, barn owls, ducks, flamingos, alligators, iguanas, tortoises, and a couple of bizarre animals such as Malayan water monitors and Madagascar ringtail lemurs.

The complex also contains a summertime children's petting zoo, an interactive audio-visual enhanced invertebrate house, a wildlife rehabilitation center for sick and injured wildlife and birds, a weekend student Discovery Room and teaching program, public restrooms, and a nice little gift shop. Over the next several years, the complex is going to be expanding even more, with a proposed 145,000 gallon reef tank, dozens of new bird, mammal, and reptile exhibits, and a tropical waterfall environments full of even more exotic creatures. Admission here is valid for all wings and exhibits throughout the complex. The hours are from 9am until 4:30pm daily, and admission is $6 per adult, $3 per child under 13, and free for kids under 5.

After spending some quality time at the aquarium, museum, and zoo complex, head back onto North Shore Road and continue for about 600

SEAL & TURTLE FEEDINGS!

During the low season, after paying your admission to the complex, you are invited to attend a series of special events. On Tuesdays there are free guided tours of the Aquarium every half hour from 2pm until 4pm, including a seal feeding at 1:15pm. On Saturdays you can watch the turtles being fed at 1:15pm.

---

meters (yards) until reaching the **Bermuda Railway Museum** on the left (north) side of the road. Housed in a former railway waiting station, this small and somewhat confused museum contains a collection of relics, photos, furnishings, and memorabilia from the yellow narrow-gauge trains that were operated by the Bermuda Railway Company.

Here you can find out more about the English-built 2 and 4 car diesel trains which ran the length of Bermuda for less than 20 years ending in 1948. The old rattle and shake, as it was referred to by the locals, had carried up to 14,000,000 fares until cars became a more common sight on the island. Public interest in rail service declined, and the old tracks and engines were sold off to Central America. Nowadays, most of the original route has been converted into the Railway Trail walking paths which still pass by this building. The museum is open from 9am until 4pm Tuesday through Saturday, and admission is free.

After leaving the museum, continue heading up North Shore Road for another 850 meters (yards) or so until reaching the parking lot for beautiful **Shelly Bay Beach**. This beautiful wide sandy roadside beach has an unusually calm and shallow basin where you can walk out in waist deep water to cool off or even fish. Since this is one of the few beaches along the northern coast, it is seldom crowded, has lots of trees to sit under, and has several facilities including a beach house with public restrooms, exceedingly cold showers, high season snack bar and snorkel equipment rental shop, and its own bus stop.

Nearby is the small but peaceful mangrove-filled **Shelly Bay Park and Nature Reserve** where you can hike about or relax and enjoy a scenic picnic on one of the wooden tables. The beach and park are both always open, and admission is free.

After getting a well-deserved tan, keep heading up (east) on the same road until reaching **Crawl Hill**. This high elevation seaside park once looked out over Bermuda's famed 17th and 18th century cedar wood boat building industry. From here you can see all the way up and down the dramatic northern coastline, and if you're lucky you might even see a Longtail nest.

About another 2 kilometers (2000 yards) further east on the same road, you should turn right (south) onto **Trinity Church Road** to get a glimpse at the exterior and adjacent graveyard of the **Holy Trinity Anglican Church**. Originally built in 1623 on the side of **Mt. Wyndham**, this peaceful and rather private church has been enlarged and updated several times since its days as a one room thatched roof parish church. The building still retains much of its former structure, beauty, and simplicity. Since the church is not open to the general public, it makes for a quick stop with great panoramic views and peaceful gardens.

CONEY ISLAND, BERMUDA - NOT BROOKLYN!

*At this point you can take a short side trip on the the small unmarked road straight ahead to reach remote **Coney Island**. This peaceful island was once the sight of an old horse ferry landing and some cottages which are all but in ruins. The most interesting reason to come here now is for its lovely park. During the warmer months, cricket matches often can be watched for free on the park's large cricket pitch. There are also a few trails that wind around the island's shoreline.*

Now head back up to North Shore Road where you will turn right (east) and continue to follow it until reaching the bend in the road. As North Shore Road bends to the south to follow the coast of **Bailey's Bay**, you will soon pass the next major tourist attraction at the **Bermuda Perfumery & Gardens**. This 18th century mansion is the headquarters of family owned Lili Bermuda, the manufacturer of naturally produced men's colognes and women's perfumes with names like Jasmine, Bambu, and Frangipani. The factory has opened a small exhibition on the age old en fleurage fragrance extraction process, and gives free guided tours every 20 minutes that take you through the factory and finish at their outlet shop.

The property also includes over 5 acres of gardens you can tour that are used to grow most of the flowers needed in the production of these scents. The factory and its gardens are open 9am until 5pm from Monday through Saturday, and 10am until 4pm on Sunday, admission is free.

At the next intersection, bear left (east) onto **Blue Hole Hill**. This small road will take you past the refreshing **Bailey's Ice Cream Shop** where you can get huge sundaes, cold shakes, frozen yogurt, chili, salads, and sandwiches. The road then leads onto a small workshop which is also the showroom of the **Bermuda Glass Blowing Studio**. Here you can watch a team of masters and their apprentices use hollow steel rods to manipulate blobs of molten glass in and out of a 2500 degree furnace. By the time the glass blower is finished, they have colored and shaped these blobs into beautiful plates, cups, statues of fish, and small figurines which sell for between $8 and $160 each. The staff take an hour off at noontime, and leave the workshop by 4pm. The studio gives special workshops to the public on the last Sunday of each month. The studio is open from 9am until 5pm daily, and admission to the workshop area is $1 per person.

A few steps further down Blue Hole Hill, you can't help but notice the **Swizzle Inn**. This is perhaps the most famous bar and restaurant in all of the country. With a logo that states "Swizzle Inn - Swagger Out," you get the feeling that their clients mean business. Besides serving the best rum swizzles in town, they offer a full lunch and dinner menu featuring everything from pub food to complete dinners. Patrons have been known to add their business cards to the walls (which have little uncovered space left). This is also a great place to buy a souvenir T-shirt.

Area Beaches & Watersports

A few more dozen yards (meters) down the same street, you will pass the entrance to the moderately priced seaside **Grotto Bay Beach Resort**, which offers rather nice accommodations, private beaches, a natural cave toswim in, and a huge assortment of excursions and facilities.

The hotel is also home to a branch of the **South Side Scuba Watersports** center which offers high season two-tank morning scuba dives for $60, an $85 beginners resort course with sea dive, and rentals of windsurfing boards for $20 per hour, Boston Whalers for $45 per hour, kayaks for $12 per hour, and Sunfish for $50 per 4 hours. For those interested, you can also visit **Island Water Skiing** to have group lessons for $60 per half hour or $90 per hour, and **Bermuda Water Sports** can take you on a 3 hour snorkelling and glass bottom boat cruise for $32 per person.

Back to The North Shore Route

Since Blue Hole Inn leaves the parish at this point, turn around and head to the last intersection (near the ice cream parlor), and turn left (west) onto **Wilkinson Avenue**. About 300 meters (yards) down the road you will find a well marked turnoff on the left (east) side of the street that leads to **Crystal Caves**. These are the most impressive of the area's many caves and were first discovered by a pair of boys chasing a runaway ball down a small hole in the ground. The hole was soon excavated to uncover a massive cavern over 100 feet below surface level. The caves include an underground salt water ocean feed lake that rises and falls with the tides and can reach up to 18 meters (54 feet) in depth. The cave's top and bottom of the caves are covered by limestone stalagmites and stalactites forming unusual patterns, including what the guides point out as the Manhattan skyline. It's important to remember that these giant formations are naturally created at the rate of only 1 cubic inch per 100 years.

Guided tours are given by shouting staff members who lead you down a long slippery staircase and onto a series of floating bridges. Don't touch the formations, or else you will be in violation of the law! *The caves are open from 9:30am until 4:30pm daily (except for low season when it may close on Mondays and for the whole month of January) and the required group tours depart about every 30 minutes throughout the day. Admission is $4 per adult, $2 for kids under 12, and free for children under 4.*

The Harrington Sound Route

At the next intersection, turn left (south) onto **Harrington Sound Road** and follow it for a few minutes until reaching the large sign for the fabulous **Tom Moore's Tavern** restaurant and its adjacent jungle and streams. This absolutely amazing formal gourmet restaurant is housed in a historic mansion, which was first erected in 1652 for the Trott family. In the early 1800's the then unknown Irish poet Tom Moore was officially assigned to Bermuda as a Registrar of the Court of the Vice-Admiralty. Soon he became a frequent guest of the Trott family and started a well documented affair with Mrs. Hester "Nea" Tucker, the wife of Moore's next door neighbor.

It has been said that he wrote many of his most famous (and deeply romantic) pieces in this very house, under the Calabash tree that sits on the heart of the estate grounds. Although it was converted into a local tavern some 90 years ago, the building was recently completely renovated and has become perhaps the finest continental structure in Bermuda. The adjacent grounds are home to streams filed with snapper, and a small Bermuda National Trust property called the **I.W. Hughes Nature Reserve**, which is a small jungle-like park (sometimes referred to as Tom Moore's jungle) that can also be visited.

After leaving the enchanting grounds around the restaurant, take a left (south) turn back onto **Harrington Sound Road**, and follow it for just a minute or two until reaching the **Leamington Caves**. Much like the

Crystal Caves, which are in fact more impressive, these caves offer guided tours down an assortment of lighted walkways that bring visitors through a series of stalagmite and stalactite formations.

Just above the caves is the colonial-style **Plantation Restaurant** which serves somewhat casual lunches and more formal dinners daily during the high season. *The caves are open from 9:30am until 4pm Monday through Saturday (except from late November until February when it they are always closed) and admission is $3 per adult, $1.50 for kids under 12, and free for chldren under 4. A special deal allows lunch patrons of the Plantation restaurant to visit these caves for free.*

Harrington Sound Beaches & Watersports

After the caves, continue south on the same road passing by the entrance road to the massive harbor front **Castle Harbour Resort**. Originally constructed in England in the 1920's and shipped over piece by piece to its current location, this impressive full service resort is now managed by Marriott Hotels. Besides a vast array of fine eating establishments in all price ranges, this huge hotel has several lounges, watersports facilities, sea excursions, pools, tennis courts, private beaches, and corporate meeting and convention rooms.

Above all, many guests come here for their famous **Castle Harbour Golf Club**. The hotel's internationally renowned Charles Banks designed private 18-hole championship par 71 course has 6440 yards of seriously challenging oceanview and inland greens with plenty of wind to contend with. The course charges $85 per person per round plus cart rental fees, and offers a special sunset rate of $50 per round after 4:30pm, but have your hotel's front desk call well in advance to reserve tee off times.

The resort's marina hosts another branch of the **South Side Scuba Watersports** center, which offers high season parasailing for $40 per person, and rentals of windsurfing lessons for $25 per hour, kayaks for $12 per hour, and Puffers for $60 per 4 hours. Also at the resort is the **Club Wet 'n' Wild** jet ski rental club with Wave Runners starting at $40 per half hour.

Back to The Harrington Sound Route

After popping in on this dramatic resort and golf course, continue on Harrington Sound Road for about 400 meters (yards) until turning left (south) at the intersection of **Paynter's Road**. I hope not to confuse you too much, but the area you will be passing through before reaching the next attraction is actually the members-only Mid Ocean Golf Club in the exclusive residential area of **Tucker's Town**, which is actually part of St. George's parish, and will be dealt with in the next chapter.

As **Paynter's Road** winds its way down for about 900 meters (yards), turn left (west) onto **South Road**. A few minutes after following South Road to the west, you are back in the boundaries of Hamilton parish and can keep your eyes open for the entrance on the right (north) side of the road for the **H.T. North Nature Reserve**, consisting of Mangrove Lake and Trott's Pond. This rarely visited area contains a sanctuary for wildlife as well as local flora and fauna.

NIGHTLIFE & ENTERTAINMENT

Most of the nightlife in this parish centers around the **Swizzle Inn**. Over at **Castle Harbour**, you can disco dance the night away at **Blossom's Dance Club**, which also features a few nights of Karioke, or eat at their more tranquil **Golf Grill** serving fantastic pizzas. **Grotto Bay** may also be offering special evening entertainment.

19. ST. GEORGE'S PARISH

Bermuda's easternmost parish of **St. George's**, named after the patron saint of England, is steeped in history and adventure. Situated on a a series of islands including **St. David's Island**, **St. George's Island**, and a small corner of **Great Bermuda Island**, the area was first inhabited when the crew of the shipwrecked *Sea Venture* landed ashore near what is now **Fort St. Catherine** on July 28, 1609.

Although most of these Englishmen and Englishwomen would only stay here for some 10 months before finishing the construction of cedar vessels to take them to Jamestown, Virginia (their original destination), a couple of them decided to remain. Two years later, a party of 60 settlers would arrive on these shores to permanently colonize the islands in the name of England, thus making the town of St. George the capital of Bermuda for over 100 years. During this time its coastline became home to some of Bermuda's major harbors and whaling ports. When the government finally moved to Hamilton in 1815, the parish was drawn into a serious economic recession.

Throughout its long and occasionally turbulent history, St. George's has seen more than its fair share of shipwrecks, hurricanes, divided loyalties, blockade running, espionage, and prosperity. Despite all of this, several parts of the parish have been able to keep their original 17th and 18th century architecture and ambiance alive to this day.

If you are visiting Bermuda during the high season, the best days to walk around this town are Monday and Tuesday when the cruise ship passengers are usually touring other parishes in the country. The feisty residents of this part of Bermuda are a bit different from most other Bermudians, especially those from the somewhat remote St. David's Island, and all have dozens of wonderful stories to tell interested visitors.

If you really want to get a good feel for this parish, expect to spend at least one whole day (if not two) to explore it. Be sure to bring some comfortable shoes and a bathing suit, because you will be doing plenty of swimming and walking along the way.

ARRIVALS & DEPARTURES

Visitors can travel between the hotels and inns of St. George's Parish and the **Kindley Field International Airport** by taking a taxi ride for about $11 each way. The ride is about four kilometers (three miles) long and takes only about seven minutes.

ORIENTATION

Almost all of the visitors to this parish will find themselves spending much of their time walking around the city of **St. George's**. The various church towers in the heart of the city can be seen from far away, and when cruise ships dock here they too are good landmarks to use while navigating around town. If you intend to visit more remote areas, like the peaceful settlements around **St. David's Head**, bring a copy of the free *Bermuda Handy Reference Map*, available at any Visitor's Service Bureau office and which will help you avoid getting totally lost.

GETTING AROUND

Getting around the attractions of this parish is no problem. St. George's Island has a series of connected roads that reach from one end to the other and are serviced by public bus routes #1, #3, #6, #10, and #11. Most of the sights on St. David's Island can be reached by public bus route #6, while the exclusive Tucker's Town section on the southeast corner of Great Bermuda Island can be accessed by public bus route #1.

Taxis are fairly abundant in most parts of this parish, and a special shuttle service is offered by **St. George's Mini Bus Service** *at Tel. 441/297-8492*, which can take people between some of the most heavily traveled parts of the parish.

Walking is the most prevalent form of transportation used by tourists in much of this area, with excellent self guided tour possibilities in the main town of St. George and its beach and fortress-laden outskirts. The final section 7 of the **Railway Trail** also cuts across the northern coast of St. George's Island.

WHERE TO STAY

ST. GEORGE'S CLUB, *Rose Hill, St. George, St. George's. Tel. 441/297-1200; Fax 441/297-8003. High season rack rate from $250 per double room per night E.P. Low season rack rate from $165 per double room per night E.P. 69 air conditioned 1 and 2 bedroom units with private bathroom. Two restaurants and one bar. Cash, Traveler's Checks, and all major credit cards accepted.*

This unique 17 acre apartment colony is located on a hillside just steps behind the heart of downtown St. George. Although is is actually a timeshare vacation property, it is entirely possible to rent unoccupied apartments by the day or week. Since the property has been in receivership, the rates have been kept fairly low and represent a genuine bargain. The most luxurious of these units are the newer 2-bedroom townhouse style apartments, but all units have full kitchens, television, radio, telephone, lots of sun-filled interior space, modern comfortable furnishings, and either a nice balcony or a lawnview patio.

The facilities here include a nearby 18 hole golf course, access to a private beach club, two restaurants, a pub, three swimming pools, shops and boutiques, a minimarket, and beautiful garden-filled grounds. I was rather impressed with this place on my last visit, and I am sure that after someone has bought the property (which should happen by the time you read this book) it will be an even better place to stay.

AUNT NEA'S INN, *1 Nea's Alley, St. George's, St. George's. Tel. 441/297-1630, Fax 441/297-1908. Internet: www.auntneas.com.bm. Low season rack rates from $110 per double room per night (C.P.). High season rack rates from $135 per double room per night (C.P.). 11 deluxe rooms and suites with air conditioning and private bathrooms. One breakfast room. Cash, Traveler's Checks, and most major credit cards accepted.*

Located in a lovingly converted 18th century mansion just a couple of minutes' walk from the center of town, Aunt Nea's Inn is a delightful place to stay while in St. George's. The historic inn is owned and operated by Delaey Robinson and his wife Andrea who together have transformed this once simple guesthouse into what has become one of the most beautiful and welcoming small bed & breakfast inns anywhere.

Aunt Nea's offers 11 stunning individually decorated rooms and suites which feature Andrea's wonderful hand stenciled cabinetry, air conditioning, four poster and canopy bedding, hand woven rattan and hand carved hardwood furnishings, granite tile lined super deluxe private bathrooms (some have glassed-in shower areas and whirlpool baths, Spanish tile floors, beautiful local paintings and photographs, mini-refrigerators, clock radios, and nice peaceful courtyard or garden views.

Besides offering several cozy sitting rooms filled with plush sofas and plenty of local charm, Aunt Nea's has a wonderful garden-view terrace that is the perfect place to glance out over their limestone Moongate and sip a warm afternoon tea. Many other more expensive hotels could learn a few lessons about providing true Bermudian comfort, charm, hospitality, and excellent value for the money from this quaint and friendly property.

Selected as one of my *Best Places To Stay* – see Chapter 10.

WHERE TO EAT

THE CARRIAGE HOUSE, *Somer's Wharf, St. George, St. Georges. Tel. 441/297-1730. Open 12noon until 4:30pm and 6pm until 9:30pm daily. Sunday Brunch from 12noon until 2:30pm. Dress code ranges from Casual to Smart Casual. Reservations suggested. Cash, Traveler's Checks, and all major credit cards accepted.*

This romantic medium-sized restaurant is housed in a former 18th century carriage house in the Somer's Wharf complex of downtown St. George. The massive structure has been beautifully converted into a series of vaulted waterview dining areas replete with old brickwork and hanging plants. In the warmer months, they may open up their wharfside outdoor dining terrace.

The restaurant has become the best in town with the help of great lunch, brunch, afternoon tea, and dinner menus offering such specialties as huge sandwiches, burgers, an unlimited salad bar, Bermuda fish chowder, the Bermuda Triangle of filet mignon with shrimp and chicken, prime rib, fresh local fillet of fish, roast lamb, vegetarian pasta, Steak Diane, and dozens of other fine selections which are quite reasonably priced. Deserts are also a treat, with a whole trolley full of tempting choices to choose from. They even offer children's menus and early bird specials. Service here is polite and prompt, with a totally stress free ambiance. Expect dinner for two to cost about $69 without wine. Highly Recommended

DENNIS'S HIDEAWAY, *Cashia City, St. David's Island, St. Georges. Tel. 441/297-0044. Open 10am until 2:30pm and 6pm until 10:30pm on most days. Call first to verify the hours of the day in question. Dress code is Informal. Reservations suggested. Cash, and Traveler's Checks cnly, no credit cards accepted.*

This is the singularly most authentic casual restaurant in all of Bermuda. If you want to see the way real Bermudians used to cook, this is the place to find out! Dennis Lamb and his son prepare an assortment of unique St. David's seafood specialties in humble surroundings on what seems to be a scene straight out of the Louisiana Bayou.

The food here is fantastic in its down to earth simplicity; you'll leave this restaurant with a life-long memory of the experience. Dennis's photocopied menu lists such wonderful offerings as incredible mussel stew, conk stew, conk fritters, a wonderful shark hash, fish sandwiches, fried shrimp and scallops, shark steak, and lobster when it's in season. For the big eater, I suggest trying any of their dinners with "the works," which includes samplings of several house specialties. Bring your own wine or beer with you as they don't have a liquor license. Expect a dinner for two to cost somewhere around $53. Highly Recommended.

WHITE HORSE TAVERN, *King's Square, St. George, St. George's. Tel. 441/297-1838. Open 11am until 10pm daily. Closed on Tuesdays in low season. Dress code is Casual. Reservations are recommended, but not always necessary. Cash, Traveler's Checks, Visa, and MasterCard accepted.*

This cozy and centrally located in-town pub and restaurant has a small inner dining room with old wooden tables complete with fireplace and maritime decorations, an upstairs pool table and dart board, as well as a harborfront dining patio. The restaurant features such offerings as Bermuda fish chowder, onion rings with spicy sauce, conch fritters, BLTs, roast beef with Boursin cheese sandwiches, vegetarian pitas, reubens, Caesar salads, burgers, hot dogs, cod fish cakes, mussel pie, fish & chips, shrimp & chips, Casava pie, grilled chicken, pasta Creole, grilled wahoo, and an assortment of great desserts like bread & butter pudding and chocolate cake. Expect a lunch for two to cost about $31 and dinner for 2 to cost somewhere around $57, before adding wine or drinks.

WHARF TAVERN, *Somer's Wharf, St. George, St. Georges. Tel. 441/297-1515. Open 12noon until 3pm and 6pm until 10:30pm daily. Dress code is Casual. Reservations are Recommended, but not always necessary. Cash, Traveler's Checks, Visa, and MasterCard accepted.*

This is a good pub style bar and restaurant that features live music on many weekends and high season evenings. The interior is rather dark and uninspiring, but the outdoor wharfside tables are one of the best spots in town to people watch.

The large menu features a huge selection of good lunch and dinner choices including New England clam chowder, chili, fish fingers, deep fried mushrooms, tuna salad plates, burgers, onion rings, fish & chips, nachos, shepherds pie, barbecue ribs, bangers & mash, open face roast beef sandwiches, pan fried Wahoo, blackened tuna steak, fried shrimp, sirloin strip steak, mixed grill, chicken parmigiana, beef kebabs, and pizzas. Expect lunch here to cost about $29 per couple, and dinner to go for about $64, without drinks.

PASTA PASTA, *Duke of York Street, St. George, St. Georges. Tel. 441/297-2927. Open 12noon until until 10:30pm Monday through Saturday. Dress code is Casual. Reservations are not necessary. Cash and Traveler's Checks only, no credit cards accepted.*

Pasta Pasta is a good spot for a quick meal when you're on the go. It is set up as a cafeteria-style restaurant, with self service tables upstairs. The menu is basic and includes freshly prepared (while you watch) pastas with a variety of sauces including cream and mushroom, garlic with white wine and vegetables, tomato with pork and olives, spinach and tomato, tomato and Cajun fish, lasagne, vegetable lasagne, mixed salads, garlic bread, and pizzas (which not so good). A filling mid-day meal for two should only cost about $24.

SEEING THE SIGHTS
Getting to St. George

To get to St. George, you must first take a combination of bridges and linkage roads not so good are somewhat difficult to walk upon. I suggest that you consider using a taxi, public bus, or a scooter for this first part of your journey. The only possible route to this parish will be to depart the Bailey's Bay section of Hamilton parish from Blue Hole Hill as it merges east onto the long and narrow road known simply as **The Causeway**.

After this narrow harborview highway has connected with the **Long Bird Bridge**, you will be merging onto **Kindley Field Road**. This road travels alongside the perimeter of the Bermuda International Airport and comes to a traffic circle where you will be bearing left (north) to take **Mullet Bay Road** across the small body of water called Ferry Reach. Continue on Mullet Bay Road for about 2.3 kilometers (a bit more than 1.5 miles) as it twists and turns to the right (east) to follow the coastline of Mullet Bay and eventually merges onto **Duke of York Street**, which heads into the heart of **St. George**.

The Town of St. George

As you enter the town, you will notice that there are many shops and restaurants lining both sides of **The Duke of York Street**. I suggest holding off the temptation to go on a shopping spree until a bit later on.

First, turn right (south) for one block before making the first left (east) turn onto **Water Street** and follow it for a block or two until reaching the town's central square. The small landfilled harborfront plaza known as **King's Square** has become the central meeting point in town. The most obvious attraction for tourists are the replica **Stocks** and **Pillory** which were once a commonly used form of punishment on the island. In the 18th and early 19th century, locals could be accused and punished for all types of offenses including swearing in public, gambling, acts of treason, robbery, murder, or even scandalous behavior.

These days the offenses are handled in a more civilized manner, although many Bermudians will privately admit that they wouldn't mind bringing back these old and rather effective deterrents. Don't be at all surprised to find young couples asking you to take their photos while they pretend to be locked up together in the stocks.

As you wander around the buildings that face onto King's Square, you should first pop into the **Visitors Service Bureau** office on the south side of the square to pick up free maps and tickets to local attractions. They can also be quite helpful with restaurant recommendations and directions for the utterly lost. The bureau is open from 9am until 1pm and from 2pm until 4:30pm Monday through Saturday during high season, and is closed on most days during the low season.

IT'S THE STOCKS FOR YE!

During the low season on Wednesdays, an excellent free guided walking tour, hosted by the mayor and led by the Chamber of Commerce, starts at 10:30am from King's Square. Besides viewing the impressive parts of town, a rather unusual ceremony takes place afterwards in the heart of the square.

The oddly dressed St. George's Town Crier stands in the middle of the square at about 12 noon and rings a bell as he shouts out high volume cries of Hear Ye! Hear Ye!, and then convenes a tribunal to pronounce the sentencing of supposed criminal offenders (usually visiting tourists) to be locked into the stocks or even worse, dunked into the sea on the nearby Ducking Stool. Additional walking tours (without the extra added bonus of the Town Crier) are held on Wednesdays at 2pm and on Saturdays at 10:30am.

Almost next door to the bureau you can't miss the early 19th century **Town Hall** whose shuttered facade is emblazoned with a bold coat of arms. This is where the elected Mayor meets with the Corporation of St. George to discuss official business. The building's fine cedar furnishings and interior have been beautifully restored, and now include a photo gallery containing portraits of previous mayors. For those interested in a 30 minute multimedia presentation about Bermuda's history and culture, you can walk up to the top floor theater to watch the Bermuda Journey.

Town Hall is open from 9am to 4pm Monday through Saturday and admission is free. The Bermuda Journey is screened from 10am until 3pm Monday through Saturday during high season with limited showings during low season, admission is $3 for adults, $2 for seniors and children under 12.

King's Square is also surrounded by several other shops, pubs, services, and restaurants including (starting from the southwest corner), the quaint **White Horse Tavern** restaurant and bar, a **Peniston, Brown & Co.** perfume shop, the town's **Taxi Stand**, the **Paradise Gift Shop**, two offices of the **Bank of Bermuda**, **O'Malley's Pub on the Square**, the

Designer Bazaar, and a telephone booth. Public restrooms can be found just behind the town hall area.

After finishing with the square, it's now time head south on the small bridge-road which takes you across the water and onto **Ordnance Island**. The first sight you will see is a full size replica of the original *Deliverance*, one of two sea vessels built by the first long-term inhabitants of Bermuda, Admiral Sir George Somers and his stranded passengers and crew from the Sea Venture.

Deliverance II displays reconstructions of scenes from everyday life aboard the ship and can be visited to view the living conditions that these brave venturers subjected themselves to while at sea. *The ship is open daily from 9am to 5pm. Admission is $3 per adult and $1 for kids 12 and under.*

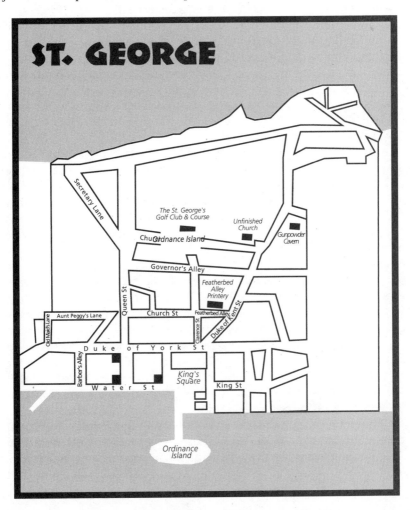

ST. GEORGE'S HARBOUR NIGHT FESTIVALS

*On Tuesday evenings during the summer from 7pm until 10pm, St. George hosts the wonderful **Harbour Night** street festivals. This event attracts both locals and tourists of all ages who wander over towards streetside vendors selling local handicrafts, stalls offering unique foods, sidewalk fashion shows, live bands, children's activities, and extended store opening hours (some close after 9pm). I strongly suggest that you experience Harbour Night if you are here during high season.*

This small island has a few more points of interest including a magnificent 1.5 ton bronze statue of **Admiral Sir George Somers** by gifted local artist Desmond Fountain, whose other fine work (predominantly life-size statues of children and naked women) is prominently displayed in several galleries in the US and England, as well as other attractions and resorts in Bermuda. In the front of the island you will find a replica of the 18th century **Ducking Stool**, which was once used to dunk suspected witches and other social misfits into the cold sea. At the back of the island there is a full service passenger ship terminal that hosts large luxury liner cruise ships during the summer season.

After the island, return to King's Square and turn right (east) at the Town Hall onto King Street. You will find a small triangle with a sculpture of famed poet Tom Moore, who resided in this town back around 1804. The building just to your left (north) is the famed **Bridge House**. Built in the early 18th century, it was once adjacent to a small bridge that carried pedestrians over a small creek which has since been landfilled. In its infamous past, this was the private residence of several Governors, as well as a much despised privateer Named Bridger Goodrich, who commandeered Bermudian ships trying to outrun the embargo placed on the rebellious colonies during the American revolution. These days this fine structure still contains cedar staircases and period furnishings, but is now owned by the Bermuda National Trust.

Also in the house is the **Bridge House Art Gallery & Crafts Shop** where you can buy prints, watercolors, crafts, and hand-made gift items by famed local artists. The house and gallery are open from 10am until 5pm Monday through Saturday during high season, and 10am until 5pm on Wednesdays and Saturdays during low season, admission is free.

Continuing east to the corner of King Street and Princess Street you can see the **Old State House**. This unusual stone building was erected in 1620 for then-Governor Nathaniel Butler to host the new colony's House of Assembly, which had been meeting at St. Peter's Church but desired more privacy. The most unusual feature of this building is that of a flat roof, something you would almost never see in subsequent Bermudian structures. The building had been used by the government for quite some time, when in 1815 the capital of Bermuda was picked up and moved lock, stock, and barrel, into the city of Hamilton. The St. George Lodge of the Grand Lodge of Scotland association later acquired the right to rent this property for the sum of 1 peppercorn per year. The building is open from 10am until 4pm on (most) Wednesdays only; admission is free.

FOR RENT - ASKING ONE PEPPERCORN!

If you are lucky enough to be in town on the closest Wednesday to April 23 each year, you are in for one of the country's most exciting events. On that Wednesday, a ceremony with much pomp and circumstance has been created for the Grand Lodge of Scotland to present the city of St. George with their annual rent of 1 peppercorn. The festivities kick off at about 11am. With the guaranteed appearance of the Governor, the Premier, the Mayor, and the Bermuda Regiment Band, the rent payment of a single peppercorn is presented to government officials upon a velvet pillow. This is one of the most spectacular old traditions still carried out in modern day Bermuda.

After the State House, the road curves upward and intersects with King of York Street where you should cross over to wander about in **Somers' Gardens**. This peaceful garden full of palm trees and shrubs is named after Admiral George Somers. After he and his men finally departed Bermuda after being shipwrecked here on the *Sea Venture*, they arrived safely in Jamestown, Virginia. Soon after, he returned to Bermuda to pick up more supplies and check up on the few men who had decided to stay behind on these islands. He unfortunately died in September of 1610 while on his return visit here, and his heart is said to have been buried on this spot, with the rest of his body being shipped back to England for burial. While wandering amidst the park and its collection of palm trees, shrubs, and benches, take note of the large stone memorial dedicated to this brave and honorable man. The park is open from 8am to 4pm daily and admission is free.

After perhaps resting in the park for a while, turn right (west) back on to Duke of York Street, and at the corner turn right again (north) onto Duke of Kent Street. After a block or so, you will see a set of stairs on the left (west) side of the street, just after the corner of **Featherbed Alley**, leading up to the **St. George's Historical Society**. This quaint 18th century colonial Bermuda-style cottage has been converted into a museum exhibiting a fine collection of early cedar furnishings, original copies of old Bermuda Gazette newspapers, an authentic period kitchen and pantry, a bible dating back to the mid-17th century, and lots of other local relics and artifacts.

The old slave quarters of this house now contain the **Carole Holding Studio** which displays and sells prints and watercolors from this famed local artist. *Museum and studio are open 10am until 4pm on Monday through Friday from April through early December. Price is $4 per adult and $2 for kids under 12 and includes admission to Featherbed Alley Printery. A special combination ticket to here and several other St. George's attractions is also available.*

When you're finished at the museum, continue walking up (north) on Duke of Kent Street for another block or so until seeing the haunting skeleton of the **Unfinished Church** above a hill at the intersection before you. This half-finished Gothic church, one of my favorite spots to visit in town, was originally built in 1874 to replace St. Peter's Church. The project was abandoned midway through construction due to a combination of funding problems, a roof collapse, and various political reasons.

These days a team of builders and landscapers can be seen occasionally renovating and strengthening the structure, which was turned over to the Bermuda National Trust. Some say that it may actually be re-roofed one day. The church is not open to the public due to safety concerns, but you can still see much of its barren interior, supporting buttresses, and facade from street level.

Once you've taken a few good pictures of the church, retrace your steps back down (south) on Duke of Kent Street, passing again by the Historical Society, and then immediately turning right (west) onto Featherbed Alley. Here you should pop into the old **Featherbed Alley Printery**. The printery contains a working model of a Gutenburg-style manual printer of the type that was once used to print the Bermuda Gazette during the the late 18th century. If the press is being utilized to print notices when you visit, ask to help in this antiquated but still effective process. *Open 10am until 4pm on Monday through Friday from April through early December. Price is $4 per adult and $2 for kids under 12 and includes admission to St. George's Historical Society. A special combination ticket to here and several other St. George's attractions is also available.*

From the printery, head up Featherbed Alley until the next corner where you will keep going straight (west) onto Church Street. You should then make your first right (north) turn onto Broad Lane to find the **Old Rectory House**. This quaint small house, built in the 17th century by a retired pirate, is now owned by the Bermuda National Trust. During the mid-18th century the house was occupied by Reverend Alexander Richardson of St. Peter's Church, hence the name Old Rectory. You can get an interesting glimpse into the life of Rev. Richardson from several antiques and personal effects which are on display. The house is open on Wednesdays only, from 10am until 5pm, and admission is free.

At the next corner, turn left (south) onto Queen Street and follow it a couple of blocks down until being able to turn left (east) onto Duke of York Street. About halfway down the block, you can't help but be drawn to the fantastic whitewashed facade and portal of **St. Peter's Church**. This beautiful Anglican church was originally erected in 1619 on the spot of a wooden thatched roof structure that dated back to 1612. After incurring severe hurricane damage, the church had to be completely rebuilt in 1713, with the side wings and clocktower being added in the early 19th century to accommodate a growing congregation.

During the course of all these construction projects, the church's original cedar altar and some old cedar pews were salvaged and are still in use today. The church's great vestry contains a collection of old Bermudian coins, and 17th century Royal English silver communion sets and chalices that should also be seen. In 1620, Bermuda's first House of Assembly session took place here.

While visiting the church, make sure to take a good look at the unusual memorial plaques that line many of the interior walls. Behind the church is a peaceful graveyard that can be visited to see the inscribed gravestones of many people including assassinated Governor Sir Richard Sharples, and American sailor Richard Dale who lost his life during the War of 1812 (St. George was a hotbed of British military activity before the naval attack on America). The church is open daily from 9am until 4:30pm and admission is free.

Almost directly across the street from the church is the next stop: the **Bermuda National Trust Museum** (formerly the Confederate Museum). This unusual house, with two huge chimneys protruding from its facade, was originally built with public funds for use by Governor Samuel Day. After his term expired, he spent years illegally occupying this pretty house as if it were his own property. After viewing its impressive interior, you'll understand why he was so damn adamant about not giving it back to the government.

Somewhere about 1850, the building was converted into the Globe Hotel. When the American Civil War broke out, local residents with relatives and trading ties to the southern states actively broke through the North's naval blockade of the Confederacy. One of the occupants here was Major Norman Walker, a Confederate agent who help organize these clandestine ammunition and equipment supply routes.

Nowadays, you can visit this house to stroll alongside its collections and exhibits regarding St. George's role in the Civil War, including scale models of the ships used in smuggling operations, historic documentation, and an antique press which stamps out foil replicas of the Great Seal of the Confederacy. *Open 10am until 4pm on Monday through Saturday. Entrance is $4 per person. A special combination ticket to here and several other St. George's attractions is also available.*

Since there are many fine shops and eating establishments along the path to your next few in-town attractions, I suggest returning to King's Square for a cold drink or a snack. After you have regained both your strength and desire to press onward, from the center of the square, turn left (west) onto **Water Street** and do a little well deserved window shopping. Keep your eyes out for the 24 hour **ATM** bank machine, the other branch of **Carole Holding Art Studios** for prints and watercolors, great deals on unique high quality jewelry and timepieces at **Crissons**, English and American shoes at **W.J. Boyle & Sons**, fine women's swimwear and fashion clothing at **Frangiapani**, a vast assortment of gifts and men's and women's clothing at the **Bermuda Railway Co.**, the **St. George's Post Office**, **Sinclairs'** souvenir and T-shirt shop, a branch of **Vera P. Card** porcelain and collectable figurine shop, and **Taylors Clothing**.

When you have walked about two blocks down this small but heavily commercial road, you will pass the **Carriage Museum** on the left (south) side. This old panel floored former carriage house contains the Wilkinson collection of restored horse drawn carriages. Since cars were not available in Bermuda until the mid 1940's, it was not uncommon for Bermudians to take a great deal of pride in their carriages. Here you can see an amusing assortment of both common and unique vehicles, all with explanatory signs, including old fringe-topped Surreys, Runabouts, and a two-wheeled child's model once pulled by a pony. The museum is open from 9am until 5pm weekdays (and occasional Saturdays). Admission is free but donations are appreciated.

The building housing the Carriage Museum marks the beginning of a new harborfront shopping mall called the **Somers Wharf**. In this center you will find the remarkable **Carriage House Restaurant**, **A.S. Cooper & Sons** china, crystal, and perfume shop, **Davison's** sportswear shop, the **Cow Polly** novelty store, a branch of **Trimingham's** department store, **Bluck's** china and crystal shop, the **English Sports Shop** with its fine selection of imported gents sportswear, the **Crown Colony** ladies clothing shop, and finally the **Wharf Tavern** restaurant that features live music on many evenings. This waterview strip of wharfs and moorings leads past the outdoor tables of various eating establishments, and heads westward towards the other cruise ship terminal.

If you retrace your steps back up to **Water Street** and turn left (west) at the Carriage Museum, on the opposite side of the street you will find the entrance to the **Tucker House**. Originally built on what was then the town's waterfront in 1711, this limestone house was later home to the infamous Tucker family. This well established and politically connected family were caught up in a legendary plot that still provokes anger in some Bermudians. When the American colonies decided to revolt against Mother England, the revolutionary Colonial Congress imposed an export embargo on all British colonies who did not support their struggle. Since the vast majority of Bermudians were rather loyal to the crown, they were subject to a cut- off of badly needed food supplies from America. Under cover of darkness, a group of men, including a couple of the Tuckers, stole several dozen kegs of gunpowder from the local arsenal on August 14, 1775, and loaded them onto ships in nearby Tobacco Bay, which were headed for Boston. The result was that food supplies were kept flowing to Bermuda throughout the duration of the supposed embargo.

The house, now owned by the Bermuda National Trust, contains a number of 18th century English mahogany and Bermudian cedar furnishings, oil paintings of prominent Tuckers, crystal chandeliers, fine engraved silver, and other family heirlooms. Downstairs, in what was once the kitchen, is an exhibit dedicated to local barber Joseph Hailey Rainey, a former slave who escaped to Bermuda during the Civil War. He would later return to the south after the war, to eventually be elected as the first black Congressman in the United States. *Open 10am until 4pm on Monday through Saturday. Admission is $3 per person.*

As Water Street keeps heading west, you will also find several more stores, services, and restaurants such as the **House of Linens**, the **San Giorgio** Italian restaurant, the **Bersalon** beauty salon, the **Moonglow** cafe, **St. George's Cycle Livery** scooter and moped shop, and a few other new shops.

Now that you have seen all the sights in St. George, you may want to head back to **Duke of York Street** to hit the rest of the shops and unusual venues. These include (from west to east): **Antiques & Old Stuff**, the **Cracker Box** gift shop, the **East End Florist**, **True Color** photo shop and film processing lab, the town's main **Bus Stop**, **the King Midas** gift and jewelry store, another **Vera P. Card** porcelain and figurine shop, the **Music Chamber** record shop, **Alice's Yarns & Crafts**, the casual **Pasta Pasta** Italian restaurant, the **H.A. & E Smith** department store, the **St. George Police Station**, the huge **Robertson's** drug, magazine, and stationary store, **Dowling Cycle Livery** scooter rental shop, **Goslings** wines and spirits, **Frith's Liquors**, **Xpressions** imported gift store, the **Bank of Butterfield**, **Constable's** woolen shop, another bargain laden **Crissons** fine jewelry and watch shop, the **Shabazz Bakery**, and **Clyde's Cafe**, and the charming little **Angeline's Coffee Shop**.

The Outskirts of St. George

After checking out the town of St. George for several hours, you can now see the many other dramatic sights of this special parish. From the town, you can take buses, taxis, scooters, or walk to most of the following attractions.

First stop: follow Duke of York Street all the way east (out of town) until it first becomes **Barrack Hill Road**, which later merges with **Cut Road**. From this scenic road, look for signs at its end on the tip of this peninsula, and go to **Gates Fort**. The restored limestone block structure was one of Bermuda's first defensive fortress. It was probably built around 1622 and is named after Sir Thomas Gates, one of the *Sea Venture* crewmen who first came ashore on this spot. He was later to become colonial Jamestown, Virginia's Governor. Since the fort later was converted into a private residence, a restoration was necessary to recreate its original ambiance. The views are rather impressive. The fort is open from 10am until 4pm daily and admission is free.

From this point, Cut Road ends and Barry Road heads north to trace the peninsula's windswept coastline. Soon you will come to a 19th century rectangular fortification known as the **Alexandra Battery**. Its three massive guns were used to defend the St. George's area from intruders off the coast, and can still be visited to climb to its turret. The battery is open from 10am until 4pm daily, and admission is free.

Almost adjacent to the battery, the first of several bays and beaches that you will now pass is known as **Building's Bay**. Besides possibly being the settlement sight of the stranded crew from the *Sea Venture*, it was also where the crew built one of the ships which would later take them safely, but not in comfort, to Jamestown. The bay and its beach are open from sunrise to sunset, and admission is free, but don't expect any public restrooms or other facilities.

About another 1350 meters (yards) further north on Barry Road is, in my opinion, the most breathtaking fortress which can be seen in Bermuda, **Fort St. Catherine**. Built on the site of an older fortification dating back to 1614, this massive restored defensive fort was actually rebuilt and expanded in the 19th century, and was the area's first line of defense against the incursion of American warships during the war of 1812.

With it high position above the bluffs where many of the *Sea Venture* crewmen first reached Bermuda after their shipwreck, the fort must have been an awesome deterrent. After crossing over the moat to enter the fort, you will be taken on a self guided subterranean tour which leads past several scale model reconstructions of scenes starting from the initial wreck of the *Sea Venture*, and continuing through the launch of the Deliverance, the repulsion of Spanish invaders in the 1600's, English sponsored privateering and local pirate activity, use of the Ducking Stool for punishment, and the theft of local gunpowder for the American revolutionaries.

Next you will descend down into the tunnels that were cut right into the bedrock, and enter the basement. You will first pass by displays of old uniforms, armaments, and lanterns until you have reached the first of several cubby hole sized exhibits with mannequins dressed in 19th century uniforms and recorded announcements. After viewing the magazines used to store the 181 kilogram (400 pound) loaded shells and the hand operated shell elevators, you will be led to a large room containing a fantastic collection of antique swords and rifles.

Now you are brought back up to the ground floor. Here you will walk past several cannons to enter the keep with its stairs and tunnels leading to the kitchen area, and finally reach the former gun room which now is used to display a replica collection of England's Crown Jewels, gem encrusted swords, orbs, scepters, and other royal relics. As you exit through the rooftop, keep your eyes out for the huge English built 10" muzzle loaded guns that face the sea. *The fort complex is open daily from 10am until 4pm. Admission is $5 per adult and $2 for kids under 12 when accompanied by an adult.*

GEORGE THE GHOST

While you are wandering through the fort, you will most certainly find out about the fort's most famous former inhabitant, **George the Ghost**. *Although it may not seem that scary to you, enough respectable people had experienced a spirit or strange noises firsthand in these tunnels that in 1978 the church performed an exorcism to remove any ghosts or evil spirits. Since then, only the electronic version of George has been confronting visitors.*

Beaches & Golf

From the top of the fort, you can see two fine beaches on either side of the hilltop. Just under the defensive walls to the right (south) is the wide and sandy **St. Catherine's Beach**, which was once the private stomping grounds of the still closed Club Med resort (it's for sale if you're looking for property!), which can be seen in a sad state of disrepair across the road. It's an excellent beach for a good suntan or quick swim, but don't go out too far here, the currents are strong! The old Club Med beach house is now locked up, so bathrooms and other facilities are not available here.

On the left (northeast) side of the fort is a small cove called **Archilles Bay Beach**, which is much smaller and also does not contain facilities.

There is, however, a nice bar and restaurant atop the bluff called the **St. George's Beach House** where you can enjoy a cool drink, sandwich, or full lunch and dinner from its seaview patio or main dining room.

At this point you can follow **Coot Pond Road** as it bears left (west) from the fort and its beaches, and twists around until reaching the sea formations and sheltered beach of **Tobacco Bay**. Here you can swim up to naturally formed sea arches and boulders in perfect safety from the current. During the summer, the beach is full of ghost-white passengers just arriving in town from the cruise ships that dock nearby, but if you get here early enough, it is a fantastic place to relax. A few small beachfront buildings will rent snorkeling gear and flotation devices by the hour in high season, as well as selling hot dogs, hamburgers, french fries, tuna sandwiches, grilled cheese, and cold sodas. Public restrooms and changing facilities are also available. The beach is open from sunrise to sunset, and admission is free.

From the beach, take the next left (south) turn off onto **Government Hill Road** which leads past the Robert Trent Jones-designed **St. George's Golf Course**. This 18 hole par 62 oceanview course has 4043 yards and only will cost you $35 during the day, and $18 after about 3:30pm, plus cart rentals. Book this one well in advance; it is a favorite among locals and visitors alike. The course also has a great pub and restaurant called the **Smugglers Green**, serving excellent breakfast, lunches, and dinners, just off the course's 18th hole.

Back to St. George's Outskirts

From here you can take Government Hill Road down (south) to pass by the **Gunpowder Cavern**. After the theft of gunpowder by the Tuckers and others in 1775, the British built this structure, as well as others, to assure that this type of incident would never happen again. The road now merges into **Duke of Kent Street** and continues into the heart of St. George.

Follow Duke of York Street out of town to the east, as it first merges with Mullet Bay Road. Now you can stop at a couple of fine seaside parks with benches and trails including Mullet Bay Park and Rocky Hill Park. A few hundred meters (yards) ahead, bear right onto **Ferry Road**. This street will lead past a few oil tanks, and into the 22 acre **Ferry Point Park**.

While in the park you can visit a couple of old cemeteries and ruined fortresses, swim, fish, picnic, and visit the **Martello Tower**. Built in 1823 to support a huge gun that could swivel to any direction needed, the tower now offers visitors a great panoramic lookout point over much of the northern coastline.

Now you should head back in the direction of the bridge that crosses over Ferry Point, but do not yet cross it. Instead, keep your eyes out for **Biological Lane** and the signs leading to the **Bermuda Biological Station for Research** which really should be experienced before departing the island. Founded in 1926, this world class scientific facility is operated as an American non-profit research organization, hosting leading scientists from all over the globe.

Besides containing a vast library of science and marine biology materials, the station offers a slew of courses, seminars, whale watching excursions, work study programs, and marine education camps to advanced international students, as well as an Elderhostel program for more mature groups. The station operates dozens of state of the art laboratories, a seagoing research vessel, a remote controlled underwater video hydrobot robot, and an on-line Internet link to the rest of the world.

Among the recent research conducted here are studies on subjects ranging on the long-term effects of oil spills on tropical marine ecosystems, to the satellite analysis of ocean biogeochemistry. The station is open to the public on Wednesdays, when they offer a free tour with refreshments starting at 10am.

St. David's Island

From St. George's Island, cross over the bridge that leads over **Ferry Reach** and take the traffic circle to the 3rd turnoff to reach **Swalwell Drive**, which heads east alongside the runways of the International Airport. You are actually on a landfill of three smaller islands joined together to form what is now known as **St. David's Island**.

This is a rather unusual island, with many of its residents voluntarily isolating themselves from the rest of the country. They even speak with their own sort of accent here. In fact, many of these humble and hard working locals are the descendants of American Indians who were brought to Bermuda as manual laborers. Much of the island is strictly off limits to the general public, as it contains NASA space tracking stations (and the facilities of the former **US Naval Air Station** complex).

Swalwell Drive will go through several name changes and bends during the approximately 4 kilometer (4000 yards) run before finally reaching the intersection of **Texas Road** where you will be turning right (south). This small street eventually leads to the foot of the **St. David's Lighthouse.** This stone block lighthouse dates back to 1879, and can be climbed to enjoy magnificent views from its panoramic balcony. The lighthouse is open daily from May through October only, and admission is free.

After the lighthouse, return to the main road and look across the way to the waterfront. This is where you will find the **Black Horse Tavern**, a local restaurant with great seafood. Turn right (east) and continue on the main road until you are able to turn right (southeast) onto **Battery Road**. Soon you will be entering into **Great Head National Park**, which among other things is the official finish line for the world famous yearly Newport, Rhode Island to Bermuda yacht race.

The park also contains **St. David's Battery**, which was built in the 1800's to house and protect 4 British made 6" and 9.2" guns that could propel shells upwards of 33 kilometers (20 miles) out to sea. The park and its fort can be visited from 10am until 4pm daily, admission is free.

If you head back to the main road, and follow it to the very end, it will merge with a small street called Cashew City Road that leads to **Little Head Park**. The park itself is just a place for boats to moor, but the small wooden buildings next to it are home to **Dennis's Hideaway**, the most authentic Bermudian restaurant in existence. Dennis Lamb, the restaurant's owner, serves up old Bermudian seafood recipes like shark hash and mussel chowder. Don't expect opulence here; it's more like being invited into someone's living room for a meal.

Before retracing your route back towards the Airport, if you are here on a Wednesday, call *Tel. 297-1376* and ask see the **Carter House**. Once inside, you can view the 17th century house built in 1640 of limestone and cedar by the son of Christopher Carter, a *Sea Venture* crewman who decided to stay behind after the rest of the crew sailed onward to Jamestown. The house is now used as a museum for Bermudian culture and US military history. The museum is open from 11am until 3pm on Wednesdays only, and admission is free.

Tucker's Town

After leaving St. David's Island via the **Long Bird Bridge** and its adjacent causeway, continue to the end of **Blue Hole Hill Road**, and turn left (south) onto **Harrington Sound Road**. After passing the entrance to **Castle Harbour**, bear left onto **Paynter's Road** and take it for about 1 kilometer (1000 yards) until reaching the intersection of South Road where you will turn left (east). The lush green landscaping that you will now see is actually the beginning of the most exclusive residential area in all of Bermuda, **Tucker's Town**.

This rather private suburb, with its multimillion dollar estates owned by American, European, and Bermudian millionaires who all seem to guard their privacy in a serious way. The area consists of a few small and winding lanes that have magnificent estates hidden on private access roads, many of which face the sea. The most notorious home owner here is H. Ross Perot, who reportedly dynamited the reef in front of his seaview estate when local authorities refused to give him permission to expand his boat dock. As long as you don't trespass onto private property, you can still do a fair amount of mansion viewing from the side of several small roads that divide the area.

More Beaches & Golf

The **Tucker's Town Road** veers off to the right (south) at just about the end of South Road and more or less leads to several semi-private beaches, including beautiful **Windsor Beach** and the nearby strange **Natural Arches** rock formations.

The nearby private **Mid Ocean Club Golf Course** was then designed by Charles Blair Macdonald to become what is still Bermuda's most expensive and challenging course. With its fine 18 hole par 71 championship course of 6547 yards, this is the sight of several PGA sanctioned tournaments throughout the year. This is a private club, and either your hotel's concierge (if they have the right connections) or a club member may be needed to get you a tee off time here.

The club also sports a fine Clubhouse restaurant, two tennis courts, private beaches, and 20 terraced rooms that are only available to guests. In any case, the non-member price for these fine links is $100 per round, or $50 per guest per round when accompanied by a member plus cart rental fees. There is also a series of semi-private beaches just south of Mid Ocean's clubhouse.

NIGHTLIFE & ENTERTAINMENT

Most of the activity in this parish centers around the pubs that line King's Square and Somer's Wharf in central St. George. On most high season nights, especially on weekends, hundreds of locals and visitors alike flock to places like the **Wharf Tavern, White Horse Tavern**, and **O'Malley's Pub in the Square** for live bands, pool, and darts.

INDEX